AFTERNOON STORY

JOHN WILDS

AFTER-NOON STORY

A Century of the New Orleans *States-Item*

Louisiana State University Press BATON ROUGE

ISBN 0-8071-0192-3
Library of Congress Card Catalog Number 76-27188

Manufactured in the United States of America
Designed by Dwight Agner

To all who cherish *The States-Item*

Contents

Illustrations

Preface

"Tell the truth," I was admonished when I was assigned, as a member of the staff, to write a history of *The States-Item* in preparation for the observance of its centennial. I have tried to do so.

I should be ungrateful indeed if I did not acknowledge the invaluable assistance of Mrs. Aline H. Morris and Miss Rose Lambert of the Louisiana State Museum Library, of Collin B. Hamer, Jr., of the New Orleans Public Library, of Mrs. Connie Griffith and Mrs. Ann S. Gwyn of the Howard-Tilton Library, Tulane University, and of David A. Combe of the Tulane Law Library.

Others to whom I am indebted include Vincent Calderone, George Chaplin, Alberta Collier, Carl M. Corbin, John Dastugue, Mrs. Leneve Davis, Charles L. Dufour, Crozet J. Duplantier, Charles East, Edward W. Evers, Louis Faust, Warren Nardelle, Marjorie Roehl, Richard Stagno, David Stern III, and Francis G. Weller.

I also want to thank Martha Lacy Hall, of the Louisiana State University Press, who used tact and wisdom in her editing.

And finally, I must offer an assurance to Walter Cowan, to Frances and Warren C. Ogden, and to my wife, Tommie Lee: They won't have to listen to any more Dominick O'Malley stories. I've told all I know.

John Wilds, February 19, 1976

AFTERNOON STORY

1

Exit Carpetbaggers, Enter *Item*

Promptly at noon on that drizzly Tuesday, April 24, 1877, Brigadier General John R. Brooke gave the order. Came the tap of a drum, the blare of the regimental band, and the five companies of the Third Infantry, United States Army, marched away from the Orleans Hotel, 133 Chartres Street, behind the St. Louis Hotel, which occupied the downtown side of St. Louis Street between Royal and Chartres. The troops in their full-dress finery tramped over the cobblestones straight to the Mississippi River levee, where waited the steamer *T. Palace.* Balconies along the line of march were filled with ladies who fluttered their handkerchiefs in a genteel gesture of jubilation. Banquettes in the area were almost deserted. Fearing incidents, police had blocked off the approaches. But the music and drumbeats carried their message to a cheering throng centered at Royal and Canal streets. The soldiers boarded the *T. Palace,* and at 12:30 the steamboat cast off. At 1 o'clock at the foot of Canal Street the Louisiana

Field Artillery under Colonel John Glynn and a detachment from the Washington Artillery fired a one-hundred-gun salute.[1]

The hurrahs and the booming cannon marked the end of Reconstruction. President Rutherford B. Hayes had ordered the Third Infantry to go away, abandoning the presence which had served to keep alive the hopes of Stephen B. Packard, the Republican pretender to the governorship of Louisiana, and his would-be legislature holed up in the St. Louis Hotel. In recognizing Democrat Francis T. Nicholls as governor, Hayes withdrew the bayonets that had backed up a carpetbag reign since the end of the Civil War. Home rule was guaranteed again for the first time since that doomsday in 1862 when Flag Officer David Farragut's fleet had steamed upriver and subjugated New Orleans under the threat of ships' cannon pointed down the streets.

April 24, 1877.

The crowd in the business district that day was celebrating the close of an era. Unknowingly, citizens also were greeting the dawn of the city's modern age; for the departure of the soldiers broke the carpetbag knot that had strangled New Orleans economically. In a hundred years the city would become a great world port. A population of 200,000 would explode past the million mark in the metropolitan area.

Even as the thunder of the guns was echoing off the Algiers riverfront, men were talking about a new daily newspaper, a journal that was to become the first forebear of the *States-Item.** Within two months, the first issue

* At various times the names of the present newspaper and the two papers which were merged after previous separate existences have been *Daily City Item, New Orleans Item, Daily States, New Orleans States and New Orleans Item, New Orleans States-Item* and the *States-Item*. In the interest of clarity and brevity, the early versions will be called the *Item* and the *States,* and the merged paper the *States-Item*.

was sold on the streets. For the next hundred years, in one form or another — earlier as two papers, later as one — the *States-Item* or its antecedents would not only record New Orleans history, but also would often help to shape it and play vital roles in events.

This account of the first century of the *States-Item*, therefore, is also a chronicle of the city's modern age.

Over the years it has been written that the *Item* was conceived in a saloon.[2] There is no reason to doubt this version. In 1877 Andrew Kreutz's barroom at 133 Gravier Street, in the block between Camp and Magazine streets, was a convenient hangout for the compositors who, before the introduction of typesetting machines into New Orleans,* performed the tedious task of setting the type by hand. Kreutz's was just around the corner from Newspaper Row, a line of four-story brick buildings on the river side of Camp Street between Gravier and Poydras. Here, for decades, most New Orleans dailies and some of the weeklies were printed. Kreutz's was near the entrance to Bank Place, later Picayune Place, an alley extending from Gravier to Natchez Street. The *Daily Picayune*, the *Times* and the *Democrat* had back doors opening onto Bank Place, making Kreutz's only a few steps away for a thirsty printer. It wasn't much farther away for employees of the New Orleans *Republican*, published at 94 Camp Street,** between Natchez and Poydras, or the *German Gazette* at 108 Camp. The French-language *L'Abeille, The Bee*, was situated across Canal Street at 73 Chartres, between Bienville and Conti.

* The *Item* on May 11, 1891, reported the arrival of the first Mergenthaler linotype machines in New Orleans. The six units were installed at the *Times-Democrat*. Printers were paid four dollars for an eight-hour workday. The overtime rate was fifty cents per hour.

** The city's street-numbering system was changed on May 31, 1894. In this chronicle the old numbers will be used in the discussion of events which took place before that date and the new numbers for subsequent developments. When the old numbers are used, the locales often will be fixed with reference to cross streets in the hope of helping the reader to visualize the scenes.

These were the daily newspapers appearing in the spring of 1877. All were morning papers, although the English-language journals offered so-called fly sheets for sale in the afternoon. A fly sheet was a four-page production containing late news and market quotations that was wrapped around the regular edition of the same morning.

In March, national administration support of the carpetbag regime in Louisiana was crumbling. The *Republican,* newspaper voice of the government, found itself in financial straits. Since the war the paper had existed on subsidies from public funds funneled in by Republican officeholders. One source of revenue had been the advertising of the texts of bills introduced in Congress. By March the flow of public dollars had dried up, and the *Republican* abandoned daily publication although it continued as a weekly into the next year. Most of the *Republican*'s employees were thrown out of work. Only a handful could be absorbed by the surviving dailies, themselves far from prosperous during the economic depression that developed out of the repressive and corrupt political administration. Most of the jobless printers gravitated to Kreutz's, where they lounged, day after discouraging day, discussing their plight. In one of the conversations the idea of starting a cooperative newspaper was suggested.[3] The seed fell onto fertile ground. The printers had little to lose except the labor they might put into such a venture. It would be a relief to be working, even if they were gambling on any return from their efforts, rather than idling the days away. The talk at Kreutz's at the time General Brooke's soldiers marched away resulted in more formal meetings.[4]

For an editor, the printers looked over the ranks of the available men and came up with a veteran of the New Orleans journalistic scene, Mark Frederick Bigney. It was a quirk of fate that a nondrinker would be the first editor of a newspaper born of barroom talk. But Bigney was a teetotaler, of whom few existed in the adult male population of a whiskey-guzzling city, and an oddity indeed in a vocation in which topers abounded. Chosen as associate editor was Edwin L. Jewell, an experienced newsman and publisher. The problem of a printing plant was solved by enlisting Charles W. Clark, partner in the printing firm of Clark and Hoefeline, in the project.

Since all of the city's dailies were morning papers, it was logical that the new journal would try its luck in the evening field. And since the newcomer would have neither the money nor the facilities for gathering national and international news, there was little argument over the decision to emphasize local news. The first issue of the *Daily City Item* was published on June 11, 1877, on the Hoe drum press of Clark and Hoefeline at 112 Gravier Street.[5]

The *Times* noted the event by saying: "The *Daily City Item* is the name of a new evening paper which made its appearance yesterday. The makeup is neat and the matter sprightly and creditable."[6] The *Democrat* was even more cordial:

> The *Item* is neatly printed, and full of live and racy reading. We welcome the new paper into the field of journalism, and we say this, not as a mere expression of courtesy, but sincerely. The journalistic field may be over full here or elsewhere, and some enterprises must fail, while others succeed; but the more that are started, and, indeed, the greater number that succeed, the stronger, abler and truer the press of the locality will be. The principle of survival of the fittest will control the result, and the energies of all are stimulated to their highest action by vigorous competition.
>
> Established newspapers which look with enmity upon new journalistic enterprises are generally superannuated institutions, or corrupt ring organs which have more to conceal from than they have to tell their readers. The one dreads the coming of the young and vigorous rival whose brains and spirit will force it to stir its sluggish blood or drive it out of its ruts, while the other trembles before a fearless and honest journal, whose eager and new-born zeal may hunt out and expose its rotten secrets. The public, however, and honest and enterprising journalism are benefitted by the birth of new papers. Our young neighbor has a hard fight before it, but energy and enterprise will win in the end.[7]

The style of the *Democrat*'s editorial will become familiar in the pages to follow. It was the work of Major Henry James Hearsey, the paper's editor, who was destined to become the founder in 1880 of the *States.* Many years later the *States* would be merged with the *Item* to create the *States-Item,* the form in which it exists today.

Indicative of the ephermeral nature of newspapers is the fact that apparently not a single copy of the first edition of the *Item* remains in existence. Newspaper publishers can give little thought to posterity; their worry is today; and whatever files remained of the earliest *Items* were not preserved. The oldest copies extant indicate the first issue was a four-page paper, somewhat narrower than today's six-column format.

The twelve men who shared the proprietorship of the *Item* learned what the *Democrat* meant by predicting a "hard fight of it" when they totted up the receipts and expenses of the first week of operation and divided the net profit among themselves. They received $2.65 each.[8]

Not until October 12, 1877, did the founders get around to obtaining a charter for the City Item Co-Operative Printing Company. Capital stock was set at $50,000, consisting of two thousand shares at $25 each. The incorporators actually subscribed to $12,000 worth of shares. Those who chipped in were Bigney, Jewell, Clark, William J. Hammond, James Beggs, Thomas C. Wilkinson, J. L. Dujarric, B. F. Harrison, Joseph C. Duster, William A. Bryan, Bernard Cunniffe, and William H. Magruder. Newsmen on the original staff were Harry S. Michel, who in 1878 succeeded Cunniffe as city editor; J. F. Barringer, Arnold Pierce, Charles O. Donnaud, and George J. Duncan. William F. Tracey handled miscellaneous tasks in the office. William Mack was distributor, John Franklin Shansy was advertising solicitor, and P. M. Joachim was organizer of delivery.[9] Clark was business manager. When the cooperative finally was chartered in October, all of the reportorial staff except Donnaud and Michel walked out; whether in protest against being excluded from the ownership or for some other reason is not recorded. Michel and Donnaud carried on by themselves until other reporters could be employed.

The third article of twenty-three in the original charter reads: "The objects of the newspaper compiled, printed and published by the corporation, shall be to promote the commercial, industrial, social and political interests of the state and country, and to give tone, vigor, point and effect to everything calculated to elevate, refine and enoble public sentiment and feeling; and to that end shall, without fear or favor, decry and condemn all frauds, peculation, corruption and crime wherever found." Noble goals, indeed, for a newspaper with a barroom beginning.

By the end of 1877 Clark was removed from his job by other board members who feared he was trying to take control of the *Item.* The printing contract with Clark and Hoefeline was ended, and on January 1, 1878, the directors arranged for publication by E. D. Elliott, printer, at his plant at 39 Natchez Street, between Camp and Magazine. The lease on the building was taken over by the *Item,* which later purchased Elliott's equipment. Oil lamps and weak gaslights provided the illumination in the building. There were wigglers in the drinking glasses, since the water came from a cypress cistern. There were no telephones. Negro copy boys acted as messengers between outside reporters and the city editor.[10]

By the summer of 1878 the *Item* had muscled into the daily newspaper ranks and was ready to square off with any of the older journals. Bigney wrote an editorial, entitled "Sunday Reading," in which he ridiculed the contents of the other papers. Of the *Democrat,* he said: "But its chief effort in the Sunday editorial line is a schoolboy essay on the tyranny of babies. The household despot is held up to the execration of mankind as 'brainless' and 'immoral,' and the stale suggestion of Sydney Smith that he should be roasted and eaten is impotently revamped. Just think of the low condition into which journalism has fallen when papers claiming to be first class present such food for babies as the Sunday reading of grown-up people."

The *Democrat* fired back promptly: "A sickly little evening sheet, which subsists mainly by puffing the lottery, has for some weeks past devoted its energies to the business of extorting a notice from the *Democrat.*" The writer told the story of a boor, who upon being kicked downstairs by Napoleon Bonaparte, had the seat of his pants framed as proof that the emperor had condescended to apply the toe of his boot. The *Democrat* said it would deny the *Item* the dignity of a kick. Bigney retorted: "Whenever a person, whether in a newspaper or out of it, boasts of his achievements in the way of kicking, he proves himself an insignificant creature, and a coward, who has learned all he knows upon the subject by an unwilling familiarity with other people's boots."

Hearsey sent Charles E. Whitney of the *Democrat* to Bigney's residence at 183 Carondelet Street, between Girod and Julia, to demand a retraction, or, as an alternative, to meet him in a duel. "I replied judging from the teaching of long experience, that duels never settled such affairs satisfactorily," Bigney reported, "and for my part I was too old to indulge in such foolishness." Bigney was warned that he might be attacked on the street. On July 25 Hearsey espied the much-larger Bigney walking on Natchez Street a few paces from Camp Street and attacked with his cane. Bigney wrested the cane away. In attempting to break it in two, he knocked Hearsey to the pavement, and could not resist the temptation to administer a kick with the side of his boot. "He was completely at my mercy," Bigney wrote. "I could have jumped on him and disfigured him, and the law would have justified me. He was down and I was not; but I could not find it in my heart to be so cruel to him as he had attempted to be to me. He had tried to degrade me, and was himself degraded." Whitney led Hearsey away and there the affair ended.[11] The encounter retains a place in New Orleans journalistic legends.

Of all the editors who wrote for the *Item* or the *States* in the nineteenth century, Bigney would have been most comfortable on today's liberal *States-Item.* The very thought of endorsing Democrat George McGovern, as the *States-Item* did in the 1972 presidential election, would have flabbergasted Hearsey and all of the others. Bigney was born in Nova Scotia, of French Huguenot descent. The original family name was D'Aubigny, which was anglicized. His mother was of Scottish ancestry, member of a Tory family that moved from New England during the American Revolution. Bigney, born in 1817, as a youth went to sea with the Nova Scotia fishing fleet. In 1849 he settled in Jefferson City, a separate political subdivision in what is now Uptown New Orleans. He established a weekly publication, the *Live Oak,* which provided an outlet for his literary talents. When the *Live Oak* folded, Bigney joined the *Picayune* and then the *Delta.* He established a reputation as a reporter. The *Times-Democrat* later said his accounts of city council meetings were as authentic as official reports. "Mr. Bigney possessed that energy, industry and enterprise which never let his newspaper get beaten on an item."[12] He left the *Delta* to join the *True Delta,* and in 1860 founded a literary weekly, the *Mirror.* After the Civil War he worked for the *Picayune,* was acting editor of the *Times,* and became connected with the *Republican.* Bigney was recognized among minor southern poets. He died of Bright's disease at his residence on April 30, 1886. The *Times-Democrat* noted that he was the third oldest of the newspaper editors in the city at the time. The only two senior to him were Robert J. Kerr, formerly of the *Courier,* and Alexander Walker, once editor of the *Delta* and later a contributor to the *States.* "Mr. Bigney was greatly respected by all classes of our people for his integrity, firmness, amiability and benevolence," said the *Times-Democrat.* "Positive in his opinions and fearless in their assertion and in all the duties of his profession, earnest and tenacious in his devotion to his craft, he was also kindly, generous, faithful to friendships and considerate and magnaminous to all men." "His labors cover a period of nearly 40 years, and what remains of the products of those days and nights of toil," lamented the *Picayune.*[13] "The work of the journalist dies with each day — its effects often durable and far-reaching. What sadder or truer epitaph could he have than those mournful words of the dying philosopher, Grotius: 'I have lost my life laboriously doing nothing.' "

Edwin L. Jewell had a unique, although obscure part in the genesis of the *States-Item.* Not only was he one of the founding editors of the *Item,* but he also was one of the original employees of the *States.* He did not linger long on either journal and left no lasting imprint on either. Jewell was born in 1836 in Pointe Coupee Parish. He learned his early newspaper lessons in the employ of his father, who was editor of the *Pointe Coupee Echo.* After his father's death in 1854, he published the *Echo* until 1862 when Union troops appeared in the parish. He fled to Port Hudson and produced the Port Hudson *News* during the siege there. Moving to New Orleans in 1865, Jewell founded the *Southern Star.* Later he was joint proprietor, along with Daniel C. Byerly and Page M.Baker, of the New Orleans *Bulletin.* Jewell served in the state Senate and later went to Washington as index clerk of the House of Representatives. In the 1870s he was editor and manager of the *Crescent City Illustrated* and in 1876 compiled the city's ordinances under the title *Jewell's Digest.* He died of consumption at his residence at 95 First Street, between Annunciation and Chippewa streets, on November 29, 1887.[14]

In 1878 the last yellow fever epidemic of disastrous magnitude in New Orleans gave the infant *Item* an opportunity to show its aggressiveness and enterprise. By the time the outbreak was on the wane on November 1, there had been 13,317 cases reported and 3,972 deaths. In July, when the situation was alarming and New Orleanians could think of little else, the *Item* began publishing a daily bulletin of new cases and deaths. The paper managed to print the names and statistics far ahead of the afternoon fly sheets and, of course, twelve to fifteen hours ahead of the morning journals.

Occasionally, a newspaper beat, or scoop, drops into a reporter's lap. Most often, it takes perspiration and planning for a paper to get on the street first with a story. This was the case in the *Item*'s yellow fever exploits. At 11:30 A.M. daily a list of new cases and deaths in the previous twenty-four hours was closed by the State Board of Health, which had offices in the St. Louis Hotel. The closing coincided exactly with the hour when the statistics for twenty-four hours were compiled at Charity Hospital, where many victims were taken. B. B. Howard, later an attorney, was the messenger for the board of health. He picked up the Charity figures at 11:30 and took them by streetcar to the St. Louis Hotel, where the statistics were combined and released to reporters. Somebody at the *Item* — it may have been Bigney but the name has been lost — devised a plan that enabled the paper to have the figures running off the presses while other publications awaited them at the Board of Health. An *Item* man was stationed at Charity and another at the St. Louis Hotel. As soon as the statistics were ready they were handed to relays of fleet newsboys who raced to the newspaper office. The *Item* did its own computation and soon had papers ready for sale.[15] At one time during the epidemic the *Democrat* posted blackboards in the business district and sent out reporters to chalk up the late bulletins.

Michel knew that opium was being smuggled into New Orleans for the numerous Chinese who came to the port city. He assigned a reporter, Peter Kiernan, to go to Tucker's place on Dauphine Street between Conti and St. Louis streets to buy a pipeful and see what was happening. Kiernan made an affidavit, and police officer John Journee, later the inspector of police, arrested several Chinese and confiscated a supply of opium. But when the case came to trial, attorneys could find no city ordinance under which vendors or users could be prosecuted.[16]

A test of a newspaper's ingenuity is the unexpected event of overriding public interest — a bolt from the blue. Any competent city editor can plan the coverage of a scheduled occurrence, assigning his reporters to specific duties and then coordinating their efforts to produce a readable, comprehensive account. Sometimes a desk man's intuition will enable him to have the right staff at the right place at the right time. But it is the response to a bombshell on which newsmen grade their colleagues.

On December 14, 1883, the *Item* faced probably the toughest challenge of its brief lifetime. At 1:30 P.M. in front of a polling place on Marais Street near St. Bernard Avenue, forty pistol shots were fired in an election-day battle. Three men fell dead, and eight others were wounded. James D. Houston,* chairman of the State Democratic Committee and state tax

* Houston shot Captain Michael J. Fortier to death at point-blank range. He said Fortier fired at him but the bullet did not penetrate his clothing. Fortier made the second notch on Houston's weapon. The first came when Houston, then a deputy sheriff, killed Arthur Guerin. Although Houston was primarily a politician, he served in the 1879-1881 period as publisher of the *Democrat*.

collector, and Robert A. Brewster, the criminal sheriff, were among the participants.[17] The afternoon deadline was nearing when a flash reached Michel in the *Item* newsroom. He dispatched to the scene five reporters, every one he could find, and then beat his competitors to the punch by getting a telephone call through to a telephone next-door to the poll. The reporters took turns on the line to relay their information to Michel, who wrote the stories for a series of extras. That afternoon eighteen thousand copies were run off on a double-cylinder press, a mechanical feat that reinforced the news staff's superlative performance with the aid of the telephone, still a relatively new gadget.[18] The *Item* came off with high grades.

"Extra! Extra!" The pulse-quickening shout was heard with regularity near Newspaper Row in those long-ago days when New Orleans newspapers already were battling for street sales.

From the start the *Item* was willing to try innovations, one of the first being the publication beginning on October 13, 1878, of a Sunday evening paper, few of which have been printed in the United States. Among the offerings was a column highlighting the features printed in the New York City Sunday morning editions. The *Item*'s Sunday evening paper was continued for years.

James Beggs, whose name is fifth in line on the *Item*'s act of incorporation, was the composing room foreman. Beggs was a city councilman in 1862 when General Benjamin Butler's occupying troops moved in following Farragut's invasion. The crusty Beggs made no secret of the fact that he kept a memorandum book that he called his son-of-a-bitch book. When Butler learned that his name was the first listed, he summoned Beggs and demanded to see the book. Beggs had no choice but to hand it over, and Butler found out first-hand how he ranked in Beggs's estimation. "I suppose you think I'm going to ask you to take my name out of here," Butler said. "Well, I'm not. The only thing you're going to do is to write your own name there, right above mine. Go ahead, write."[19]

The *Item* was only a year old in June, 1878, when Major William M. Robinson entered Bigney's office with a tiny, shabbily dressed, half-starved figure in tow. "Mr. Bigney, I've brought you 'round a man after your own heart; you're a literary fellow and he's a literary fellow, too," said Robinson.[20] Thus was Lafcadio Hearn introduced into the New Orleans editorial world. He had drifted down from Cincinnati eight months earlier and become fascinated with the sights and sounds of the Creole city and its conglomerate population. He could not find a job, fell victim to dengue fever, which almost finished him off, and was at a point where he did not know how he could obtain his next meal. Bigney took him on at ten dollars a week, a hardly munificent wage even then but nevertheless the going rate for some newsmen.

For three and one-half years Hearn was a major contributor to the *Item.* He wrote some of the editorials, devoured the out-of-town newspapers for pick-up articles, put together some of the "Wayside Notes" that remained a fixture long after his departure, and translated such French works as caught his eye. He also wrote vignettes, some depending on dialect for their touch of humor and others glossy pieces that enabled New Orleanians to see their city through a poet's eye. Hearn was deft with a sketching pen and illustrated many of his "fantastics," as he called his sketches of life. Woodcuts of the sketches were made by the engraving firm of Zenneck and Bennett. It was Hearn's own idea to do the sketches, and later he wrote: "The pictures are not magnificent, but the experiment paid well, for the adoption of my suggestion put the journal on its feet at a time when it was on the verge of dissolution."[21] He may have overestimated the importance of his contribution, but there is no question but what the *Item* had lean early years.

In December, 1881, when the *Times* and the *Democrat* were merged, Hearn was hired away from the *Item* and given the job of literary editor at $30 a week, $10 more than he earned. Page M. Baker, editor of the *Times-Democrat,* recognized Hearn's literary potential and lent encouragement. It was during Hearn's tenure on the *Times-Democrat* that his first book was published. His translations, which appeared in the Sunday *Times-Democrat,* attracted so much public attention that the *Picayune* and *States* put their own translators to work. The *States* challenged the *Times-Democrat* to a competition between translators for a sizable side bet. "We can scarcely consent to ask our translator, whose ability as a French and English scholar is known and appreciated in literary circles throughout this country, and who has won, from competent critics, both in Europe and America, the highest ecomiums, to enter into a purely local contest with rivals who have yet their spurs to win," loftily replied the *Times-Democrat* on June 16, 1886. Hearn left New Orleans in June, 1887, eventually settled in Japan, and went on to establish a literary reputation that was at its brightest seventy-five years ago. His death was reported by the *States* on September 28, 1904.

Hearn's days on the *Item* overlapped those of John P. Weichardt, who earned the nickname Quicksilver because of his seeming omnipresence and the flashing speed with which he operated. Weichardt also was called the King of the Flowers in recognition of the boutonniere he seldom was without. He set a standard of diligence and audacity that few, if any, succeeding reporters have been able to match. Some mornings Quicksilver would get to the mayor's office before the arrival of the incumbent, General William J. Behan. Presuming on the chief executive's friendship, he perused the official mail. He even wrote suggestions for replies and blithely printed news stories based on the smug assumption that Behan would follow his advice.[22]

Although it is true that in the beginning the *Item* steered a precarious course, the fact should not be forgotten that it was the first evening paper to make the grade in New Orleans. On October 24, 1879, Bigney was saying in an editorial: "The success of the *Item,* which from the first has been conducted on the cooperative principle, should prove the applicability of the system to our social and industrial situation. An honest, self-sustaining newspaper, by no means an unimportant entity in the history of a community, has been triumphantly established, and is now capable of holding its own with the oldest and best of our daily journals. In local circulation it is greater than the greatest." Noting the third anniversary of the *Item* on June 11, 1880, the rival *States* said: "We frankly confess that but for the struggle made in its first year by the *Item,* we would have had to have made it. . . . The heavy underbrush had been removed before this paper was planted."

Although Bigney was crediting the cooperative principle with the early strides made by the *Item,* the newspaper's days as a true cooperative were numbered. The ranks of the original partners began to break within a few months after the incorporation. By early 1878 Jewell and Hammond had hypothecated their shares to John W. Fairfax, a stock and bond broker, in obtaining loans. Harry Michel and Lafcadio Hearn made a visit to Fairfax's office at 171 Common Street and offered to buy the stock. Years later Michel said Fairfax's interest was whetted because he reasoned that the newspaper must have bright prospects if employees wanted to risk their own money in it.[23] At any rate, Fairfax kept the stock and by the fall of 1880 was demanding that he be put on the payroll in order that he could share in the revenue. Several communications were exchanged between Fairfax and the board of directors, the climax coming on December 14 when the secretary, William Bryan, indited a note to Fairfax in which he said:

> I am sorry to see that you misapprehend the subject had in view of the formation of the City Item Co-Operative Printing Company. It was organized solely for the benefit of its charter members — each one being assigned a special duty, with the understanding that a faithful performance of said duty would be exacted on the part of his associates. You were not one of the originators — therefore you were never assigned to any duty. Your stock was acquired by purchase and we continue to pay that same party to represent your interest. The mere fact of a person holding stock in a bank, insurance company or railroad does not entitle them to be president or secretary or treasurer, or any other paying position. It simply entitles them to a share of the net profits. If there are no profits it is a bad investment. Your contributions to the *Item* were volunteered. You were never employed until recently, when you were placed on the payroll, with the distinct promise in writing that you would increase the receipts sufficient to justify this additional outlay. Our books show that you have not done so. If you will come to the office and take the place of an employee and do his work, there will be no objection to your drawing the same salary as the balance.[24]

Perhaps Bryan would have been less forthright if he could have foreseen the future. Wilkinson died of yellow fever in 1878. On May 14, 1880, Cunniffe wrote to the board, saying he was ill and offering to dispose of his interest for six hundred dollars. It eventually was bought by Frank West. Magruder sold his stock to Michel. Bryan moved to Iberville Parish and established the *Iberville News.* By 1881 the *Item* fell under control of a triumvirate: Bigney, Fairfax, and Michel. After Bigney's death in 1886, Fairfax and Michel continued to run the paper until Michel left in 1889 to become manager of the Boylan Detective Agency. Michel sold his interest to Fairfax in 1892.[25]

For nearly a dozen years Fairfax was a powerful figure in *Item* councils, and toward the end of that period his was the lone voice of authority. Born in New Orleans in 1840, he worked as a youth as a printer for the Cincinnati *Enquirer.* Returning to New Orleans, he became a printer and assistant editor for the *Delta.* He entered the Civil War as a member of the Chasseurs au Pied. By 1870 Fairfax was a reporter for the *Republican.* He acquired wealth as a stock and bond broker. He married Virginia Washington of Virginia. They observed their sixtieth wedding anniversary on April 27, 1924. Fairfax died a few days later, on May 18, at his residence, 1535 Henry Clay Street.[26] In his later years he explained that he wanted to own the *Item* because he intended to give the paper to his elder son, H. W. Fairfax. But the latter decided to go to New York and become a broker. After his son passed up a publisher's career, Fairfax apparently lost interest in the *Item* and began looking for a way out.

The circumstances are not clear, but first he took steps that resulted in the appointment of the *Item*'s first and only woman editor. Her name was Julia Kendall, surely one of the most neglected of all New Orleanians who achieved distinction in their lives, but who were allowed to sink into obscurity after their deaths. Despite all of her activity, there is a dearth of records concerning Miss Kendall. She was a schoolteacher and principal, who may have been in her late thirties or early forties before she began a career in journalism. She was listed in the 1874 city directory as principal of the Webster and Jefferson schools, and in the 1877 book as principal of the Lower Girls High School. By 1879 she was principal of Peabody Normal, a state school for Negroes that operated in New Orleans between 1877 and 1888 with support from the Peabody Educational Fund. She was described as an excellent teacher.[27] In 1891, when she was forty-three years of age, the directory had her as a member of the editorial staff of the *Item,* and the next year finds her listed as associate editor. Word of her promotion to editor and general manager appears in the 1893 directory.

The first public intimation that Fairfax was contemplating changes appeared in the *Item* of December 11, 1892, in the form of a pickup note from the *Delta* saying he had severed his connections with the paper and was going on a trip north. On December 13 the *Item* published a special notice dated December 9 which said a meeting of the City Item Co-Operative Printing Company was held that day and a board of managers named, including Julia Kendall, H. C. Chaplain, J. R. Wells, James J. McGinty, and J. H. Heslin. It said a meeting of the board of directors followed and Julia Kendall was elected editor and general manager. Apparently Fairfax had put the operations into the hands of a group of his employees. He went off to Washington, New York, and Chicago, sending back a series of dispatches signed J.W.F. By January 26, 1893, he was back home, and the *Item* was printing on page one a long interview with him. The dispatches and the interview suggest he had not given up his ownership.

There were no drastic changes in the *Item*'s makeup or content, nothing to demonstrate a feminine touch at the controls, if, indeed, Miss Kendall busied herself with supervising the gathering and display of news or the formulation of editorial policy. No echoes from her regime reverberated over the years. She was seldom mentioned in later *Items.* On the twenty-fifth anniversary, June 11, 1902, the historian had this to say: "It was during the administration of Col. Fairfax that Miss Julia Kendall, a brilliant New Orleans woman and one of the first in the country to adopt newspaper work as a profession, was placed in a responsible position on the editorial section of the *Item.*" Even so, she was a Jane-come-lately to the

New Orleans press scene. Long before, Eliza Jane Poitevent had come out of Mississippi to marry the boss and, through inheritance, become owner and publisher of the *Picayune.* The boss was Alva Morris Holbrook, who died in 1876. His widow carried on and later married George Nicholson, business manager of the *Picayune.* She was the mother of Leonard K. Nicholson, who was president of the Times-Picayune Publishing Company in 1933 when the *States* was acquired and made the company's evening paper.

Miss Kendall died on February 20, 1915, at the age of sixty-seven. A four-line obituary notice appeared in the *Times-Picayune.* There was no mention in the *Item.* She left an estate of $15,229, most of it in utility stocks.[28]

Another early woman employee at the *Item* was Linda Bensel, a reporter who married James J. McGinty, the city editor.

Fairfax finally sold the *Item* to Eric W. Talen; Charles Burkhardt, Talen's brother-in-law, and printers George Kern and John Lagroue. Talen's name first is listed in the masthead as president and managing editor on November 13, 1893. It was the only inkling of the sale to be found in the paper. On April 13, 1894, Henry Dufilho's name was added to the masthead as associate editor. Little more than a month later, the *Item* was sold again, and entered its most flamboyant, most outrageous, and in some ways most successful period.

2

Lottery Switch-About

It was the end of 1879, and the Louisiana State Lottery Company was riding high, heading into the period of its greatest prosperity and power. Behind lay a victory in the 1879 Constitutional Convention which appeared to protect the company from the assaults of its enemies until its charter expired in 1894. Behind lay court decisions which gave reason to believe the company had nothing to fear from the judiciary. Behind — a clear warning to other journalists who might get out of line — lay the revenge wreaked upon two New Orleans newspapermen who dared attack the company. Publisher George W. Dupre and editor Henry J. Hearsey had been bilked out of their interests in the New Orleans *Democrat* by the machinations of the lottery, and the paper now had joined all of the other dailies in the city in a solid front of support.

Too far in the future to be seen through the golden haze lay the shoals on which the lottery would be wrecked. Charles T. Howard and John A. Morris, the lottery mil-

lionaires, knew their operation was controversial, but they had no reason then to suspect that in the years ahead the president of the United States himself would line up against their company. They had no foresight which would enable them to know that Hearsey would start a new newspaper with a respectful following, or that Dupre would join Hearsey as coproprietor. And certainly they could not know that in the lottery's desperate hour, with the end fast approaching, Hearsey and Dupre would play surprising roles. The details make a strange chapter in the story of the *States.*

As early as March 6, 1810, the legislature of the Orleans Territory approved a lottery to raise $10,000 for Christ Church (Episcopal) in New Orleans. In 1822 a legislative act sanctioned a lottery to provide $30,000 for the Presbyterian Church. And in 1826 St. Francis Church (Roman Catholic) was permitted to conduct a lottery which would bring in $20,000. In 1833 the Louisiana General Assembly prohibited lotteries. The ban was repealed in 1841. However, the state constitutions of 1845 and 1852 prohibited drawings and the selling of tickets. But the Constitution of 1864 authorized the legislature to license lotteries and gambling houses. Act 21 of 1866 licensed the vending of tickets and appropriated $50,000 from the lottery tax to Charity Hospital. In 1868 the carpetbag legislature granted a charter for a lottery operation to Charles T. Howard, who had been agent in New Orleans for the Kentucky State Lottery Company. Howard joined with John A. Morris, wealthy New York racetrack owner, and others in founding the Louisiana State Lottery Company.[1]

The company established headquarters in a bank building at St. Charles and Union streets, and held its first drawing on January 2, 1869.[2] Between 1870 and 1892 various efforts were made in the legislature either to rule out lotteries or to charter other companies that would challenge the Howard monopoly, but only once in this period did the company lose its control of state senators and representatives.[3] On that occasion a friendly federal judge saved the lottery.

The Louisiana lottery established a reputation for honesty in its drawings and prize payoffs. It won prestige by hiring Confederate Generals P. G. T. Beauregard and Jubal A. Early to preside at the major drawings, and saw to it that every winning ticket holder was given his money immediately, even when shares of capital prizes running as high as $300,000 were involved. It was the biggest business enterprise in the state, and by far the most profitable. By 1890 Representative Orren C. Moore, in a speech to Congress, reported that the company netted $8,232,800 in a single year on the sale of $28 million worth of tickets for ten regular and two special drawings. Representative H. Clay Evans said the profit actually was more than $13 million because all of the expenses for the twelve major drawings were paid by the smaller daily lotteries conducted by the company.[4] With such a gold mine, it is no wonder that Howard, Morris, and their successors wanted to silence critics.

Nowadays, when sovereign states run lotteries, churches raise money with bingo games, betting is legal at racetracks and the casinos at Las Vegas and Reno run night and day, the furor over the Louisiana lottery may seem overdone. The moral issue was important in the nineteenth century, however, and clergymen were among the leaders of the opposition, although the early history of lotteries that benefited churches was thrown up to them. Another factor in a growing swell of antilottery sentiment was the feeling that despite the purity of the drawings, the lottery actually was a fraud because of the astronomical odds against a ticket buyer. One compilation showed the chance of winning to be 1 in 76,076 in the major drawings.[5] Said the *Democrat*: "The man who buys a ticket every day at every drawing will have only one chance in eighty-four years to draw even the $243.35 prize. Old Methusaleh himself had he bucked up against the lottery from his earliest childhood to the day of his death and bought a ticket every day, would have found himself winner of $2678.85 after having spent about $250,000 on the lottery."[6] In the early days there were 108 policy shops in New Orleans. These were operated or controlled by ward bosses or other politicians who became beholden to the lottery.[7] Yet only 7 percent of the tickets were sold in Louisiana. The pipeline into the company's treasury stretched from every state in the Union.

There was another, overriding reason why some Louisianians hated and feared the lottery. The company had become a colossus which opponents said was corrupting government. One of the incorporators, Jesse R. Irwin, made an affidavit in 1886 which said Howard had used company money "for bribing members of the General Assembly of Louisiana. The sums paid out amounted to $300,000 during the first seven years of the company's existence." F. F. Wilder, another incorporator, corroborated the allegation.[8] In its anxiety to win public goodwill, the lottery spent considerable sums for activities that were the rightful responsibilities of government. For instance, on March 27, 1890, Wright Schaumburg, secretary to Mayor Joseph A. Shakspeare, wrote to M. A. Dauphin, lottery president, asking for immediate payment of $50,000 pledged by the company to help combat a flood that threatened the city. Schaumburg said the sum was needed to pay the workmen, and Dauphin sent a check by messenger.[9]

On December 19, 1875, a new daily newspaper appeared in New Orleans — the *Democrat,* published in the plant at 74 Camp Street formerly occupied by the defunct *Delta.* George

W. Dupre was principal owner of the paper, which he and associates had conceived as a Democratic organ to offset the influence of Republican publications. The first editor was Robert Tyler, son of President John Tyler.[10] Tyler soon was replaced by Henry James Hearsey, whose vitriolic editorials in the Shreveport *Times* in behalf of white supremacy and the Democratic party were earning him a reputation. The *Democrat* was begun as an evening paper, but on January 23, 1877, it moved into the morning field.

The lottery had found a foe. On March 8, 1878, the *Democrat* reported a national movement for enforcement of federal laws against the sending of gambling material through the mails:

> There is a very stringent Federal statute against the circulation of lottery matter through the United States mails, but the Louisiana State Lottery, which for nearly eight years owned State and Federal judges, newspapers, Governors, and legislators of this State, learned to entertain a very supreme contempt for laws of any sort. . . . This overgrown and arrogant monopoly assumed that laws were only made to enable courts and public officials to make money by accepting bribes. . . . Sometime ago we called attention to the fact that Mr. J. M. G. Parker, the Postmaster of New Orleans, was a large stockholder of the lottery, and was conniving at this gross violation of a very wise and beneficial law.[11]

The warm endorsement of the mail law by Dupre and Hearsey should not be forgotten as later pages in this chapter are read.

The lottery was jealous of its sole-licensed-operator status and moved promptly against agents of outside companies that sold tickets illegally. "On Monday," reported the *Democrat* on May 15, 1878, "Mr. Stanislas Plassan, an estimable gentleman and reputable merchant of this city, was arrested at his office and dragged before Recorder Smith, by Gaspaid J. Schreiber, one of Charles T. Howard's pimps and private detectives, on a trumped up charge of selling Havana lottery tickets. The charge is an infamous lie as Mr. Plassan has no more connection with selling Havana lottery tickets or any other lottery tickets than Howard and his brother thieves have with decency and honesty." The lottery countered with a $25,000 libel suit against Albert C. Janin, one of the proprietors of the *Democrat.* The *Democrat* claimed the suit was an attempt to crush the newspaper. On January 19, 1879, the *Democrat* said:

For months and years we have labored to show that the Lottery Company was a potent factor in State and city politics; that it debauched public as well as private morals, and that it is a powerful engine against the welfare of the people, inasmuch as it corrupted public sentiment, traded in public officers, and controlled public interests to its advantages. . . . It (the *Democrat*) recognized the fact that no party could remain pure which harbored this corrupting element, and no measure for public good was safe as long as it was hostile to such measures.[12]

The editorial campaign of the *Democrat* must have been a factor in a shift of public opinion which resulted in the passage by the legislature in January, 1879, of an act to revoke the charter of the lottery. The company countered with a suit in federal court, before Judge Edward C. Billings, a former attorney for the lottery, in which it was claimed that the company had a vested right until its charter expired on January 1, 1894. Said the *Democrat:*

That it will be sustained and the injunction prayed for perpetuated, we assume at the outset. When we take into consideration the litigants, a rich and unscrupulous corporation, fighting for very existence, on one side and a mere nominal defendant on the other, State officials having no actual issue, any other hypothesis would be unreasonable, with such a judge as Billings occupying the bench. . . . There must be a limit to the continued oppressions of the Federal courts and if that limit has not been reached in this instance, then the State may as well relinquish her autonomy and turn over the administration of her domestic affairs and the enforcement of her laws, civil and criminal, to the Federal judges and United States marshals.[13]

Then Hearsey wrote: "The Lottery Company owns Billings,

body and boots, by right of purchase and . . . he will certainly obey implicitly the instructions of the company and its attorneys in all matters which come before him, and which interest that institution."[14] As forecast, Billings granted the injunction that kept the lottery in business.

As a reward for the support of the Democratic party in the election and installation of Francis T. Nicholls as governor in 1877, Dupre was named state printer, using the facilities of his newspaper's composing room and press to produce such documents as the legislative journals. The award was regarded as a plum; but it proved to be poisoned fruit. Dupre and Nicholls had a falling out over patronage, and the strain was exacerbated when the *Democrat* favored a constitutional change which would have cut short the governor's term of office. At the same time, the lottery company was waging war against the *Democrat.*[15]

H. W. Green, who had been production superintendent of the suspended New Orleans daily, the *Republican,* was given a job in the composing room of the *Democrat,* then was fired. Threatening vengeance, he offered to sell to the *Item* information which he said would ruin the state printer.[16] His complaint that the printer had overcharged the state was investigated by the attorney general, a grand jury, and a special legislative committee. Gerard Stich, foreman at the *Picayune,* was named an umpire to determine whether the state had indeed been overbilled. He reported "a great diversity among printers as to what constitutes price and a half matter," a key point in Green's allegation. Finally, Stich concluded that the state had been undercharged $92.13 and overcharged $164.23, a difference of $72.50 instead of $800 as a grand jury reported. Governor Nicholls in his annual message said the facts did not warrant criminal prosecution.[17]

The legislative committee, by unanimous vote, exonerated

Dupre, and even recommended that he be paid $5,000 for printing for which he had not billed the state. The committee also reported that Dupre should have been paid $42,000 in cash for his work, as specified in his contract, and added that he actually had received only $1,900 in cash and $40,100 in state warrants. The committee told the legislature: "Your committee believes that the witness Green was procured to give the evidence that he did." The report cited Green's "splenetic and malicious motive," and included these quotations from a public hearing:

Q. How come you to bring charges against the State Printer, based upon the prices charged for the work?

A. (Green) I didn't bring any charges, the bill was brought to me.

Q. By whom?

A. That's a private matter.[18]

Green flatly declined to name the instigator. After the exoneration, the lottery company published in the *Picayune* an advertisement complaining that the committee was packed.[19] There can be little doubt that the company had a hand in Green's effort to discredit Dupre. Later Dupre was indicted for perjury in the presentation of printing bills to the state treasurer. He won a directed verdict when it was developed that the bills had not been delivered under oath. In the long run, Dupre was cleared of every charge brought against him.*[20]

The dispute over the warrants led to a clash between Dupre and Nicholls which might have resulted in a duel, although it never did. While Green's charges were pending, the issuance

* On December 16, 1878, George Dupre, Henry J. Hearsey, John Augustin, and Albert C. Janin of the *Democrat* brought a $25,000 damage suit in federal court against Mr. and Mrs. George Nicholson and George W. Lloyd of the *Picayune*. The plaintiffs contended that the *Picayune* maliciously published charges that fraudulent claims were made for superfluous state printing. They dropped the suit on January 27, 1880.

of state warrants to the printer was held up, and Dupre paid a visit to the governor's office. Nicholls, it will be remembered, was a Confederate war hero who lost an eye, an arm, and a leg in battle. Nicholls told Dupre he had not instructed the attorney general to tie up the warrants in the treasury. Dupre replied that he regarded the withholding of the warrants as an act of the Nicholls administration.

"I can say that your statement is a falsehood," retorted the governor.

"I cannot answer that," said Dupre. "You are Governor of the state and a crippled soldier. To an insult such as you have inflicted upon me there can be but one response, and that is a blow. I refrain, because you are governor of the state and a cripple."

"I will waive all that, sir," replied Nicholls. "I shall soon retire from office, and I will be responsible to you then."[21]

In spite of the legislative committee's report clearing Dupre, the state Senate declared the post of state printer vacant and authorized the governor to appoint a new man. On March 8, 1879, Nicholls named George Nicholson of the *Picayune*.

By now the lottery had found a means of putting Dupre and Hearsey out of business. Dupre had used $40,000 worth of state warrants as collateral for bank loans to provide operating funds for the *Democrat*. A suit was brought in federal court by a British citizen challenging the validity of the warrants. A court decision left the warrants valueless. Then the banks foreclosed, and Dupre and Hearsey lost their interests in the *Democrat*.[22] Said the *Democrat* of the lottery:

> That rotten and corrupt concern has already initiated two suits against the *Democrat* for libel, each for $25,000. In addition to this, the company has picked up some adventurer by the name of Benjamin, claiming, at the instigation of his masters, to be a citizen of England, and to have an interest in state warrants, who has applied to the United States Circuit

Court for an injunction to prevent the payment of $40,000 of warrants held by the *Democrat* on the general fund. These warrants discredited and our cash money expended for the material and work conscientiously done and delivered to the state, necessarily the resources of the *Democrat* would be crippled and its credit damaged to such an extent that bankruptcy and the suspension of the paper would be the issue. This was the calculation of the Lottery Company and their calculations were well made."[23]

On April 24, 1879, this editorial appeared in the *Democrat*:

One of our associates, the state printer, was actually assailed by two stacked grand juries and indicted by a third. Every ring, monopoly and bondholder in the state combined and arrayed themselves against us. And finally, with all the warrants the state owes us, for a year's work done and thousands of dollars of materials furnished out of our general business, enjoined by a Federal court, presided over by an infamous judge, the tool and property of the rings we have fought, the Democratic governor of the state, when for the only time in the career of the paper we needed credit and official support, arbitrarily and against his own construction of the law, took from us the state printing and gave it to the New Orleans *Picayune*, a journal that, in its forty years of experience, never struck an honest blow for an honest cause in the state, and which has been the persistent enemy of the Democratic party.

Under these burdens and without capital — with only the affection and support of an impoverished people — we have been forced, at the very opening of the Convention alongside of which we had hoped to fight for the redemption of the people and State and for the final triumph of all the issues we had raised, to surrender the *Democrat* into the hands of other parties. With these explanations the proprietors of the *Democrat,* who have conducted it during the past three years, withdraw and bid a journalistic adieu to their readers.[24]

The reference was to the Constitutional Convention of 1879, which allowed the lottery's charter to continue in force until January 1, 1894, but which tried to take away the company's monopoly status.

Not long after the names of Dupre and Hearsey disappeared from the masthead of the *Democrat,* the federal court reversed itself and restored the value of the warrants. The name of E. A. Burke, an adventurer with lottery connections, now appeared as managing editor of the *Democrat.* He was the same Edward A. Burke who, elected state treasurer, sold $827,000 in worthless state bonds for his own gain and later fled into exile in Honduras in order to escape trial.

Hearsey's editorial pen was idle for only a few months. On January 3, 1880, he produced the first issue of the *States.* The new paper soon was involved in a new lottery wrangle, this time over a proposal to charter a second lottery, the New Orleans Lottery Company. "We have always regarded the policy of granting lottery charters as pernicious," wrote Hearsey, "but the constitutional convention took a different view of the question; confirmed the charter of the Louisiana Lottery Company on condition that it should renounce its monopoly privilege and authorized the legislature to grant other similar charters. The new company will pay $40,000 into the treasury, $10,000 for the Charity Hospital at Shreveport and the residue for the benefit of public schools. This money will be of great use to our hospitals and schools, and the charter should be granted."[25] Later Hearsey said:

> It is too late now to discuss the moral phase of this question and it is idle to say that the establishment of other companies will aggravate the evil. The present company, with its Briarens-like hands, reaches out to every corner of the land. Its offices are found in almost every square of the city. Indeed, the first thing that strikes the attention of the stranger visiting New Orleans is all the pervading character of the Louisiana Lottery Company. It has become almost a part of the city; its tickets are for sale in, we may say, thousands of windows. Its power and its influence are felt everywhere. If it is permitted to hold its exclusive privileges until 1895 it will be to the State what it is now to the city, and will be able to perpetuate its power indefinitely.[26]

When the *Times* suggested Hearsey had not been consistent when he supported establishment of a new lottery after he had fought the Louisiana State Lottery so strenuously, he wrote an editorial. The editor of the *States,* he said, "believes that there is a vice of consistency as well as a vice of inconsistency, and that both are injurious to truth and calculated to mar the usefulness of public men and journals." He said he had opposed the existing lottery because the company held its charter "by a notoriously corrupt act of a corrupt legislature." "We assailed it as a pernicious monopoly, and we assailed it as a demoralized institution." But, he continued, the Constitutional Convention "in consideration of the surrender of its claim to monopoly rights, rescued the lottery company from the courts; ratified its contract in the Constitution, and rendered any further attacks upon it, or efforts to destroy it, futile, puerile and factious." The question of morality was outdated.[27]

Thus did Hearsey justify his turnabout, which reached the full 180 degrees by 1890 when the Louisiana state lottery, which had managed meanwhile to exclude any competitors, began a campaign to continue its existence after the expiration of its charter. When the Mississippi River flooded in the spring of 1890, the lottery company sent a relief boat to the affected area. Aboard was a *States* reporter who wrote that flood victims "were one and all profuse in their expression of thanks to the Lottery." And Hearsey came forth with an editorial which must be read in amazement when the writing of his *Democrat* days is recalled. "There are a great many persons," he said,[28] "who are denouncing the Louisiana Lottery Company as a very wicked institution, seemingly forgetful of the fact that during the dark days of Reconstruction the Louisiana Lottery came forward in the hour of need and sore trial just as it has done during the present floods, and helped the people with its money and its influence to establish home rule in Louisiana and to throw off the yoke of negro domination which was fast debauching and ruining the state." The *States* said a former generation considered the lottery an innocent pastime. Lottery owners were pictured as public benefactors and patrons of the arts, as well as constructive businessmen.

"With a record thus marked with charitable deeds and munificent benefactions, they come before the General Assembly and the people to offer to share their gains with the state to the extent of half a million dollars a year, for a period of twenty-five years. . . . They ask that the question may be put to the people, and the people have a paramount right to vote upon it, being the sole and final arbiters and judges of the fundamental law." This was the expression of an editor who a dozen years earlier found the lottery "rotten and corrupt," an editor who had lost his share of a newspaper because of the ruthlessness and chicanery of the company.*

Although the lottery company since 1869 had paid a state license fee of only $40,000 a year, John A. Morris now proposed that the 1890 legislature submit to the electorate a constitutional amendment which would permit his enterprise to operate for an additional twenty-five years, and he offered to pay $500,000 a year for the extension. Eventually he raised the offer to $1,250,000 a year, a windfall which was enough to tempt the lawmakers and voters of the state.

On May 12, 1890, opening day of the legislative session, the Anti-Lottery League published the first issue of a new daily newspaper in New Orleans, the *New Delta*, with C. Harrison Parker and John C. Wickliffe as coeditors. It was the only antilottery daily in the city. Of all the newspapers in the state, daily and weekly, there were 173 in favor of the lottery and 28 opposed.[29] The lottery spent $2 million a year on newspaper advertising.[30]

High drama marked the passage of the lottery bill through the legislature. The measure was passed by both houses, but Governor Nicholls vetoed it. The House overrode the veto.

* The *States* was indignant when another paper reported that Emaniel Bohner remarked, just before shooting himself to death, "The Louisiana Lottery has been my curse." Responded the *States* in an editorial on January 2, 1891: "The causes of suicide, indeed, are as numerous as the passions of human nature; and we doubt if there is a single incentive to this sad work less potent than lottery playing."

When the matter came before the Senate, floor leaders of the lottery found they were one vote short of the required two-thirds majority. Lying ill in his apartment at the Mayer Hotel, several blocks from the State Capitol, was Senator J. Fisher Smith of Many, in Sabine Parish, a staunch supporter of the lottery. When his condition deteriorated and he was unable to go to the Capitol to cast his vote, although a carriage was kept waiting outside his hotel, Smith suggested that the Senate convene in his apartment in a maneuver that would make his ballot legal. A parliamentary snarl prevented this, and the next day Smith died. Commented the *States*: "His sense of obligation to his people triumphed even in the very presence of the grave and he demanded, nay pled, to be accorded the privilege and opportunity of casting as his last act on earth, his vote for what he conceived to be the most sacred interests of the state."[31]

It was the *New Delta,* however, which provided a memorable account of events:

> The closing scenes were of that marvelous character to impress themselves not only upon the State of Louisiana, but to the entire nation.
>
> The origin of debauchery had been stricken by the hand of death. The carriage which stood so long at the door of the dying senator's hotel gave place to the hearse. The hand of God had stayed the last vote that was to override the veto of the chief executive. The elements had predicted the fatal end. When the lottery debate opened in the House of Representatives a black canopy covered the heavens. The voice of the Lottery leader in the opening speech was drowned by the voice of nature, and as he closed a blinding flash fell athwart the sky, followed by a crash, as if the very ribs of the globe had been split asunder. Members cowered in their seats and a shudder went through the vast assembly at the supervening darkness. The lightning had extinguished the lights and the same fiery breath had left its halo in the Senate chamber at the other end of the building, and the little glass bulbs that hung in the chandelier then gave forth a light that came not from the dynamo governed by the hand of man, but straight from its reservoir in the bosom of the Divine Master. The light of God's truth had

gone out in the hall where Shattuck* stood and He had placed his seal upon the Senate chamber. Following the lightning came the grim message of death to invade that hall, and snatch away the vote that was to place the capsheath upon this iniquitous legislation. He had been there before and He came again.[32]

The Louisiana Supreme Court eventually decided that the legislation had been properly passed, and as a constitutional amendment was not subject to gubernatorial veto. It was placed before the voters in an election on March 22, 1892, and was overwhelmingly rejected. The vote was 4,225 for the lottery and 157,422 against it.[33] The result was an anticlimax; the fate of the Louisiana lottery already had been sealed.

In 1890 President Benjamin Harrison asked Congress to pass a stringent, easily enforceable law to take the place of existing federal legislation which did not serve its purpose of barring lottery material from the mails. A bill was passed on September 16, 1890.[34] Earlier the *States* had complained that the measure "attacks the press, as it excludes from the mails all newspapers containing lottery advertisements."[35] On September 19, 1890, Hearsey and Dupre, now joint proprietors of the *States,* along with J. Pinckney Smith, business manager, announced that their newspaper would begin to print lottery advertisements. "'The *States,* until this day, has never held any relations whatever with the Louisiana State Lottery," said an editorial on that day. "Our columns never contained its advertisements, even after we had determined to advocate the extension of its charter conditioned upon the payment of a high license to the state of Louisiana."

On September 29 the *States* reported that its September 27 editions had been barred from the mails because they contained lottery advertisements. The September 29 issue put the

* The reference was to Representative S. O. Shattuck of Calcasieu Parish, a lottery floor leader.

following announcement into the space where the lottery advertisement had appeared: "Lottery advertisements excluded from this space in obedience to the law of Congress recently passed. For copies of the *Daily States* containing lottery advertisements apply to express agents everywhere."[36]

The *States* joined other newspapers in publishing editions containing lottery advertisements which were not mailed. Mail subscribers received otherwise identical editions from which the offending matter had been deleted. On November 12, 1890, Inspector W. T. Sullivan, of the Eastern District of Louisiana, swore out the first affidavit charging violation of the new law. He accused Pinckney Smith of knowingly mailing to Waco, Texas, on September 27, copies of the *States* including lottery advertisements. Smith surrendered[37] but never was indicted, and the government did not pursue the case. On February 13, 1891, Dupre deliberately courted arrest in a test of the law. Postmaster S. M. Eaton made an affidavit which said Dupre mailed a *States* edition containing lottery matter, and also sent a letter with a lottery ticket enclosed. The letter was addressed to A. J. Bachemin at Baton Rouge and said:

> Enclosed you will find one-twentieth of lottery ticket No. 40296 of the Louisiana State Lottery, of the February 17th drawing. Price one dollar.
>
> That ticket, among others, I bought of the widow whose name she, herself, stamps on all tickets she sells, for you must know that she supports herself and her several children on the commission of 15 per cent which the Lottery allows her on all tickets she can sell.
>
> I want you to help her, yourself, besides, you must get such of your friends, who do not believe that to play lottery is to play with Hell fire, to club with you and order lots of tickets through Mrs. Pasley and I will risk the penalty of law, myself, and transmit, at my own expense and risks by mail, your monthly orders.
>
> Read the circular enclosed. I will send you a similar one after every drawing, hereafter.[38]

Dupre was arrested on February 17 for depositing at the

post office another letter containing lottery tickets. On February 18 he was indicted by a federal grand jury for mailing a newspaper containing lottery advertising. On February 27 Dupre was locked in parish prison when he declined to post a surety bond pending determination of the case against him. On March 2 attorney Hannis Taylor of Mobile asked the United States Supreme Court for writs of habeas corpus for Dupre and for John L. Rapier of the Mobile *Register,* who had been arrested on a similar charge.[39] They were released pending court action, and the charges later were dropped.

The *States* editorialized:

> Mr. Dupre has no apology to make for his action in this matter. He is prompted in his move to test this law in the courts by the spirit which should animate every citizen in a free government; a spirit which, while it pervades the hearts of the people, is the best security of liberty, and without which the forms of constitution and laws, however admirable they may be, are but as dust and cinders in the pathway of the enemies of free institutions. . . . It is the determination of Mr. Dupre to test this law to the very utmost. Indeed, when the courts get through with him or he gets through with the courts, the country will know whether the police powers of the States can be usurped by the federal government and whether or not the liberty of the press can be hampered and restricted whenever some sect or faction shall set themselves up as the dictators of what is public morality.[40]

The *New Delta* was not impressed by the arguments of the *States* and other prolottery newspapers:

> A free press is one that is at perfect liberty to express itself upon any side of any question affecting the public welfare. It is one that is under no obligation to any man or set of men. Can any lottery paper in the State of Louisiana honestly and truthfully declare that it is in that condition? Can any of them open their money drawer without having the dollars of the lottery company staring them in the face? . . . There is not one in the whole gang that has not "seen" the lottery magnates before it espoused the lottery side. . . . That is our "free press" in Louisiana.[41]

Hopes that the lottery could continue to distribute its tickets nationwide and collect its revenues by using express company delivery instead of the mails were short-lived. The attorney general ruled that the postmaster general had the right to prevent express companies from carrying lottery material, and the U.S. Express Company and Adams Express decided to refuse such shipments. The sale of tickets fell off rapidly, and on December 1, 1890, the Chicago *Tribune* was saying: "The Louisiana Lottery is in a moribund condition. . . . Before the postal law was passed the Louisiana State Lottery Company stock was worth $1,400 a share, and now it goes begging at $400."[42]

The death blow was delivered on February 1, 1892, when the United States Supreme Court upheld validity of the postal law. On February 3 Morris withdrew the company's offer of $1,250,000 a year for a new charter. "It is my purpose and that of my associates to respect the law and abstain from violating it in any manner," he said.[43] The last drawing in New Orleans was held in December, 1893. The company moved to Spanish Honduras and used fast boats to smuggle tickets into the United States. Even this source of revenue dried up when the federal government eventually put on a drive against lottery agents.*

During the years when the lottery was a potent force in Louisiana affairs, as well as a big advertiser, the *Item* was one of its more outspoken journalistic adherents. From Honduras the company no longer could exert its influence. In 1894 the *Item* asked in an editorial whether four New Orleans banks were cashing tickets of the Honduras Lottery Company, the name under which the old Louisiana firm was operating. "A wonderful thing this great lottery company," said the *Item*.

* The Honduras National Lottery Company continued its clandestine activity in the United States until June 3, 1907, when thirty-two men, including fifteen New Orleanians, were reported by the *States* to have been fined a total of $284,000 in federal court at Mobile on charges of conspiring to cause interstate circulation of lottery advertisements. The defendants agreed to break up the company, which had been operating a printing establishment at Wilmington, Delaware.

"Changed in name it may be, but in nature, methods and general rottenness it is the same old thing which the people of Louisiana got rid of only after twenty-five years of the hardest kind of struggle, and at an expense of hundreds of thousands of dollars. However, it was finally whipped, but it lingers under cover and continues to possess itself of many a hard-earned dollar for which no return is known to come. It must be killed; it has only been scotched. The *Item* will take pleasure in assisting in its slaughter."[44]

The *Item*'s change of heart could be attributed to a new owner, one Dominick C. O'Malley. He was the same O'Malley whose name was listed as one of the operators of an illegal lottery which sprang up after the departure of the Louisiana company, and one which had to compete with the tickets shipped in from Honduras.

But why did Hearsey and Dupre switch their attitudes so drastically? Hearsey's explanation that the 1879 Constitutional Convention cloaked the lottery in a garment of legality is not completely satisfactory, especially in view of the fact that the company managed to remain a monopoly until the end.

It must be remembered that the *States* published lottery advertisements for only a few weeks. The *New Delta* charged that every prolottery paper had "seen" the lottery magnates before it espoused the cause. The *New Delta* offered no date and place as proof. Of course, a subsidy could be subtle. A few years later an editor, Joseph Mark Leveque, wrote as though it were accepted fact that the lottery bought subscriptions in wholesale lots to some papers. He used the plural, but he did not name the *States*.

The most believable explanation for the *States*'s turnabout lies in the fact that Hearsey lost ownership control to Dupre, who held half interest at the time of the last crisis, while Hearsey and Pinckney Smith each had one-quarter. Somewhere along the line Dupre made his peace with the lottery company, as did Smith.

The respect with which Hearsey was held by his contemporaries supports a disbelief that the peppery major was a bribe-taker. Bigoted? Certainly. Mercurial? Yes. Inconsistent? Obviously. Reckless? Demonstrably. Irresponsible? Of course. Vindictive? Highly. Imprudent? He could not hold the reins of the paper he alone founded.

Venal? Never.

3

Hearsey Sires the *States*

His editorials provided more heat than light.

His preoccupation with the Civil War and the Lost Cause helped to keep old wounds from healing, and contributed to the let's-live-in-the-past mentality that was so costly to the South.

His racism was unreasoning. So was his scorn of Italian immigrants. His belief in Judge Lynch was shocking.

But Henry James Hearsey was a man who would not be silenced, who could not be ignored.

For twenty years the *States* was his voice.

After the Louisiana State Lottery Company maneuvered Henry J. Hearsey's ouster from the *Democrat,* he decided to publish his own paper, and on January 3, 1880, Number 1 of Volume I of the *Daily States* appeared on the streets. Hearsey invested $2,250 in the venture.[1] In an editorial in the first issue he explained the choice of a name. He said he had considered *Herald, Sun, News, Post, Crescent,* and other designations, but all were rejected because in each case "some unfortunate journal bearing it in this city" had perished. "We are devoted to the rights of the States and the preservation of the principles of the constitution which guarantees these rights," he continued, hence the name *States.* The title was changed to the *New Orleans States* on March 19, 1916.[2] The *New Orleans States and New Orleans Item* was the lengthy masthead designation for a period after the two papers were merged on September 15, 1958. This was shortened to the *New Orleans States-Item,* and finally on September 21, 1970, to *The States-Item.*

Hearsey's first edition was produced in the job-printing shop of M. Sagendorph at 90 Camp Street, on the uptown, river corner of Camp and Natchez streets, the site now occupied by the Dameron-Pierson Company's office supplies store, the present address being 400 Camp Street.[3] The edition of three hundred two-page papers was run off on a one-cylinder press turned by a blind and elderly Negro.[4] The first floor of the building was used as an auction mart and was crammed with furniture and bric-a-brac. A passage and stairway on the right led to the printing office. Sagendorph allowed Hearsey to use the passageway for a business office, and a room twelve by fourteen feet on the second floor for the editorial quarters. Alexander Walker, Jr., who served as cashier and clerical assistant, had a long, high bookkeeper's desk in the passageway. Facing the street was a three-foot-long counter over which Walker did business with the public. The windows of the upstairs room looked out onto a rubbish heap on one side and a damp, brick-paved courtyard on the other. Hearsey wrote at a flat-topped desk. Judge Alexander Walker had a rolltop desk, and Edwin L. Jewell sat in a corner. He had no desk and worked as best he could with newspapers piled around him.* When the *States* began to gain circulation and advertising linage the auctioneer moved, and the newspaper took over the entire first floor. A new press was ordered, and Huey McManus was installed as pressman in charge. While waiting for delivery of the new press, the *States* had to announce it could accept no new subscriptions.[5]

On the editorial page of the first issue was a note in which Hearsey showed a humor that was not always evident in the years ahead. "We are not surprised by the complaint that New Orleans newspapers are lacking in enterprise," he wrote. "Thursday morning, for instance, there was not a single journal in the city that contained a single item of news of later date than last year." Thursday, of course, had been New Year's Day, and the morning papers, as always, were covering the events of the day before.

A few days later the joke was on Hearsey. He published an editorial, "Degraded Journalism," in which he said:

> That this community is patient to a fault, as witness its toleration for over a year, of so-called "society" columns in two of the leading journals of the city, wherein are dragged into public notice every week the names of ladies and gentlemen who have no connection whatever with public life, and certainly neither seek nor desire notoriety at the hands of the press. There was a time indeed when the Journals of New Orleans were conducted with the spirit of chivalry and refinement of which the South is justly celebrated and justly proud, but the era seems to have passed. Now every week is observed the vulgar practice of publishing column after column of "society" news in which the names of modest and retiring women are handled with familiarity—all their movements noted—their very dresses described—the list of their gentlemen friends published—in fine, are held up to public gaze as freely as are those of second rate actresses in the flash papers of New York.
>
> Witness the weekly departments in the *Picayune* and *Times*. The writers, evidently unacquainted with the majority of those described in

* Veteran employee George C. Blackwell exhibited in 1924 old payroll records showing that the *States* pressroom wages in 1880 totaled eighty dollars a week, and the composition costs were only slightly higher.

them, publish therein the name of every lady who may happen to appear in public, coupling it with those of gentlemen, larding it with adjectives intended to be complimentary and dogging her through the walks of private life, and hold up to the world her every word, look and movement. Refinement and delicacy are thrown to the winds in these wholesale "society" advertisements, and the privacy of homes is invaded for the purpose of glutting the public with the "news". . . .

Ah, it makes the papers sell? True, it does. It gratifies the gossip and scandal monger, and furnishes a vehicle for many a shaft of nicely feathered malice, prepared by anonymous contributors to the columns. And then—to be sure—when a lady hears that her name has appeared, clothed in dubious flattery and connected with perhaps that of some gentleman, she buys a copy — of course she does. So, too, do her indignant friends and triumphant enemies. Yes indeed — it makes the papers sell! But at best it is a puerile toadyism that degrades the journal from its legitimate and undignified position.[6]

The reaction must have been immediate and vehement. Eleven days later Hearsey wrote an editorial captioned "Our Society Column":

Complaints are frequent that the "society" columns of our contemporaries, the *Times* and *Picayune,* do not give the news accurately, are full of errors in their description of toilets, etc., and frequently omit notices of the most recherche entertainments given in the city. The *States* therefore will now assume the leading position in the matter, and will give an accurate and minutely detailed summary of all social events occurring in New Orleans. The initial step will be taken tomorrow, when we will publish a careful description of the most elegant entertainment given this winter, with names and toilets in full.[7]

The editor knew how to get divorced from a position, and quickly when it was politic to do so.

From the earliest days the *States* took a crusading interest in municipal problems. Its first campaign, in March, 1880, was concerned with the disposal of night soil in the period before indoor plumbing and sewerage systems. "How We are Poisoned," was the headline over an interview with Mr. Horter of the Sanitary Association, who inspected the nuisance wharf at Robin Street.[8] From the contractor it was learned that he was paid fifty cents a load for disposing of about 250 loads a day of the matter collected by wagons making their rounds through the city. Horter complained of carelessness. "The stuff was spilt all over the wharf, on the top and sides of the boat, and a great deal into the water. I discovered that frequently the valves of the boat are opened, and the night soil is dumped into the river right there at the wharf. At times the boat is taken only as far as the middle of the river and there emptied." He noted that the nuisance wharf was in the heart of the city, "where many a good ship would be lying, but for its presence. As it is, no vessels can lie within two hundred yards of the place, as the captains and their families and crews cannot stand the effluvia." Horter said there was an odor as far away as Annunciation Street when the wind was wrong. "Even at the distance the vessels are placed, the water is doubtless very foul, and yet the water casks of these vessels have to be filled with this river water. Is it a wonder some dreadful sickness often breaks out on shipboard?" The inspector said he was told that because of an eddy, foul water from the wharf sometimes backed up to the point from which the waterworks took its water.

The next day the *States* followed up with an account from its own reporter. He said the boat was supposed to be taken below the city and emptied twice a day, the discharge of a full load requiring an hour or longer. The *States* reported that on a recent evening Martin O'Rourke, policeman assigned to the wharf, sat on the wheel which opened the valve for half an hour while a large portion of its contents was discharged on the spot. "When it is understood that fifty cents to a dollar is paid for every load taken on the boat, the philosophy of discharging a portion at the wharf, thus enabling the boat to receive a greater number of loads in one day, also is understood," the reporter wrote.

By April 16, 1880, Hearsey was writing: "The evening

newspaper, with its numerous and rapidly succeeding editions, has become one of the institutions of the age. New Orleans is perhaps the only great city in the Union in which this branch of journalism has been neglected, and this neglect is not flattering to the enterprise and activity of our population." He added:

> Undoubtedly the scrawny evening editions of our morning contemporaries, springing up before their time into this breathing world, unfinished and half made up, have done a great deal to delay the full and perfect development of evening journalism by presenting it to our public more as a sort of catch-penny fraud than legitimate and useful enterprise . . . the day is near at hand when our evening newspapers will assume their proper importance and become far more valuable to the business community than the large, expensive, cumbersome and unprofitable morning sheets. Our excellent evening contemporary, the *Item,* was the pioneer in true evening journalism in this city.

It was the period in which the morning papers produced the so-called fly sheets for sale in the afternoon.

By June 7, 1880, the Baton Rouge *Sugar Planter* was saying the success of the *States* was unparalleled in newspaper history. The circulation had reached 5,200 daily by May 21, and by September 6, with 6,114 sales, the *States* said it was the largest daily edition published in the city.

For nearly twenty-one years Hearsey provided the heartbeat of the *States.* In 1900 Joseph Mark Leveque wrote in the *Standard History of New Orleans,* edited by Henry Rightor, that Hearsey was "the most conspicuous editor of the State. He has made himself so by his singular genius of bitterness, sarcasm and ridicule in controversy. No one approaches him in invective and some of his editorials during heated political campaigns are remarkable pieces of work. Not in the history of the country possibly has there been a man with greater power of fierce sarcasm and ridicule. Single editorials have frequently been the talk — the sensation of the city." Leveque said the *States* started "with little pretension to a newspaper," and its chief claim to attention was its editorial page "and the courage and resolution with which it approached its chosen task of reform." He reported the paper became "one of the most substantial newspaper properties in the South."[9]

The historian William Ivy Hair, whose research into Hearsey's character and philosophy has not been approached in thoroughness and perception by that of any other scholar, has written that "in lasting influence no Louisiana Bourbon rated above Henry J. Hearsey. . . . Major Hearsey was a man of many hates. But he displayed an ardent love for at least two things: the Lost Cause and whiskey. Florid-faced and goateed, Hearsey perfectly played the role of a Dixie Don Quixote; with his circa 1830 nullification rhetoric, his pistol duels and mint juleps, he seemed like an out-of-date burlesque on Southern manners. Yet his ability to mold public opinion was no laughing matter." Hair said Hearsey "considered it to be one of his special missions to teach the new generation to hate; he was keenly determined that men too young to remember the Civil War and Reconstruction should learn to revere the 'old war whoops and cries.' If they did not, it would be 'better that such boys should have died in their infancy.' Hearsey was equally firm in his opposition to Negro schools because 'the very worst nigger for a voter is an educated nigger.' "[10]

Edward Larocque Tinker related that "although every night of his adult life he was intoxicated, his speech never thickened nor did his floriated manners ever become less punctilious. At a certain point in his potations, his friends always put him on one of the little mule drawn street cars. When it arrived at his corner, if he were able he got out under his own steam and steered a scolloped *(sic)* course home. But if he were not, the driver always deserted his car and, with the help of some passengers, carried him a half-block and deposited him on his doorstep, after carefully ringing the bell."[11]

Hearsey was born on November 21, 1840, near Thompson's

Creek, West Feliciana Parish, the son of James Price Hearsey and Caroline Generelly Hearsey. As a youth he started the *Feliciana Constitutionalist* and showed such promise that he was appointed editor of the established and influential Woodville *Republican.* At the start of the Civil War he joined the Wilkinson Rifles as a private, serving as part of the Sixteenth Mississippi.[12] He progressed to the post of regimental brigadier assistant quartermaster, being discharged with the rank of major. After the war he established the *East Texas Bulletin* at Marshall, then moved to Shreveport, where he helped start the *Times.* His work in Shreveport prompted George W. Dupre to bring him to New Orleans as editor of the *Democrat.* Hearsey was married in 1878 to Martha Mary Morris. The couple was childless. He died of Bright's disease on October 30, 1900, at his home at 929 Dorgenois Street.

The *States* was only twenty-four days old when Hearsey fought a pistol duel with Major E. A. Burke, who had taken his place on the *Democrat.* They exchanged insults in editorials, a challenge was delivered and accepted, and at 2:20 P.M. on January 27, 1880, the principals and their seconds entered carriages and set out for the rendezvous at the old Beard place on Metairie Road, about halfway between the New Canal and the Mississippi River. The carriages made detours in order that there would be no police interference. They arrived at about the same time, Hearsey accompanied by Captain Leon Jastremski and Guy Carleton, his seconds, and Burke by Page M. Baker and Richard Weightman. While the principals waited some distance apart at the nearby house, their seconds picked out a spot in a field at the rear which was shaded by a large oak tree. Hearsey and Burke showed no nervousness. Burke wore a glove on his left hand, and had a pink carnation in his buttonhole. Hearsey, attired in a dark suit, had the slender cane which was his usual companion on the street. The seconds measured off ten paces, and the two parties moved to the scene of combat. In the group were two surgeons, Doctors Joseph Scott and D. C. Holliday. While the principals smilingly conversed with their friends, the smoothbore dueling pistols were loaded. Hearsey and Burke were placed in the positions they had drawn, both in the shade of the tree. The pistols were put into their hands and they were instructed not to fire before the count of *one* or after *three.*

Page Baker called out, in a clear, ringing voice, "One," and the antagonists fired simultaneously. They remained motionless in their positions, neither having been hit. The seconds met, those representing Hearsey asking Burke's friends whether their principal was ready to make an apology. It was decided the combat should proceed. The editors were allowed to leave their positions while the pistols were reloaded. They walked about, each chatting with his supporters, until the weapons were ready. Then they took their places and fired again, the pistols making a single report. The result was the same. This time the seconds agreed the duel would end with the provision that Burke would declare he did not doubt the honor and bravery of Hearsey. Then the two men advanced toward each other and shook hands.[13]*

In the first few weeks of the *States's* existence Hearsey, who had no stomach — and certainly no head — for the business side of newspapering, found himself in financial difficulties. He kept the paper alive by selling a part ownership to Erwin B. Craighead, who must have had an inheritance or some other source of funds because only two years earlier he had started his apprenticeship on the staff of the *Times* at ten dollars a week. For nearly two years the *States* masthead list-

* In an editorial in the *Item* on January 28, 1880, Mark Bigney regretted that his "esteemed friends," Hearsey and Burke, fought an illegal duel. "We understand it to be the intent of some of our legislators," Bigney added, "to so amend the duelling laws as to protect duels from police interference; to make it an imperative condition of all such meetings that the fight must continue until one or both are killed, and to hold the survivor, in case there be one, to a rigid accountability for the blood he sheds. This would give an air of serious solemnity to such affairs of honor."

ed Hearsey and Craighead as proprietors, the latter being manager. Craighead later wrote, referring to himself in the third person: "In this period he found out that it was a position not suited to his taste or capacity. So he sold his interest and retired, leaving the paper free of encumbrance of any sort and in position to be advanced by his successor, Mr. J. Pinckney Smith. What the writer gained from the association was experience, which he has always thought well worth the money he paid for it — experience which taught him that his vocation was that of an editor and not that of a business manager."[14] He went on to become editor of the Mobile *Register.*

Smith was a silent partner for the first period of his connection with Hearsey. After Craighead's departure the *States* masthead began to list the proprietors as Hearsey and Elmore. The Elmore was Minor Martin Elmore, son of Hearsey's longtime friend, Judge William A. Elmore. Elmore, who served as city editor, was only twenty-five years old when he died of an intermittent fever on September 20, 1883. "We do not feel prepared today to pay the tribute to our young and beloved associate's memory that his gentle and manly characteristics deserve," wrote the sorrowing Hearsey.[15] Details of Elmore's share in the *States* are obscure. The paper was operated as an unchartered company for its first thirteen years, and records of the ownership arrangements are lacking. It may have been that Elmore purchased an interest with $1,000 that he borrowed from his father on November 1, 1880. However, the inventory of his estate listed total assets of $1,125 and included no mention of stock in the *States.* Among the assets listed was a $500 promissory note issued by Pinckney Smith on August 28, 1883, in payment for shares in the paper.[16] Elmore was connected with the *States* for about two and one-half years.*

* The estate inventory reflects the economics of the times. Elmore owed $8.35 for ten days' board at the City Hotel, Common and Camp streets; $17 for a boardinghouse room from August 17 until September 20; and $5.50 for eleven days' board for a nurse. The undertaker

Born at Natchez, Mississippi, on September 25, 1840, Smith was taken to Louisiana as a child and eventually settled in Carroll Parish, where his first job was in the sheriff's office. He was present at the secession convention at Baton Rouge on January 26, 1861, which took the state out of the Union. As a recruiting officer, he raised three infantry companies in Carroll Parish, but was rejected for active service himself because of physical disabilities. Undeterred, he demanded permission to form a cavalry company, and was elected a lieutenant. He commanded the company in the Battle of Shiloh.[17]

Smith relieved Hearsey of the fiscal burdens which the editor regarded as a nuisance. He tried to build a solid financial foundation for the *States,* "the idol of his eye," in the words of an associate. "Every now and then the interest of the news and business offices would clash, but the Captain was always amendable to argument and the local room won most of the time," recalled the one-time city editor, Theodore D. Wharton.[18]

George Washington Dupre, Hearsey's fellow victim in the lottery company's rape of the *Democrat* in 1879, rejoined the major in 1886 by acquiring an interest in the *States.* An editorial on April 1 announced the transaction and said that Pinckney Smith had retired from proprietorship but would continue as manager. For seven years Hearsey and Dupre maintained a tranquil partnership. According to office legend, the two never had a quarrel.[19] They saw eye to eye on political, racial, and economic issues and must have had a mutual fondness; otherwise, Newspaper Row would have witnessed one more duel or at least a fistfight. For whereas Hearsey's urbane manner was gloss on a prickly, thin-skinned personality, Dupre was a pugnacious brawler. In public repute, Hear-

charged $7 for washing, dressing, and shaving the body, $3 for preserving the remains in ice and $6 for a set of crepe scarves for the pallbearers. A dollar was a dollar.

sey was a testy but high-minded representative of the Old South. Dupre, on the other hand, had his detractors, among them John C. Wickliffe of the *New Delta.* During an editorial dispute, Wickliffe wrote that Dupre was "a person who cannot be engaged in a serious difficulty on the streets, as is evidenced by the fact that in the last one in which he engaged he lied to induce his adversary to disarm. . . . With just enough boldness to commence a difficulty and not enough to continue it, with just enough courage to give an insult and not enough manliness to apologize or fight for it, this eunuch in head, conscience and heart is beneath the notice of a gentleman, save such notice as may be given to any other cur which might bark at your heels — to kick him when he becomes too annoying."[20]

Dupre was born in New Orleans on March 19, 1844. At the age of eighteen, he ran away from the Jesuits College and started to Virginia to join his brother, Adolphe, with the Washington Artillery in General Robert E. Lee's army. George was made to return home but was then allowed to enlist in time to join his brother at the Battle of Gettysburg. Adolphe was shot through the lung, and George stayed with him when they were captured and held on Governor's Island, New York, until they were exchanged.[21] George returned to action in the fighting around Petersburg in the last days of the war and again was captured, this time being held at Point Lookout, Maryland, until hostilities ceased. Back in New Orleans, Dupre was a cotton dealer until he organized the *Democrat.* He was elected to the legislature in 1874. As a captain in the White League, he commanded Company H during the battle of September 14, 1874, in which New Orleanians rose up against the Carpetbag government. From 1880 until 1887 Dupre was clerk of the Louisiana Supreme Court.[22] He got rid of his interest in the *States* in 1893. Meanwhile, Pinckney

Smith had renewed his part ownership, and Robert Ewing was acquiring stock. Dupre died on August 12, 1907, at his home, 2024 Carondelet Street.

The ownership of the *States* was questioned by the *Picayune* on April 24, 1887, in an editorial written by C. Harrison Parker in answer to an attack on the *Picayune*'s advocacy of the Cotton Seed Oil Trust. "A few years ago Henry J. Hearsey came from the pine hills of Louisiana down to New Orleans to seek a field in journalism here," said Parker.

He was then an alleged rank Reformer, and stood in that position before our community for some years. With a limited education and little knowledge of the world he flourished in his capacity as a "pine top" regulator. Time rolled on and he went through various stages of metamorphosis until he appeared finally as a full fledged henchman of the corrupt rings that have controlled our state government, and seek to control the destinies of Louisiana in the future.

His paper, the *States,* entered into a contract with Mr. James D. Houston, the tax collector of the upper district of the city, to publish the delinquent list of taxes. Upon this "official pap" the *States* and Mr. Hearsey have been living. The legislature has supplemented the "pap" from the old tax rolls as drawn from individuals and appropriated some $40,000 for the benefit of the *States* and the alleged "Pine Woods Reformer," who came down here to run an honest journal.

Of course Mr. Hearsey did not get this fat contract all by himself and enjoy the emoluments alone. He is not the only beneficiary. It is not the habit of "the state ring" to give these favors without security.

There was associated with him in the *States,* Pinckney Smith, than whom, if common report is worth anything, no more corrupt man lives. Such jobs on journalism always require a very corrupt man to put them through. Smith has evidently gotten his share of the spoils. What he has left to Mr. Hearsey we do not know.

Then another phase comes over this evening journal which it is our duty to record. A half interest was sold to some parties. Mr. George Dupre appeared as an editor and representing that new interest. We all know him as a "professional" "pap sucker" *(sic)* and chronic incubus on public patronage. What he represents in the *States* we cannot say positively. We can remark, however, that wherever he is the "Ring" is dominant.

It is said, and without any contradiction, that the brokerage firm of

Fazenda & Seixas, of Carondelet street, gave the check for the money which purchased Mr. Dupre's share in the paper. This firm has an excellent standing financially, but they have never been accused of representing anything like reform. Exactly what Dupre represents in this alleged "Pine Top Reform Ring Journal," the *Daily States,* we leave for this brokerage firm to say.

It was a period when column after column of delinquent tax notices appeared in the *States,* which obviously was drawing a large part of its advertising revenue from this source.

The *States* called Parker a "hired bully and would-be assassin." Parker in effect dared the paper's owners to challenge him to a duel, but the *States* replied that under the code "no hired bully of a corrupt newspaper can force honorable men to recognize him."[23] The *Mascot* said "the youthful David got the best of the Philistines. His sling contained no doubt too much *(sic)* truths for the *States* to have hurled at it and so it retreated from the contest. The claim of the *States* that the editor of the *Picayune* had no standing under the code is a shallow pretext to evade responsibility and is in effect a square backdown."[24] Five years earlier State Treasurer E. A. Burke considered Parker gentleman enough to challenge, and was wounded in a duel fought on June 7, 1882, near the slaughterhouse in St. Bernard Parish.[25]

The *Picayune*'s editorial introduces an element of mystery to the ownership of the *States* before December 27, 1892, when the Daily States Publishing Company, Ltd., was chartered.[26] The charter revealed that Dupre was the principal owner. The company was authorized to issue $50,000 worth of capital stock, five hundred shares at $100 par. Dupre was listed as owning 250 shares, Hearsey and Smith 125 each. Hearsey was designated as president and Smith as secretary.

During the next year Dupre divested himself of his stock and retired from coproprietorship. It was about this time that

Robert Ewing was playing an increasingly important role in the direction of the paper. Court records do not show to whom the Dupre shares were sold, or whether Dupre himself collected the $25,000 which they were worth at par. It is interesting to note that when Dupre died he left a net estate of only $188.75 to be divided among his three surviving sisters. His assets included $1,455 worth of books and furniture and $163.16 in cash.[27] Of course, he could have spent the proceeds from the *States* stock for living expenses in his last years, or he could have given the money to relatives before he died. The figures prove nothing, but do allow a suspicion that Parker and the *Picayune* were correct, that the *States* stock in Dupre's name might have been owned by somebody else.

Sooner or later, all of the Dupre stock ended up in Ewing's possession. After Smith's death, an inventory filed April 3, 1899, showed his only assets to be ninety-eight shares of *States* stock valued at $9,800.[28] Ewing also acquired these. After Hearsey's death, Ewing gradually picked up all of the founder's holdings. Memoranda found in Ewing's safe after he died in 1933 showed that on March 26, 1903, he bought one block of twenty-six shares from Hearsey's widow, and on the same day gave her a promissory note for $2,500 to cover the purchase of twenty-five additional shares. There is no record of a Hearsey estate inventory showing how much of the *States* he owned when he died. Eventually, Ewing possessed all of the five hundred shares issued when the company was chartered. The inventory of Ewing's estate valued the stock at $242,652.13.[29] The charter of the Daily States Publishing Company, Ltd., finally was dissolved on December 11, 1958.[30]

Two years after its debut the *States* had transformed the old auction room into an elegant office, "more resembling a bank than a newspaper," in the editor's words.[31] A huge sign caught the eyes of passengers on the mule-drawn streetcars which passed on Camp Street. Two editions were put out, one at 1 o'clock P.M. and the second at 2, 3, or 4 o'clock, depending on news breaks.* On May 21, 1882, the first Sunday edition, an eight-page paper, was printed. The *States* name appeared on a Sunday paper every week afterward until September 14, 1958. After the daily was bought by the Times-Picayune Publishing Company in 1933 the Sunday edition was entitled *The Times-Picayune New Orleans States.* After the merger of the *States* and *Item* on September 15, 1958, the Sunday edition became *The Times-Picayune,* and the *States-Item* appeared as a six-day evening paper. Few, if any readers, may know that from November 18, 1885, until March 6, 1886, the *States* was a morning as well as an afternoon paper. The morning *States* had a 4 A.M. press time.[32] The street sales price of the daily edition has varied over the years from five cents, to two and one-half cents, to two cents, to three cents, back to five cents, and then to ten cents. The two-and-one-half-cent price caused monetary complications which Hearsey tried to solve by issuing scrip good for two and one-half cents to be given as change when a buyer proffered a nickel. Newsboys scorned the scrip, and finally by January 11, 1881, the *States* listed its price as five cents on the street and two and one-half cents in the office.

Over the early years the *States* and *Item* competed in cut-throat fashion for the city printing contract, the arrangement for publishing official proceedings as paid advertising. Sometimes one paper won, sometimes the other, but the requirement for awarding the prize to the low bidder cut into the potential profit. In late 1894, someone suggested the papers get together with an agreement from which everybody could

* On October 15, 1880, the *States* published the first of its weekly editions in which articles and editorials from the daily paper were picked up and made available to out-of-city subscribers. Later the weekly became a semiweekly, which lasted into the present century.

benefit. But instead of making all publishers happy, the plan led to a wordy squabble on Newspaper Row and a fistfight and a threat of gunplay in City Hall at a council committee meeting.

Pinckney Smith of the *States* and Dominick C. O'Malley, proprietor of the *Item,* tossed a coin — a silver dollar — for the right to enter the low bid. Smith won, and the terms of the agreement were carried out. The *States* bid fifty cents a square (one hundred words), while the *Item* offered to do the work for fifty-two and one-half cents. Peter Kiernan, publisher of the other evening paper, the *Truth,* came in with the previously agreed bid of seventy-five cents. In return for being allowed to win, the *States* agreed to pay the *Item* one-half of the net profit from the advertising, and to pay off Kiernan with a one-thousand-dollar donation.

"Fraud," complained the *Times-Democrat,* and Editor Page M. Baker demanded grand jury action. The *Picayune* suggested an investigation by the city council. Hearsey was wrathful over Baker's stand. "This Harlequin in reformation as in egotism stands, in this matter, alone, wrapped in the solitude of his own ragged and bedraggled infamy," wrote the major. "Let the editor of the *Times-Democrat* make the most of this and make the most of it in such manner as he chooses,"[33] Hearsey was mentally oiling his dueling pistols.

At a hearing held in City Hall by a council committee, Kiernan called Hearsey a liar and the editor went after him. Joseph C. Aby of the *States* was closer, and struck Kiernan with his fist. Ewing yanked out his revolver, and a shooting scrape was narrowly averted when bystanders disarmed Ewing.[34] Kiernan, who in the meantime had substituted the *Evening Telegram* for the *Truth,* attacked the *States* representatives in an editorial:

They were alike loaded with whiskey or beer, malice, vituperation, cowardly thoughts and deadly weapons. Utterly contemptible, the actions of both Hearsey and Smith are in keeping with their natures and only exceeded in puerility by the conduct of their hirelings and tools, Aby and Ewing, who under ordinary circumstances would be beneath being spitted upon, but for their pre-arranged attack on Mr. Kiernan. Like the bloated, water-blooded and white-livered puppy that he is, Ewing was glad to be relieved of his weapon of death, to sit subsequently on the verge of collapse, trembling with fear and afraid to make an answer to the not particularly polite terms hurled at him.

Ewing sent a challenge. Kiernan was hot tempered, but he was not foolhardy and he let the gauntlet lie. Ewing then published a card: "I hereby denounce Peter Kiernan as a coward and a poltroon, who has placed himself outside the pale of honor by refusing to place himself in a position to accord satisfaction for insults offered." Hearsey, Ewing, and Aby were fined $2.50 each for fighting at the hearing. The city council decided there were no grounds for bringing suit to abrogate the contract,[35] and there the matter ended.

Hearsey's racial views were extreme, even for his time. Typical of his editorial expressions was this one on July 25, 1899:

We bulldozed the negroes; we killed the worst of them; we killed carpetbaggers; we patrolled the roads at midnight; we established in many localities a reign of terror. Why? Not to suppress or restrict the freedom of the ballot. The Republicans had the niggers, the Carpetbaggers, the federal army and navy united in an effort to crush the white people out of our state. We had only our undaunted hearts and fearless arms to defend our liberties, our property and our civilization, and we defeated our oppressors with such resources as God and nature had placed in our hands, and we redeemed our state. Stand forth, ye white-livered cowards and recreants who now seek to dodge the responsibility.*

* In view of Hearsey's violent prejudices, a paragraph in the *Mascot* of July 3, 1886, is astonishing. "The *States* has something that no other journal in this city can boast of and that is a Negro reporter, and who takes in the second recorder's court. If he was a man or an intelligent boy, we would say nothing, but he is only an annoyance to every reporter who goes to that court." A black reporter in New Orleans in 1886? And on the *States,* of all papers?

With glee, the *States* reported on May 26, 1900, that the Reverend Henry Frank, pastor of the Metropolitan Church in New York, said in a sermon that "a free negro often becomes a brutal beast, more dangerous to a community than a wild bull," and suggested a return to slavery. Hearsey commented that "the white people of the South would not, if they could, re-establish an institution that was abolished by one of the bloodiest wars in the history of the world." But he took the opportunity again to advocate repeal of the Fifteenth Amendment. The *States* had much to atone for when, under more enlightened direction, it became in the latter half of the twentieth century an outspoken advocate of racial justice.

Hearsey's opinions on education matched his racial ideas. In 1883 when the community was hard put to finance schools he wrote: "When the State has given its children free instruction in the elementary branches, it has fully discharged its duty to the people, and at that point a public education should stop."[36]

He also had his shortcomings as a prophet. In 1896 he wrote that some newspapers on the West Coast had been gulled into reporting the successful flight of an airship invented by a San Francisco scientist. "Thousands of people," he said, "will cling to and be governed by the belief that if the creator of the universe intended that they should fly bird-like through the air He would have caused wings to sprout on their shoulders."[37] Was this the first written expression of a die-hard thought that would be heard many times in the early days of aviation?

Forgive Hearsey his trespasses. Make allowances for the pressures that undoubtedly caused him to change his tune on the lottery. Understand that he was the child of another environment, another era. Forget his faults and give him his due. In the two decades of the little editor, the *States* had a character, a style, a pungency. It would be years, once he was gone, before some of these qualities would reappear.

4

Journalistic Jungle

In the last quarter of the nineteenth century and first decade of the twentieth, New Orleans looked like a promised land to venturesome men who yearned to own daily newspapers. The city turned out instead to be a journalistic jungle.

Of the five dailies that already existed on April 24, 1877, and of the twenty-seven that were launched in the hundred years since, only three remain, one the *States-Item.* An attrition rate of greater than 90 percent.

What happened? Why did high hopes give way to disappointment and failure? What kind of community was it that beckoned then to would-be publishers? How has it changed since? What of the papers that perished? What of the journals that once circulated by the thousands, then vanished into a limbo, even their names lost in the passage of time?

Are they not entitled at least to a brief requiem in a chronicle of one of the survivors, the *States-Item?*

It was the relief of getting Carpetbaggers' boots off their necks and the hopes for the future, rather than immediate economic prospects, that made April 24, 1877, a gala day for citizens of New Orleans. Perhaps some had an instinctive feeling they had reached a turning point. Indeed they had. There were other obstacles to hurdle in the years ahead, but after the end of Reconstruction the road stretched straight ahead to prosperity and greatness.

The Civil War and the vengeful aftermath imposed on the losers had been costly. In 1840 New Orleans was the third largest city in the United States. By 1877 it had slipped to ninth place. The population was 191,418 in the 1870 census and 216,000 in 1880,[1] indicating that about 200,000 persons lived in the city in 1877. Slightly more than one-fourth were Negroes,[2] most of them illiterate and, of course, poor prospects as newspaper subscribers. A combination of circumstances had led New Orleans into an economic depression. "The city was decaying," wrote Norman Walker in Rightor's *Standard History of New Orleans,* explaining that business was bad in the 1877 era because of war, flood, and pestilence. The city government had lost control of the waterworks and surrendered the Mississippi River wharves to a private company. Municipal bonds were selling at less than twenty-three cents on the dollar. "A low condition of political morality was prevalent, which, while it was far worse in the State government, yet more or less reflected itself in the municipal government," Walker commented.[3]

New Orleans reached the peak of its prewar prosperity in the period when the jaunty steam packet carried a large portion of the nation's goods. The city was the hub of the waterways system. In the expansion of the railroads after the war, New Orleans was sidetracked. Steamboats still were tied up, two and three abreast, alongside the levee when the *T. Palace* moved downstream with the Third Infantry aboard; yet the glory days of river traffic were over, and most of America's goods moved by rail.

The ever-present threat of yellow fever was a handicap that would not be overcome until a quarter-century later when the mosquito finally was recognized as the carrier of the germ. It developed that 1877 was a comparatively feverless year, but in 1878 the last of the major epidemics was devastating.[4] On January 10, 1880, Dr. Samuel Choppin, president of the Louisiana State Board of Health, reported that in the eighty-four years since yellow fever first appeared in New Orleans in 1796, at least 100,000 persons had died of the disease in the city, and probably another 75,000 in the nearby towns and countryside.[5] There were occasional outbreaks until 1905. In their ignorance of the disease and its causes, New Orleanians tried to combat its horrors with such medieval measures as shooting cannon and lighting bonfires on street corners. Indicative of the popular misconceptions, in 1897 when there was a minor upturn in the number of cases, the *States* ran this notice every day on its editorial page: "Readers of the *States* will please take notice that every copy of the paper sent beyond the limits of New Orleans is thoroughly disinfected under the personal supervision of the United States Marine Hospital Surgeons. The paper can be accepted with confidence that it is entirely free from infection and publishes the truth about the health situation in New Orleans."

Soldiers of the Third Infantry whose departure on April 24, 1877, officially ended Reconstruction undoubtedly had mud on their boots. In a city where the rainfall averages about five inches a month there were only 94 miles of paved streets, compared with 472 unpaved miles. Gutters were open drainage ditches, and sidewalks, called banquettes, mostly were planks laid with haphazard design. New Orleans still was truly the Crescent City, almost all of the populated area being confined to the half-moon formed by the meandering Mississippi. Residents tended to hug the riveer levee. Beyond Claiborne Avenue were dairy farms and gardens, beyond Broad Avenue mostly swampland all the way to Lake Pontchartrain. There was an advantage to newspaper distributors, of course, in the concentration of population. The large majority of residents who could not afford horses and buggies depended for transportation on street railroads, which ran on 140 miles of track. There were 313 horse cars and 1,641 horses or mules to pull them. In addition there were 60 small passenger coaches for which 20 dummies, or steam engines, furnished motor power.[6]

Frustrations of the Carpetbag regime finally caused New Orleanians to take up arms. Hundreds of them, mostly members of the Crescent City White League, fought a battle on Canal Street against the Metropolitan Police on September 14, 1874. The citizens won the battle, but lost any immediate advantage in the uneasy peace that followed. As recently as January 9, 1877, some three thousand citizens marched on Jackson Square, seized the Cabildo, kicked out the Republican state Supreme Court, and flaunted their might in front of the St. Louis Hotel where Stephen B. Packard's pretenders cowered behind the Third Infantry's sentinels.[7] Of course, a town peopled by trigger-tempered Creoles and brawling Kaintucks always had its share of shootings. But one of the by-products of the carpetbag days was a precedent for gun-toting, violence, and summary justice which persisted into the early 1900s. Among the citizens who habitually stuck pistols into their pockets before they walked out onto the streets were some of the newspapermen.

Even while New Orleanians fretted through the depression months of 1877, bemoaning the decline of river traffic, events were underway that would provide the foundation for future prosperity. In early times, small sailing vessels from Europe and the West Indies had no difficulty entering the Mississippi River and making their way a hundred miles upstream to the city's port. As sails gave way to steam and ships grew larger, the passes at the mouth of the river no longer were deep enough. The Corps of Engineers tried to maintain a channel by dredging, but was overwhelmed by the silt deposited by the river. If a ship had a draft of more than twelve feet, it had to be lightened by removing cargo before it could negotiate the passes. The unloading was costly and time consuming, and unless a solution could be found, foreign trade was destined to be diverted to more accessible ports. James Buchanan Eads, an engineer, suggested a plan: Build a jetty on each side of the Southwest Pass so as to confine the flow of the river, and the current would be strong enough to flush out a channel and keep it open. His idea was challenged. In February, 1874, he went to Congress with a "no cure, no pay" proposal. He offered to build the jetties at his own expense, with the agreement that he would be repaid if he provided a twenty-eight-foot channel. After long debate, Congress accepted his proposition. On July 10, 1879, Eads announced the approaching completion of the project, and it was obvious he had won. By August, 1880, the pass had a thirty-two-foot channel.[8] Belatedly, New Orleans was given connections to the coast-to-coast railroad grid, and by 1880 the city had established itself as a deep-water trading center. In that year 915 ships cleared the port, carrying exports totaling $90,238,503 — including cotton valued at $75,552,195. The city was on its way. There would be no spectacular growth, such as occurred in the decade between 1830 and 1840 when the population leaped from 29,737 to 102,193.[9] Not until 1904 would the 300,000 point be reached.[10] But once the modern age dawned, development would be steady and sure.

Five daily newspapers in New Orleans recorded the departure of the Third Infantry.

L'ABEILLE DE LA NOUVELLE-ORLEANS

The oldest was *L'Abeille,* the *Bee,* a French-language morning paper which was established on September 1, 1827, by Francois Delaup. The first editor was Baron Rene de Perdreauville, who had served as a page to Queen Marie Antoinette and as governor of pages under Napoleon Bonaparte. *L'Abeille* ran into hard times after the legislature in 1914 repealed a law that provided for publication of paid legal notices in French as well as English. It finally went from daily to weekly publication, while friends endeavored to save it. The *Times-Picayune* bought *L'Abeille* in 1921 and operated it until it was allowed to succumb on December 27, 1923. The *Bee* always was printed in the French Quarter, first at 94 St. Peter Street and later at 323 Chartres Street. The peak circulation of the daily edition was 5,500 in the 1886 era.[11]

DAILY PICAYUNE

Next oldest of the dailies was the *Daily Picayune,* which first appeared on January 25, 1837. It continued an independent existence until April 6, 1914, when it was merged with the *Times Democrat* to become the *Times Picayune,* the dominant New Orleans paper of the twentieth century. In 1877 the *Picayune*'s plant was part of Newspaper Row, at what is now 326 Camp Street. The circulation was 6,000.

DEUTSCHE ZEITUNG

The New Orleanser *Deutsche Zeitung,* the *German Gazette,* was founded by Joseph Cohn on August 1, 1848, and was the only German-language daily south of the Ohio River. Jacob Hassinger was editor-publisher in the late years of the nineteenth century and early in the twentieth when the *Zeitung,* with a circulation of 3,800 daily and 7,500 on Sunday, exerted considerable influence. The *Gazette* ceased publication in 1907. It fell the lot of the *Gazette* to be burned out twice, a misfortune that was shared by the *Evening Telegram.* The first occasion was on April 15, 1897. Flames destroyed the Moresque Building, on the uptown lake corner of Camp and Poydras streets, and leaped across Camp Street to engulf the structure at 504 Camp which was occupied by the two newspapers. On February 20, 1899, a fire that swept through the St. Charles Theater, on St. Charles Street near Poydras, spread to the building at 437 Camp Street to which the *Gazette* and *Telegram* had moved.[12] The *Gazette* transferred its operations to 534 Poydras Street.

TIMES

Thomas P. May and Company took over the plant of the *Crescent,* two doors above the *Picayune* on Camp Street, after military authorities suppressed the former, and on September 20, 1863, printed the first issue of the *Times.* By 1877 the *Times* had a circulation of 6,000. Edward A. Burke acquired the paper and on December 4, 1881, merged it with the *Democrat,* the new name being the *Times-Democrat.* The *Times* started life as a paper friendly to the Union cause in the still-raging war.

DEMOCRAT

George W. Dupre was the principal organizer of the *Democrat,* which was founded on December 19, 1875, as an organ of the Democratic party in the troubled days when citizens were hoping to expel the Carpetbaggers. Beginning as an evening paper, the *Democrat* switched to morning publication. It was first printed at 74 Camp Street, moved to 109 Gravier Street, and shortly before the merger with the *Times,* returned to Newspaper Row at 62 Camp Street. The circulation was 3,000.

As noted, all three English-language dailies which were in business on that April day in 1877 when the cannon boomed have survived, although in merged form as one paper. Both of the foreign-language dailies became casualties of changing times.

It was the fate of twenty-seven newspapers introduced later that proved how great were the odds against the entrepreneurs who ventured into the daily publication field in the next hundred years. Only three of these still roll off the presses, two of them merged into the afternoon journal which is owned by the Times-Picayune Publishing Corporation. This is the *States-Item,* now the city's only evening paper. The daily has an unbroken publication record dating all the way back to the birth of the *Daily City Item* on June 11, 1877, and of the *Daily States* on January 3, 1880. Neither the *Item* nor the *States* was immune to the virulent economic disease that claimed the other newspapers. Both received timely, lifesaving transfusions.

While New Orleans has been a graveyard for daily newspapers, some of the corpses have vanished. Nothing is left of a few of the publications that once blanketed the city, nothing except a listing in a directory, a brief mention in a history book, or a casual reference in a contemporary publication. The tombs for others are library storage rooms where bound volumes have been preserved. Now the yellow, brittle newsprint flakes at the touch.

Competition was intense. In 1892 a reader who was familiar with three languages could choose from among no fewer than nine dailies. These were *L'Abeille* and *L'Orleanais* (French); *Deutsche Zeitung* (German) and the *Item, New Delta, Pica-*

yune, Truth, States and *Times-Democrat* (English). In other years as many as eight newspapers appeared on the streets daily. A painstaking check into likely sources produces a list of the dailies published in New Orleans in the past century. There is no guarantee that the roll is complete, but there could have been few, if any, others.

DAILY CITY ITEM

The *Item* was the first new daily to be introduced after the ouster of the Carpetbaggers.

COURRIER DE LA LOUISIANA

On December 6, 1878, the *Item* reported that a new French-language daily newspaper "came to us this morning." It was the *Courrier de la Louisiana,* "organ of the Creole-American population." "The *Courrier* is and will remain Democratic," Chief Editor Andre L. Roman was quoted as promising. "Not to be a Democrat is to play into the hands of those who lie in the dark, watching for an occasion to enable us to appreciate anew the beauties of midnight orders and returning boards." Bigney remarked in the *Item*: "If our French contemporary can maintain the excellence of its contents at the point apparent in its first issue, it will deserve to realize all its hopes." The paper was published at 41 Natchez Street, next door to the *Item.* But its days were numbered, and after a listing in the 1879 city directory it ceased to exist.

EVENING NEWS (original)

On April 12, 1879, the *Evening News* bowed in. "No rash promises are made," said the *Democrat* the next day, "but there is an air about the new paper which unmistakably evidences that it has come to stay and is determined to fill a field of afternoon journalism in New Orleans which is full of promise and there is plenty of room for success." The paper was published at 11 Commercial Place. "No ring or monopoly can control the *News,*" said an advertisement, which announced that the paper was edited by "experienced New Orleans journalists."[13] The promise was not realized and the *Evening News* went out of business.

LE PETIT JOURNAL

A French-language morning daily, *Le Petit Journal,* published by Le Petit Journal Cooperative Association, was listed in the 1879 N. W. Ayers and Sons' directory for the only time. Charles Bleton was editor. On August 19, 1879, the *Item* commented: "The *Petit Journal* has completed its first half-year, and may today be considered as the most brilliant little sheet in New Orleans." But on October 21 of the same year the *Item* reported that the paper had ended its career in a somewhat mysterious manner. "Its fate confirms our former prediction — that a second French daily will never be successfully established in New Orleans. The old Colonial tongue is dying out." Library catalogues show no copies of the paper in the files.

DAILY STATES

Next in chronological order appeared the *Daily States.*

NEW ORLEANS REFERENCE JOURNAL

Although the *New Orleans Reference Journal* made no pretense of covering spot news, the paper was printed in the 1883 period in competition with the other dailies. It was a single sheet of standard newspaper size. On the front page were advertisements of the classified type, grouped by location: Canal, Gravier, Decatur, and other streets. The back page was filled with "Gems of Thought," poems, facts and figures, useful hints, and other material such as is found in the family sections of papers today. The *Reference Journal* advertised a subscription price of eighty cents a month, and scorned subscriptions of less than one month.[14]

EVENING CHRONICLE

The *Evening Chronicle,* established in the spring of 1883, copied an idea from the Item and printed a journalistic oddity, a Sunday afternoon edition. The paper abandoned the Sunday field in 1886 and settled down to six-day publication until its demise in 1888.[15] It first was published at 23 Bank Place, and the masthead listed Elliott, Sagendorph and Company as proprietors and T. H. Ryan as editor. By 1886 the *Chronicle* had moved to 43 Natchez Street and was produced by the Chronicle Printing Company.[16] In the latter part of 1884 the *Chronicle* was advertising itself as "The Best Paper, the Brightest Paper, the Cheapest Paper," and claimed a circulation as large as that of any other evening publication in New Orleans. Joseph Mark Leveque, author of the chapter on newspapers in Rightor's *Standard History of New Orleans,* said the *Chronicle* was the first publishing venture of Peter J. Kiernan.[17] Kiernan was the gadfly of the city's newspaper proprietors. He and his wife, Bertha Miller Kiernan, were involved in the ownership of no less than six dailies between 1883 and 1905. Once or twice they created a new paper simply by changing the name of an existing one. The *States* twitted the *Chronicle* for its lack of success in raising funds for a monument to the philanthropist John McDonogh. Several months of effort produced contributions totaling only $65.95, and the *States* said: "It is safe to say . . . that after the *Chronicle* has finished building the McDonogh monument it will feel very much as the man who attempted to butt the bull off the bridge, and if there are any more monuments to be erected, it will be perfectly satisfied to hold some other fellow's hat and let him do the work."[18]

LEDGER

"A new Richmond has appeared in the field of journalism in New Orleans," reported the *Mascot* on November 21, 1885. "It is called the *Ledger* and it is published daily by the Ledger Publishing Company. It is a neat and tasty sheet and has our best wishes for success." The *Ledger*'s days were few in number. Libraries list no volumes in the archives.

MORNING CHRONICLE

The name of Robert Ewing, which will loom ever larger as this account moves along, first appears on a masthead as business manager of the *Morning Chronicle*, which was owned by the proprietors of the *States* in the 1887-1888 era. Frank A. Bartlett was editor and publisher of the daily which was printed at 43 Natchez Street. The *Mascot* told the story[19] of the Yankee sutler who opened up a tent offering lager beer at fifteen cents a glass. The price was too high and business lagged. The canny sutler got a friend to park another tent next to his and advertise beer at five cents a glass. "The ruse took and both tents had their patrons — both supplied with very poor beer from the same barrel with a faucet in each tent. If the *Chronicle*'s faucet aint plugged into the rear of the *States*'s beer barrel, well, the flavor is very misleadin'."

TRAIT-D'UNION

A new French-language paper printed on weekday evenings and Sunday morning made its debut on January 16, 1887. "The *Trait-d'Union* is intended to be the organ of the Creole population and of the Franco-Louisiana element of this city," reported the *States.*[20] "It professes independence in politics and will endeavor to treat of all subjects, including politics, literature, arts, science and miscellany. . . . Of handsome typographical appearance, newsy, interesting, full of advertisements, with a complete telegraphic and local news service, the first number produced a most favorable impression on the public." Officers of the Creole Publishing Company, which operated at 80 Chartres Street, were Andre L. Roman, president; educator Alcee Fortier, vice-president; J. Emile Rivoire, secretary, and John Augustin and Lamar C. Quintero, directors. Roman was editor-in-chief and Rivoire business manager. Available records do not show when the paper folded.

L'OPINION

"Our sprightly contemporary, *L'Opinion,* which has for some time been issued as a weekly paper, has changed its character to publication of a daily morning paper," reported the *States* on October 21, 1888. "We wish our friends the success their talent and enterprise merit, and welcome *L'Opinion* to the ranks of daily journalism." The lifetime of the French-language daily apparently was brief. Louis Arnauld was editor-in-chief and A. G. Nicolopulo business manager.[21] The paper first was printed at 45 Toulouse Street, and in 1888 moved to 114 Royal Street.

L'ORLEANAIS

Still another French-language daily, *L'Orleanais,* began publication, apparently in 1888, at 136 Royal Street. L. L. Bouby, a stalwart defender of the Creole ways, was editor and publisher. "Liberty" and "Progress" were the twin mottoes printed on page one. The evening and Sunday morning journal still was in operation in 1892,[22] but was not included in the Ayer directory in the following year.

DAILY NEWS (original)

The first of two dailies bearing the name *Daily News* lasted for about two years in the 1887-1889 period. A reference to the paper appeared in the *States* of November 2, 1887. Leveque said the paper was established by Kiernan.[23] The first address was 139 Poydras Street. The 1889 Soards' city directory listed W. A. Kernaghan as proprietor, and the address as 114 Camp Street. The 1889 circulation was 5,500.

EVENING NEWS (second version)

The *Evening News* came out late in 1889, published every day except Sunday at 34 Magazine Street by L. R. Simmons, J. H. Glintz and A. C. Lindauer. By August, 1890, the paper claimed the largest circulation of any evening daily in the city, its distribution being 5,500 copies. The *News* featured large advertisements of the Louisiana State Lottery Company, and also printed numerous "cards," a type of classified advertisement, in which agents or runners proclaimed that they were paid promptly by the lottery company for the winnings of their clients. By 1892 Simmons and Glintz were the proprietors, and the paper had moved to 139 Poydras Street.[24]

NEW DELTA

When the state's citizens became divided over the issue of continuing the lottery, forces opposing a new charter established on May 14, 1890, a daily called the *New Delta*. C. Harrison Parker, former editor of the *Picayune*, and John C. Wickliffe were coeditors of the morning paper, which was printed at 41-43 Natchez Street. The *New Delta* achieved a circulation of 14,267 daily and 17,926 on Sunday. It was absorbed by the *Picayune* on May 7, 1893, after it had served its purpose of helping the antilottery element win a victory.[25]

DAILY TRUTH

The *Daily Truth* was founded by the Kiernans on October 12, 1891. By March 17, 1894, a headline was boasting: "The *Daily Truth* is delivered to more homes than any other city paper," and an advertisement claimed a circulation of 12,001. "The *Truth* is Always Fair," proclaimed the journal.[26] In 1892 it was published at 114 Camp Street and in 1894 was at 106 Camp Street.

DAILY CRUSADER

A Negro newspaper, the *Daily Crusader,* first was offered in the spring of 1894. The issue of July 10, 1894,[27] said it was the "only Republican paper south of the Mason-Dixon Line." An advertisement boasted: "The *Daily Crusader* is the wage-earner's friend. Every workingman takes it." L. A. Martinet, prominent political figure, was managing editor of the Crusader Publishing Company, Ltd., 412-414 Exchange Alley. The *States,* which yielded to no other southern paper in race-baiting stridency, paid a compliment to Martinet: "A man head and shoulders above the mass of his race in this city in point of intellectuality and education." By 1898 the *Daily Crusader* was defunct.[28]

EVENING TELEGRAM

In late 1894 Kiernan scuttled the *Daily Truth* and launched the *Evening Telegram* in its place. By 1900 the paper called itself "The Only Louisiana Newspaper for a Dime a Week," and said it circulation was twenty thousand. Kiernan still was connected with the *Telegram* in 1900, but in 1902, when C. O. Wilcox was appointed to take over affairs of the bankrupt paper, L. A. Hoffman was identified as president of the New Orleans Telegram Publishing Company. The Diamond Paper Company sued the *Telegram* in 1901 in an effort to collect $3,000 due for newsprint. The paper company won a judgment but could find no property of the *Telegram* that could be seized.[29] The fires that ruined two plants undoubtedly contributed to the downfall. The *Telegram*'s last days were spent at 617 Poydras Street.

ITALO-AMERICANO

After twelve years of weekly operation, the Italian-language paper, *Italo-Americano,* became a daily on August 1, 1896.[30] At the time Paolo Montelepre was owner and Dr. A. B. De Villeneuve managing editor. The paper, which had its offices at 129 Decatur Street, was circulating 2,500 copies daily by 1900. Its last appearance in the Ayer directory was in 1901.

DAILY NEWS (second version)

The Kiernans were in action in 1902, this time with Mrs. Kiernan as publisher and her husband as editor of the *Daily News,* produced at 445 Camp Street. The afternoon paper in 1905 counted a circulation of 17,500, a figure which almost equaled the distribution of the *States* and was less than 3,000 behind the *Item.* The *Daily News* continued until it was abandoned on June 17, 1911. For the last six years the paper was printed by Robert Ewing's New Orleans Publishing Company. Kiernan sold the *Daily News* to Ewing on July 20, 1905. Edward Larocque Tinker wrote that before turning over the

News plant to Ewing, Kiernan looted it of most of the equipment needed to put out a paper. Tinker said the sales agreement contained a goodwill provision which Ewing expected would keep Kiernan out of competition in New Orleans for years.[31]

NEW ORLEANS AMERICA

Almost immediately following the sale of the *Daily News,* the *New Orleans America,* was issued evenings and Sunday from a building at Camp and Natchez streets. It ostensibly was published by the New Orleans America Company, Ltd., but Tinker reported this was a front for Kiernan. New Orleans' only penny paper certainly reflected Kiernan's flamboyance and belligerence. An editorial in the October 4, 1905, issue[32] was typical: "The yellow fever was deliberately introduced in New Orleans for a purpose. Since then the fever scare has been kept up with the object in view of spending the money contributed for the purpose." The *America* failed to make the grade, and the Kiernans faded out.

MORNING WORLD

The *Morning World* was printed for about six months in the latter part of 1907 and first part of 1908. Joseph Mark Leveque, the editor, persuaded many businessmen and other citizens to subscribe to stock, and the *World* was launched with a splash that must have worried rival publishers. The paper was printed at 212 Camp Street, the pressroom being in the front part of the ground floor in order that passersby could peer through the show window and watch editions come off the press. Some of those who promised to buy stock reneged, and the *World* floundered for lack of capital. Henry Rightor, who compiled the *Standard History of New Orleans,* was one of the editors.[33]

LA GUEPE

Count J. G. de Baroncelli founded a French-language paper, *La Guepe,* the *Wasp,* on October 11, 1902, as a rival to the *Bee.* The journal changed from weekly to daily publication in 1912 in order to take advantage of a law requiring the publication of legal notices in French as well as English. When the law was repealed in 1914 *La Guepe* went back on a weekly schedule. De Baroncelli died on June 30, 1934. Later the name of the paper was changed to *La Courrier de la Nouvelle Orleans,* which continued publication into the 1950s.[34]

NEW ORLEANS AMERICAN

From 1914 until 1917 the *New Orleans American,* a morning daily, was published by union printers organized as the Southern Publishing Company, Inc. Dominick C. O'Malley, the most controversial figure on Newspaper Row a decade earlier, was editor for one period. E. H. Merrick was publisher and treasurer. The paper, which sold for two cents, was printed at 741 Poydras Street. The 1917 circulation was 12,976. Robert Ewing was the prime target of the *American,* which developed out of a labor dispute between the International Typographical Union and three dailies of the time, the *States, Item,* and *Times-Picayune.*

DAILY SPOKESMAN

The *Daily Spokesman* was listed as a daily and Sunday paper for Negroes in the 1915, 1916, 1917, and 1918 Ayer directories. It was produced by the Daily Spokesman Publishing Company, Ltd., Pythian Temple. The 1915 Soards' directory gave the address as 1131 Gravier Street.

MORNING TRIBUNE

The *Morning Tribune* was published by the *Item* from December 16, 1924, until January 12, 1941. It was begun as a standard-sized paper but was turned into a tabloid. The *Tribune* was put into the field at a time when the *Item* was challenging the *Times-Picayune* for first place among New Orleans publishing firms. It folded when the *Item* encountered hard times after losing the battle.

DAILY RECORD

In April, 1973, the *Daily Record* became a six-day morning newspaper produced for general readership after having been printed since 1897 as the *Daily Court Record,* which reported legal proceedings. Louis J. Roussel, banker and financier, acquired the *Court Record* and converted it into the first new daily of general circulation to appear in New Orleans in forty-nine years.*

The compilation of the thirty-two different dailies which either continued publication or came into being after April 24, 1877, omits two other journals which left the daily field earlier that year. One was the *Daily Call,* first printed by the Franklin Printing House, 98 Camp Street, on December 21, 1876, with E. C. Wharton as editor and John G. Wire as business manager. The last issue on file is that of January 6, 1877.[35] As previously noted, the *Republican* lost its daily status in the collapse of the Carpetbag government. In the early months of 1877 the paper was on an irregular schedule, sometimes appearing daily and sometimes two or three times a week. For a

* The *Jefferson Parish Times,* a weekly since October, 1944, began publication on October 6, 1975, of a five-day-a-week afternoon newspaper for circulation in the Jefferson Parish suburbs of New Orleans.

few issues in March, the *Republican* did make it to the streets every day. The last edition as a daily was that of March 11.[36]

Why did dailies spring up like daisies late in the nineteenth century and early in the twentieth? And why did they fade away? It was a time made to order for the printer or editor who wanted to cut a swath in the community, but had little money. A small press and a few fonts of type were the basic necessities in a newspaper plant, and even after the typesetting machine was introduced by the *Times-Democrat* in 1891, production was an inexpensive process. Major Henry J. Hearsey established the *States* with only $2,250 at his disposal, and the group that founded the *Daily City Item* subscribed a total of only $12,000 for their shares. In 1887 the total capital investment in all the printing houses and newspapers in New Orleans was $1,179,000[37] of which by far the greater part was represented by job shops doing commercial printing. The *Item* operated for years in quarters rented for $20 a month.

A newspaper was a nickel-and-dime operation in an age of small business — the day of the corner grocery store, mamma-and-papa restaurant, neighborhood barroom, one-druggist pharmacy, livery stable, cobbler's shop, regional market where meat and vegetables were offered in tiny stalls, horse-and-wagon peddler. It was an economy that could exist without newspaper advertising. Much later would come the merchandising revolution: the result of a multiplying population, the automobile, and the transformation of cities into metropolitan areas with vast and prosperous suburban developments. Years would pass before department stores, supermarkets, shopping centers, automobile dealers, real estate brokers, chain drug outlets and other establishments geared to high volume would depend mostly on newspaper promotion to attract their armies of customers. In the first part of the modern age the number of advertising dollars for which the city's dailies scrambled was limited. Even the established morning papers ran ten-, twelve-, or fourteen-page editions, and the newcomers had to make do in the four- or eight-page range. True, production costs were low, to the point where it might have been possible to conduct business profitably on circulation income alone if enough copies could be sold. Yet when nine daily newspapers were competing for the patronage of the literate segment of a population of some 250,000, it was too much to expect that any one publication could win the requisite lion's share of the sales.

Under the circumstances, failure was almost inevitable for the publisher who gambled in the daily field. Later, when a growing city offered the possibilities of adequate circulation and when newspaper advertising supported the merchandising structure, a daily was far beyond the reach of the small investor. Publishing became big business, with huge capital expenditures required for facilities to produce and distribute hundreds of thousands of papers in a few hours. S. I. Newhouse paid $42 million for the *States-Item* and the *Times-Picayune* in 1962, then spent another $16 million to build and equip a new plant for the two papers which was opened in 1968.

Not one of the twenty-seven dailies which bowed in between 1877 and the end of 1973 would have made a success on its own. The *States* and *Item* continued only because they were rescued at critical periods.

Grotius' words quoted by the *Picayune* in its obituary for *Item* editor Mark F. Bigney in 1886 may be the best epitaph for all of the hundreds of men and women who devoted their energies over the course of a century to New Orleans newspapers that could not make the grade: "I have lost my life laboriously doing nothing."

5

Extra! Who Killa de Chief?

Rise in your might, people of New Orleans!

Alien bands of oath-bound assassins have set the blot of a martyr's blood upon your vaulted civilization! Your laws, in the very temple of justice, have been bought off, and suborners have caused to be turned loose upon your streets the midnight murderers of David C. Hennessey, in whose premature grave the very majesty of our American law lies buried with his mangled corpse — the corpse of him who in life was the representative, the conservator of your peace and dignity.

Rise, citizens of New Orleans! When Murder overrides Law and Justice, when juries are bribed and suborners go undetected and unwhipped, it is time to resort to your own natural indefeasible right of self-preservation.

Rise, outraged people of New Orleans! Let those who have attempted to sap the very foundations of your Temples of Justice be in one vengeful hour swept from your midst. Peaceably if you can, forcibly if you must!!

Major Henry J. Hearsey's exhortation to a lynching was delivered in a *States* extra timed for distribution at a mass meeting at 10 A.M. on March 14, 1891, at the Clay statue, Canal and St. Charles streets. Impending was the climax of a series of events set into motion a dozen years earlier in far-off Sicily.

In the latter part of the 1870s a wealthy British citizen, J. Forrester Rose of London,[1] was vacationing in Sicily with his wife. While riding through the tiny town of Lecrero he was kidnapped by members of the Leone gang of brigands who were commanded by a Leone lieutenant named Giuseppe Esposito.[2] The next day Mrs. Rose received a note demanding $25,000 ransom. Along with the communication came one of Rose's ears. Mrs. Rose did not respond immediately, and soon she received the other ear and a threat that her husband's nose would be next. This time the money was sent as directed and the mutilated Briton was freed. The Leone outlaws had been operating with only token interference from Italian authorities. But the indignity to Rose aroused the British government, which brought pressure upon the Italians. A reward of $5,000 was offered for Esposito's capture, and police forces set out in an apparently determined effort to find him. One account[3] said Esposito and fifteen members of the gang fought a battle with police in which nine of the bandits were killed. At any rate, the danger of capture became too great, and Esposito — who took over leadership after Leone was betrayed — fled to the United States. He settled in New Orleans.

Only five feet, four inches in height, Esposito was a broad, deep-chested, powerful man whose full black beard would have been treasured by a pirate. He had funds, perhaps some of the Rose ransom money, and bought a lugger in connection with a fruit and vegetable business which he established on Customhouse Street, between Burgundy and Rampart. In New Orleans he used the names Radzo and Randazzo. He named his lugger the *Leone,* and even flew the bandit's flag until cautious friends persuaded him to desist. He married a widow with whom he lived at 237 Chartres Street, between St. Philip and Dumaine. Thomas Byrnes, New York police inspector, said that in New Orleans Esposito "gathered together the scattered members of the Mafia that had been forced to flee to this country, and molded them into a very formidable organization."[4]

The reward for Esposito's arrest still was being offered in 1881. Possibly it was the prospect of sharing in the reward that brought David C. Hennessey and his cousin, Michael Hennessey, into the case. Both were aids, as detectives then were called, on the New Orleans police department. The Hennesseys arranged for an artist named Hoeppner to make a sketch of the unsuspecting Esposito as he sat in his hangout, Raphael's cafe at Burgundy at Customhouse streets. One of the kidnap victims of the Leone gang in Sicily was an artist who had drawn a likeness of Esposito on the envelope of a ransom letter.[5] The Hennesseys also managed to get a photograph of the man. The pictorial identification set the wheels into motion, and Marshals James Mooney and D. Boland were sent from New York to arrest Esposito. David Hennessey asked the chief of police, Colonel Thomas N. Boylan, to allow him and Mike to help in the actual capture.[6] Boylan agreed and warned that the only way Esposito could be taken out of New Orleans without arousing resistance by his allies would be secretly by ship.

On Tuesday, July 5, 1881, the New York marshals and the Hennesseys surprised Esposito as he was walking in the vicinity of Jackson Square. They collared him before he could resist, and hustled him to the Second Precinct police station, where he was held incommunicado overnight, then spirited aboard the steamer *New Orleans* before the vessel cast off for New York. During the voyage Esposito told fellow passengers his name was Vincent Rabello, and he had been mistakenly identified by the marshals because they wanted the reward. When the steamer docked officers escorted Esposito through a crowd of Italians who awaited his arrival. They took him to the

Ludlow Street jail.[7] He eventually was deported and in December, 1881, was sentenced to death for eighteen murders and a hundred ransom kidnappings. King Humbert I commuted the sentence.[8]

Esposito's arrest stirred the New Orleans Italian colony which was made up mostly of Sicilian immigrants, many of whom lived in the French Quarter. Decatur Street, between Dumaine and St. Philip streets, was known as Vendetta Alley because of the knife fights and shootings that took place there. Six former members of the Leone gang who came to New Orleans with Esposito reportedly learned of his capture and made their getaway, three taking passage on a lugger down the river, one fleeing over the lake, and two heading for St. Louis.[9]

Gaetano Ardetto, a lemon peddler, accused Tony Laboussa of betraying Esposito. Harbor police broke up an encounter between the two men that threatened to become a gun fight.[10] A week later, on the night of July 15, Laboussa went to Coliseum Hall, 52 Bienville Street, to attend a meeting of what the *Picayune* called the "better element" of Italians[11] who planned to form a society to protect themselves against the depredations of their countrymen who were beholden to Esposito. Laboussa was standing at Bienville Street and Exchange Alley directing men to the meeting room. Ardetto was seen in Exchange Alley on the upper side of Bienville Street. Suddenly there was a blast from a carbine and immediately afterward a pistol shot. Laboussa fell, mortally wounded, in front of Zimmerman's Coliseum Saloon, 51 Bienville Street. Ardetto was found in Exchange Alley, a pistol wound in his back. He had shot Laboussa, then become the target of a man who stood in the shadow of a doorway on Bienville Street. Ardetto was convicted of killing Laboussa but obtained a new trial and, unexpectedly, the charge against him was dropped.[12]

During efforts to prevent Esposito's deportation from New York, Italians in New Orleans sent a purse of $5,000 to help him, but an agent absconded with the money. David Hennessey insisted that he and Mike did not get any reward for their efforts. This was disputed by the *States,* which said the Hennesseys were hired by a New York detective to help.[13]

In view of later developments, the *States*'s attitude is interesting, demonstrating that Major Hearsey never let himself become restricted by consistency. "The Esposito Out-Rage" was the title of an editorial which said: "The kidnapping of the Italian fruit dealer Esposito and his removal by violence to New York, where after an unsatisfactory investigation, a subordinate official in the State Department at Washington, without the slightest authority, signed the extradition papers which consigned the captive to the tender mercies of the Italian authorities, is a most remarkable affair and ought to arouse the indignation of the country." The *States* later commented: "Esposito is languishing in jail at Palermo, Italy, and his identity as the brigand has been clearly shown, even if his own confession were not enough to establish that fact. The confession and proof of the identity of the so-called Sicilian Brigand Esposito Randazzo, do not by any means vindicate or justify the wrong and outrage of the mode of his capture and deportation from this city."[14]

The Hennesseys were back in the headlines in October, 1881. Mike was charged by Thomas Devereaux, chief of aids, with conduct unbecoming an officer. While drunk, he assaulted a man in a house of ill repute at 40 Basin Street and created a scene in another house at 186 Customhouse Street. Mike and his cousin went gunning for Devereaux, and on October 13 found him in the brokerage office of John W. Fairfax, one of the owners of the *Item,* at 148 Gravier Street, between Camp and St. Charles streets. Mike started a gunfight with Devereaux. David walked up behind the chief, put a pistol to his head and pulled the trigger. Even as he fell, fatally wounded, Devereaux got off one last shot at Mike. David helped Mike into a cab and took him to Charity Hospital for treatment of his wounds.[15]

When, almost a decade later, Major Hearsey was extolling the virtues of David Hennessey, he must have forgotten two editorials he had written after the Devereaux shooting. "The fact is patent that neither of the two murderers nor their victim were proper men to hold any position on the police much less the responsible positions they did hold," said one. "Mr. Devereaux had himself killed two men in his time, while the Hennesseys are desperate men; Mike, it is alleged, escaped a prosecution for robbery by a noll pros *(sic),* and no one can read the story of yesterday's terrible tragedy, conflicting as the reports are, without a conviction that Dave Hennessey is a murderer." The verdict of acquittal at the trial "met the eyes of an astounded community," said the other.[16] "We are astounded that a jury in a Christian and enlightened country would return such a verdict as 'not guilty' in this case. . . . Not even the savage tribes of the western plains would recognize such a mode of seeking protection or revenge as the Hennesseys resorted to when they murdered Thomas Devereaux, for even savages will not tolerate assassination; and all the facts proved, beyond question, that this was a deliberate and bloody assassination."

Mike moved to Galveston, then to Houston, where he was shot to death on September 29, 1886. There were reports that the killer had been sent from New Orleans. David was born on March 4, 1857, the son of a policeman who was slain in 1869 in a coffeehouse on St. Ann Street. In 1870, when he was thirteen, David became an office boy for General A. S. Badger, chief of police.[17] He rose through the ranks to become chief of aids and finally superintendent after taking time out as a private detective. On the way up, David Hennessey made enemies, as well as friends.

Sicilians continued to flow into the city, until by 1890 there were 25,000 to 30,000 of them. All were poor, many illiterate, few English speaking. Strangers in a not-too-friendly land, scrounging for an existence, they were ripe for exploitation by leaders who came from an environment in which terrorist gangs and secret societies flourished. As early as his first administration (1878-1880), said Mayor Joseph A. Shakspeare,[18] a prominent Italian begged his protection from blackmail and murder, "but as he was afraid to give me any names I could do nothing for him." By 1890, Shakspeare continued, "it is believed that these horrid associations are patronized by some of the wealthy and powerful members of their own race in this city, and that they can point out who the leaders of these associations are. No community can exist with murder associations in their midst. These societies must perish, or the community itself must perish."

Whether Esposito actually started a Mafia organization which continued to operate after he left New Orleans, nobody now knows. Some New Orleanians were convinced there was such a society; others doubted it. Without question, there were factions among the Italians, and there were rivalries. A simmering feud existed between the Provenzano and Matranga factions. The families vied with each other for stevedoring contracts on the wharves, both recruiting their workers from the Italian colony.

In 1890 David Hennessey, now superintendent of police, called leaders of the two factions together in the Red Light Club one night and told them they must curb the enmity between them. "I mean business," he said.[19] "This thing must stop. The Mafia cannot flourish while I am chief of police.

You must make up your minds to live in peace. You know me and I know you. If there is any trouble between you I pledge you my word I will send every one of the offenders to prison." George W. Vandervoort, Hennessey's secretary, made those who were at the meeting shake hands.

On the night of May 1, 1890, members of the Matranga faction were riding from the riverfront in a wagon. They had reached the corner of Esplanade and North Claiborne avenues when they ran into an ambush. A fusillade of bullets raked the wagon, and Tony Matranga was wounded. Members of the Provenzano clique were arrested, and tried on charges resulting from the attack. At this point there reenters the picture one Dominick C. O'Malley, then a private detective. Charles Matranga, who believed Hennessey's sympathies lay with the Provenzanos, hired O'Malley and the latter's lawyer-associate, Lionel Adams, to assist the district attorney in the prosecution. O'Malley later said Hennessey was angered by Matranga's move, and told friends he would have nothing further to do with the case. At the first trial, police furnished no witnesses for the prosecution. As a matter of fact, policemen made efforts to provide alibis for the Provenzanos. A grand jury investigated this surprising development but took no action. After the Provenzanos were convicted, O'Malley said, Hennessey employed counsel who won a new trial.[20]

Before the new trial could be started, New Orleanians read in the morning papers and then in the *States* and the *Item* the details of a news story rivaling in public impact the Battle of New Orleans and the capture of the city by Farragut's fleet. On the night of October 15, 1890, a windblown rain turned the unpaved streets into quagmires. The weather caused cancelation of a political rally in Algiers for General Adolph Meyer, who was running for Congress. Meyer and friends crossed the ferry and stopped for a late-evening snack at Fabacher's Restaurant at Royal and Customhouse streets. There they exchanged greetings with a party of Italians who had been to the theater and later would stop off to drink wine in a nearby house of prostitution.[21]

Shortly after eleven o'clock Superintendent Hennessey left his office at Tulane Avenue and Gasquet Street in the company of Captain William J. O'Connor of Boylan's Private Patrol. They stopped at Virget's, 156 South Rampart Street, corner of Poydras, and ate oysters, then walked along Rampart to Girod Street. Here they parted. O'Connor turned on Girod toward the river. Hennessey went in the opposite direction, walking on the downtown side of Girod toward the home which he occupied with his mother at 275 Girod, between Rampart and Basin streets. As he neared the house and was getting out his door key, shotgun blasts from across the street tore into his body. The wounded superintendent pulled out his pistol and fired several times at his assailants. J. C. Roe, a policeman who had been detailed to guard the Hennessey residence, tried to shoot at the attackers, but his revolver jammed. He was struck in the ear by a slug, and retreated. O'Connor had reached the corner of Girod and Dryades streets when he was startled by the sound of gunfire. He raced to the scene, heard Hennessey call: "Oh, Billy. Billy." He found the superintendent on the stoop of a frame house on Basin Street between Girod and Lafayette streets. "They have given it to me and I gave them back the best I could," gasped Hennessey. "Who gave it to you, Dave?" asked O'Connor. "Put your ear down here," the wounded man directed. O'Connor was quoted in the newspapers as relating that Hennessey whispered, "Dagoes." Hennessey was taken to Charity Hospital. Mayor Shakspeare gave this order to police: "Scour the whole neighborhood. Arrest every Italian you run across." Hennessey lived until 9:10 the next morning, remaining conscious to the end, but efforts to get a statement from him failed. "I'm not going to die," he said. "I'm going to get over this. Those people can't kill me. God is good, and I will get well." [22]

Five sawed-off shotguns were found near the assassination site, obviously ditched by the fleeing slayers. Italians were arrested by the dozens as Hennessey's death caused a profound emotional shock to the community. On the day of the funeral, Thomas Duffy took a look at the body, then hurried to the parish prison and asked to see Antonio Scaffidi, one of the Sicilians who was being held. When Scaffidi came to the gate Duffy shot the defenseless man in the shoulder. Duffy was convicted of assault but given a token sentence of only six months' imprisonment.[23]

The *Item,* along with an undoubtedly considerable proportion of the population, hastened to put the blame for the assassination on Italians. In an editorial entitled "Vendetta,"[24] the paper commented: "How bold impunity has made the oath-bound brotherhood of assassins, the tragical event of last night shows. Heretofore, the unlawful operation and expressions of the Carbonari have been confined to men of their own race and class; but in the very face of Justice that is dragging along a late terrible instance of their lawlessness in the tangle of the state's delays, the murderers strike down the executive of the law himself." The reference, of course, was to the Provenzano case.

A Committee of Fifty, composed of business and professional men, was formed and provided with city funds to help in the investigation. Nineteen Sicilians eventually were indicted in connection with the shooting. Ten were charged with murder and with shooting while lying in wait with intent to murder. These were Peter Natali, Antonio Scaffidi, Charles Traina, Antonio Bagnetto, Manuel Polizzi, Antonio Marchesi, Pietro Monasterio, Bastian Incardona, Salvador Sunzeri and

Loretto Comitez. Nine were indicted as accessories before the fact. These were Asperi Marchesi, Joseph P. Macheca, James Caruso, Charles Matranga, Rocco Gerachi, Charles Patorno, Frank Romero, John Caruso and Charles Pietza.* All of the latter group, with the exception of Asperi Marchesi and Charles Pietza, were connected with the Matranga faction.[25]

The start of the trial was delayed until the retrial of the Provenzanos could be held. This time the Provenzanos were acquitted. O'Malley was careful to point out later that he did not participate in the second trial.[26] It should be noted that attorneys who assisted in the prosecution of the Provenzanos became defense lawyers in the Hennessey case, and those who defended the Provenzanos joined in the prosecution for the assassination trial. A defense fund was raised through contributions from Italians in New Orleans, New York, and other cities. Lionel Adams was paid $10,000 and O'Malley $5,000 for their efforts.[27]

Finally, on February 16, 1891, the trial began in the criminal court then housed in St. Patrick Hall, at Camp and Lafayette streets, the site now occupied by the building which first was the postoffice and later headquarters of the Fifth United States Circuit Court of Appeals. The scene was described by a *Times-Democrat* reporter: "The corridors, at no time very clean, were yesterday converted into a colossal spittoon, and used as such by all who entered to such a degree as to make it filthy in the extreme. . . . The atmosphere of the place was scarcely fit to be breathed by human beings and the incessant hum of voices of the loungers penetrated even to the tribunal of justice itself."[28]

District Attorney Charles H. Luzenberg sprang a surprise

* The spelling of the Sicilians' names varied from paper to paper. Even the official records such as the death certificates are unreliable guides because they were handwritten and the scrawl is difficult to decipher. The practice in this chapter will be to follow the spelling in the newspaper cited, and to acknowledge that there will be discrepancies.

on the first day by obtaining a severance and putting on trial only nine prisoners: Macheca, Scaffidi, Bagnetto, Polizzi, Incardona, Antonio Marchesi, Asperi Marchesi, Monasterio and Matranga. One theory was that the state wanted to cut down on the number of preemptory jury challenges available to the defense, each defendant being entitled to twelve.

Selection of a jury proved to be a time-consuming process as one venire after another was exhausted. "This slow progress is very discouraging to counsel on both sides," commented the *States* by February 20. "It has by this time become evident that it is the desire of public spirited citizens to avoid, if possible, serving on the jury. The report spread around the courtroom that the case will last six weeks has caused every man summoned as a tales juror to stop at nothing but direct perjury to be released from taking a seat in the jury box. The jurors have gotten on to the fact that the only thing necessary to be challenged is to say that they oppose capital punishment." In the early days the *States* was giving prominent, but objective, coverage, with no hint of what was to come. On the eleventh day, February 28, the jury box finally was filled.

Apparently the assassins who ambushed Hennessey were waiting somewhere in the area of a cobbler shop operated by Monasterio in a shed next to the Petersen residence at 272 Girod Street, almost directly across the street from Hennessey's home. An early witness, C. Marcave, testified he passed the shop at about 11 P.M., heard voices, and recognized Scaffidi and Monasterio in a group standing outside. J. J. Driscoll, who operated a grocery store at Rampart and Girod streets, said most of the shots which felled Hennessey were fired from outside the shop. Zachary Foster first identified Scaffidi, Monasterio, Antonio Marchesi, and Polizzi as the four men who he said he saw firing guns. But on cross-examination he backed down and said he could not swear that they were the four he saw coming out of an alley next to the shop. Rosa Walton, who had a room at the rear of the shop, said she heard men talking in the place, then a door slammed and the shooting began.[29]

James Price said he heard shots, raced to the scene, and saw two men running out Girod toward the cemetery which was in the area where the Domed Stadium now stands. Price testified that one man slipped and fell into the gutter, dropped his gun, and left it when he regained his feet and fled. He pointed to Polizzi as the man. Denny Corcoran said that during the day of October 15 he saw Polizzi take two guns out of a sack and give them to another man. M. A. Peeler, a painter who lived at Girod and Basin streets, said he saw the shooting and recognized two of the assailants, motioning toward Scaffidi and Bagnetto. W. J. Leppert, reporter for the *Times-Democrat,* said that when he interviewed Peeler on the day Hennessey died he was told Peeler was on a protracted spree.[30]

Mrs. Theresa Petersen, owner of the building in which the cobbler's shop was situated, testified that on August 13, 1890, she rented the place to Macheca, who she said used the name P. Johnson. James Keyl said he heard Macheca remark at the Red Light Club that Hennessey "had better keep his hands off" the Provenzano case. There was a stir in the courtroom when Fannie Decker, "a tall and handsome young woman, dressed in a stylishly fitting brown plaid coat and black hat," took the witness stand and told the jury she was the proprietor of a house of prostitution at 11 Burgundy Street. At about 2 o'clock on the morning of October 16, she related, Macheca and Matranga came to the house in a party of six or seven men. They drank wine. When the Hennessey shooting of two hours earlier was mentioned, she said, Macheca told her: "These are all Dave Hennessey's enemies."[31]

The state put onto the stand Amos Scott, a young Negro

who sold chickens at the Poydras Market. He said he saw the sixteen-year-old defendant, Asperi Marchesi, at the market on the Saturday after the shooting, and asked him how he managed to win his release from jail. "I told on the old man," he quoted the boy, the son of Antonio Marchesi, as saying. Scott testified young Marchesi confided in him that his role was to watch for Hennessey, run ahead of him, and alert the men who lay in wait.[32] The signal was the so-called Mafia whistle — two short notes, followed by two long notes and then two more short notes, all in the same key and at the same volume. For years afterward the whistle was used by New Orleans urchins to harass Italian fruit vendors.

There was no challenge by the defense to testimony that a group of Italians — variously identified as Macheca, Matranga, John Caruso, James Caruso, Patorno and Gerachi — attended a performance at the Academy of Arts on the night of the slaying, then went to Fabacher's for supper and later to Fannie Decker's house. General Meyer testified that he saw them in Fabacher's when he stopped there after his Algiers rally was called off.[33] The state's theme was that these men paid the others to do the actual shooting, and made themselves conspicuous in order to establish an alibi.

The defense introduced Italian witnesses from Chicago to testify that Natali had been in Chicago the night before the slaying, the implication being that it would have been impossible for him to reach New Orleans in time to take a part. Henry Iff said he saw Bagnetto at the Poydras Market at the time the killing was taking place. Thomas Carey, a keeper at the parish prison, said Rosa Walton and Emma Thomas were shaky in their corroboration of Mrs. Petersen's testimony that Macheca rented the cobbler shop. Corsa Pattina, a midwife, joined Josephine Scaffidi, sister of one of the defendants, in saying he was at home throughout the night because his wife was having a miscarriage. Salvador Matranga, father of the defendant, said he knew the Marchesis, father and son, both were at home during the shooting. There were numerous character witnesses for Macheca, a prosperous businessman.[34]

By March 1 the *States* had abandoned any pretense of objectivity. Major Hearsey and his writers were determined to convict the defendants. "The evidence adduced is not calculated to give the accused much comfort," said the paper. "The defense will be put to its best efforts to offset this testimony." "Good for the State," said a headline on March 3. The venom welled up in Hearsey's brain and on March 4 spilled over onto his editorial page. He said he had withheld comment until the jury was selected and sequestered, and now he wanted to speak to citizens generally:

> Our gates are open to all who seek entrance, conditioned only upon their becoming Americans in the truest sense of the term when they cast their lot among us. One — the chiefest danger to our social system — is that of engrafting upon its stem the vagaries of other nationalities. Unfortunately the most inconsiderate of these we have found to be the Sicilians. In numbers they are a dangerous proportion among us. No people, probably, by instinct and education are more foreign to American ideas than they. . . .
>
> The crimes that distinguish them at home are their chief characteristic here. The vendetta — the highest law of their own lands — is in most instances the only thing they bring with them to the country of their adoption. Few among them are producers. They seldom follow laborious occupations. Choosing either to be, with singular unanimity, vendors of fruit and fish or peddlers of the product of other's hardy toil. Trades among them seem to be confined to two — the tinker or the cobbler, and it is worthy of note that these two are the only trades taught in their Sicilian penitentiaries. . . .
>
> Names with them are not designations. They change them as occasion or their interest may dictate. As a political factor they are especially dangerous, for the reason that they are in all cities or communities absolutely under control of their "padroni." . . . To the ward boss then this lot of cattle becomes very valuable. He need not deal expensively with the individual, he buys the lot at wholesale from the "padroni," and is always sure the goods will be delivered. . . .
>
> The defense will be — can only be — an alibi. Practised as this race has

ever shown itself in lying, with witnesses made timid lest they be assassinated with immunity to their murderers, with all of the technicality of the law in their favor; with nearly every man intelligent enough to read a newspaper "challenged for cause" — and with all of these odds in their favor, we say, we believe that the direct testimony so far adduced, will, this time, demolish the Sicilian lies and all the machinations of their hired so-called private detectives, and cause their contemplated alibi structure to tumble about the heads of the architects.

It is an open secret that the thousands of dollars which have flowed into the coffers of the "Sicilian protection fund" came from American cities and from Sicily have been placed where they would do the most good by ready and experienced hands here. Not Italian hands, either. If we know our people, and we think we do, we would offer those ready agents a word of advice. If the evidence in this case is of such character as to justify conviction and the dagos are acquitted or a hung jury follows it would be well for these American agents to seek the "lake shores" or other safe climes, lest when the vengeance comes they may be partakers of its results.[35]

Lynching, anyone?

Soon the *States* was saying: "The State has wrought the last link in the chain of evidence which may send nine men to the gallows or to the penitentiary for long terms of imprisonment. As far as it applies to some of the accused, at least, there is not a single flaw in that chain, by which the accused are as completely environed as it is within the province of the State to do so."[36]

Public excitement mounted as the trial moved toward a climax. A crowd on Camp Street greeted the wagon that brought the prisoners every morning from parish prison, then situated in the square bounded by Orleans, St. Ann, Treme, and Marais streets. A Sewerage and Water Board pumping station now stands on the site behind the municipal auditorium. It took a squad of deputies sheriff to open a lane from the wagon to the courthouse door. "Who killa de chief?" This was the taunt frequently and loudly flung at the defendants. Reaction to questions and answers in the courtroom left no doubt of the spectators' desire to see the Sicilians hanged. The memory of the shooting of Scaffidi at the prison was another reason for the defendants to fear for their safety. Under the strain, Polizzi broke. He leaped from his chair in the courtroom and shouted a stream of Italian at Judge Joshua B. Baker. The judge excluded the jury, summoned an interpreter, and had Polizzi brought into his office. The *States* and other newspapers reported he had tried to make a confession implicating all of his fellow defendants. District Attorney Luzenberg never introduced the statement, whatever it was. Polizzi showed apprehension that the others would punish him, and officers kept him separated, even bringing him from the prison in a different van. He created scenes in the courtroom, and tried to kill himself by starting a dive through a window in the sheriff's office. He complained that he was being persecuted because he was "a poor Dago." The *States* was not sympathetic. "Around the court the opinion was expressed that Polizzi was simply shamming and that he has not lost his mind," the paper reported. The *States* printed his name as *Polietz* in the early part of the proceedings. On March 8 the paper had an editorial noting that the *Italo-Americano,* an Italian-language weekly, said the name was *Polizzi.* "We publish this fact in justice to the accused," wrote Hearsey, "because he does not care, we think, to go sailing into eternity under a Spanish or Austrian name." Iama Roma, Polizzi's mistress, said he was at home at the time of the assassination.[37]

On March 6 the *States* published, under the headline "Grave Reports," a news story which said:

> This morning a representative of the *States* heard, in a public place, a man say "The State has made a magnificent case, the accused have been identified, but there are some men in the jury box whom I don't think will find a verdict according to the facts brought out." The *States'* man asked why, and he replied: "Because I, as a tales juror, was approached and told that there was $3,000 in it for my wife if I testified in a certain way and was accepted as a juror." He would not name the person or persons who

approached him. This is one of the many rumors flying around about how the jury was made up. The Mafia, after the Hennessey killing, seems to exert its influence beyond the race who have adopted it as an arbiter in their disputes.

The next day a headline, "Fixing the Jury," was printed over a story quoting another anonymous tales juror as saying he was offered $500 to favor the defendants. An editorial on the same day gave a grim foreboding of impending tragedy. Wrote Hearsey, under the heading "Those Ugly Rumors": "It is to be hoped, however, that the jury has not been tampered with because if the people are convinced that such has been done scenes of violence are pretty sure to be enacted on the streets of this city. The people are not in a mood to be trifled with." Not if the *States* would lead the way.

The newspaper's stories about the tampering reports led to a grand jury investigation. This resulted in indictments against Thomas McCrystol and John Cooney and later O'Malley.[38] Only McCrystol ever was convicted.

Coverage of the trial by the *Item* was not nearly so voluminous, nor as biased, as that of the *States*. By March 3 the *Item* was saying in an editorial: "Aside from the confession that Politz (Polizzi) is said to have made, the testimony of witnesses has been of such a distinct nature, so far as concerns certain of the accused, that on the surface it would appear as though the defense will experience much difficulty in breaking it down." An enterprising *Item* reporter managed to talk with Polizzi, and wrote: "In his imperfect dialect he went on to state that Matranga and Macheca are the grand moguls of the Mafia society. It is a sort of religious organization under the patronage of St. Joseph. Sunzeri, Geraci, *(sic)* Monasterio and the others are mere tools in the hands of the stars of a greater magnitude."[39]

The prosecuting attorneys had the spectators roaring and

stomping their feet with emotional summations to the jury. W. I. Evans exhibited the sawed-off shotguns abandoned by the slayers, calling them the "terrible engines of murder." Defense attorneys pointed to the inconsistencies in the district attorney's case. In his closing argument District Attorney Luzenberg abandoned the case against Incardona with the admission that evidence against him was insufficient. Judge Baker instructed the jury to acquit Matranga because the charge against him had not been proven.[40]

At 6:15 P.M. on March 12 the case went to the jury. At 2:53 P.M. on March 13 the verdict was read. "Outrageous," stormed one *States* headline. "Indignation," shouted another on the same front page. The jury reported itself unable to agree on the charges against Polizzi, Monasterio, and Scaffidi, and a mistrial was declared insofar as these three were concerned. The other six defendants were acquitted. Other charges still pended against all of the men, and they were hustled through a dense crowd outside the court building to a van which waited to return them to parish prison.

"Who killa de chief?" The refrain swelled to a roar as the disappointed throng surged against the cordon of deputies. Soon after the verdict was pronounced, a group of citizens crowded into the office of attorney W. S. Parkerson at 7 Commercial Place, across Camp Street from Newspaper Row. They met again at 9 P.M. in a hall near Royal and Bienville streets.

At midnight, a notice signed by sixty-one men, whose names were recognized by most residents of the city, was handed to the *Picayune, Times-Democrat,* and *New Delta* for publication in the morning editions. "Mass Meeting," it said. "All good citizens are invited to attend a mass meeting on Saturday, March 14, at 10 o'clock A.M. at Clay Statue to take steps to remedy the failure of justice in the Hennessey case. Come prepared for action." Clay Statue, now in Lafayette Square, at that time stood in the neutral ground of Canal Street at the intersection with St. Charles Street.

"We trust and believe," said a *Picayune* editorial, "that the object of the meeting is wholly in the interest of peace as in the interest of justice. The names of the gentlemen who have signed the call would seem a ready guarantee of peaceful intentions, and so we accept them." "This failure of justice creates a grave and threatening situation," chimed in the *Times-Democrat,* "and it is entirely meet and proper that good citizens should assemble to discuss the gravity of the situation and the steps necessary to remedy the wrong complained of." The paper cautioned against turning the assemblage into a mob.

The *States* was not so naive. Hearsey and his staff prepared an extra edition for distribution to the thousands who would attend the mass meeting with vengeance in their hearts, "Rise in your might, people of New Orleans!" thundered the page one editorial (quoted in the preamble to this chapter). There was another editorial, on the same page, in which the *States* asked:

> How much longer will the people of New Orleans continue to be a long suffering one? The outrageous travesty on justice, which the jury in the Sicilian assassination case has just enacted, would drive any other community to uncontrollable fury! But New Orleans juries have long since so familiarized us with such damnable vagaries, that a few red-handed Sicilian assassins, more or less, turned loose to repeat their deeds of midnight Mafia horrors, will no doubt prove the mere object of a few days' wonder. Our murdered Chief of Police Hennessey will little reck, now, in his prematurely and fouly *(sic)* filled grave, that New Orleans is become the haven of murderers, and the safe vantage ground for the Sicilian Mafia and their hired agents of American birth, who murder officers of the law, and who buy jurors and suborn witnesses, under the hooded eyes of blinded justice, that the murderers may go unwhipped!
>
> WHO BRIBED THE JURY? If there a single spark of manhood in the

anonymous tales jurors who have heretofore written to us, now is the time for them to come forth and help the authorities to vindicate the majesty of American law which the jury in the Sicilian Mafia case has just dragged in the mire.

And with that, on page one, the *States* published the names — and not only the home addresses but also the business addresses — of members of the trial jury. Was Hearsey only trying to make it easy for New Orleanians to send Easter cards to the jurors? The season was approaching.

At Clay Statue a crowd — who can say whether there were two thousand or ten thousand — heard brief talks by Parkerson, Walter D. Denegre and John C. Wickliffe, coeditor of the *New Delta*. By 10:15 the citizens streamed toward the parish prison, some stopping to pick up rifles and shotguns cached the night before. There is no record to show whether Hearsey joined the mob to see with his own eyes the results of the savagery which his newspaper had helped to stir up. If he stayed in his office, he could engage in the vicarious sensation of watching the Sicilians whom he despised perish like animals cornered by hunters. All of the daily papers ran voluminous accounts and the weekly *Mascot* on March 21 published a chilling eyewitness report.

Denied admission to the prison, the throng battered down a door on the Treme Street side. Inside, the Sicilians were turned out of their cells and allowed to seek any hiding place they could find in the gloomy old bastille.* The heavily armed mob surged through the corridors and yards, paying no attention to the other prisoners as they searched for their quarry.

They first came upon the screaming Marchesi boy, racing up and down a ground floor corridor in an effort to find his father. He was spared, and allowed to hide under a bed.

* On September 9, 1880, the cells of the gloomy old building were fumigated. The *Item* of June 11, 1902, reported that one hundred barrels of dead bats were taken out.

Macheca, Scaffidi, and the elder Marchesi were spotted crouching behind a brick pillar in a small gallery off the condemned cell. The doors were locked. Through the bars of a window a rifleman got a shot when Scaffidi was exposed for an instant, and killed him with one bullet. Marchesi stumbled over Scaffidi's body, fell headlong, and was wounded with buckshot before he could regain his feet. Macheca pounded with an Indian club on the lock of a door through which he might escape the trap, if only temporarily. He had knocked the lock loose and was opening the door when an avenger shot him in the back of the head. Blinded by blood, Marchesi was leaning against the wall when the lynchers finally got into the gallery. A man put a shotgun to his chest. Marchesi grasped the barrel, and his hand was torn off by the charge. He covered his face with the stump as another of the mob members dispatched him with a load of buckshot into the chest.

"Down the stairs the crowd flocked, their guns still warm with their recent discharges and their feet dyed with the blood of their victims," wrote the *Mascot* reporter.

Six prisoners had found momentary haven in cell Number 2, but were discovered and ran into the prison yard. There they huddled together against a wall. "The men begged for their lives," said the *Mascot,* "and got bullets in return." Romero received a fatal wound from a shot through the brain. Comitez was next. As he started to collapse from a head wound, four more bullets ripped into his body. Traina was put away with buckshot. James Caruso tried to reach a protective post and shuddered under the impact of balls which made forty-two wounds in his body. Geracchi succumbed to a chest wound. Monasterio was shot in the back of the head.

Outside, several thousand citizens, frenzied by the screams and sounds of gunfire from within the prison, demanded their share of blood. Polizzi and Bagnetto were dragged out for public executions. Polizzi was shoved through the crowd to the corner of St. Ann and Treme streets, where a youth had climbed atop a lamp post and adjusted a cord over the cross-bar. A noose was placed around Polizzi's neck and the other end of the cord pulled by eager volunteers. The cord broke and the victim fell to the banquette. A clothesline was rigged up, and Polizzi was swung above the heads of the mob. He grasped the rope with his free hands. The youth kicked him in the face and made him let go, but the struggling man again managed to hold with his hands. He was lowered to the ground and his arms pinioned. Once more he was pulled aloft. This time shots rang out; his body quivered under the impact of bullets, and after a moment of convulsive shudders, Polizzi was dead. Within ten minutes every thread of his shirt had been cut away by souvenir seekers.

Bagnetto, a noose around his neck, was kicked and cudgeled as his prone form was pulled through the main entrance to a dead tree on the uptown side of the Orleans Avenue neutral ground. The rope was passed over a limb, which broke on the first attempt to hang the unconscious Sicilian. Bagnetto was almost dead as a result of the kicks and blows, and he struggled for only a brief instant when he was suspended from a stronger limb. As the man who adjusted the rope was descending from the tree he gave the dying Bagnetto a kick on the forehead with the heel of his boot.

Thus ended the most shameful day New Orleans ever knew —an example of lynch law that would haunt a city for decades.

Soon after the last spasm of Bagnetto the *States* was on the street with another edition and another Hearsey editorial: "Citizens of New Orleans! You have, in one righteous upheaval, in one fateful gust of mighty wrath, vindicated your laws, heretofore, desecrated and trampled under foot by oath bound aliens who had thought to substitute Murder for Justice, and the suborner's gold for the Freeman's honest verdict. Your vengeance is consecrated in the forfeited blood of the assassins. Stop there! Return to your homes, resume the peaceful pursuit of your avocations."

The *Item* also applauded the mob's action: "When the ordinary means of justice fail, extraordinary means are resorted to. This is a characteristic of the American people and has been illustrated once more in a most impressive manner. Red-handed murder, made bold by successful crime, struck at the Law itself, and the agencies of the law were found impotent to punish the foul deed. But the people, the source of power, resumed temporary control and meted out swift and summary vengeance for the outrage upon justice."[41]

Late in the day, the *States* started a news story in its final edition with this smug paragraph: "The editorial in the first edition of the *States,* calling on the people to quietly return to their homes and places of business and leave the committee any further disposition of the other parties connected with the Hennessey case, had a good effect, and the irresponsible crowds that were gathering heeded the advice." If Hearsey could boast that the influence of the *States* persuaded the mob to disperse, then certainly by implication he admitted that his newspaper was a factor in inciting mass murder. The *States* did not stand alone; all of the city's other dailies condoned the lynching. A dissenting voice came from the *Mascot,* which said:

> That public opinion is all one-sided in the premises is far from being the truth, and, already, since the reaction of sober second-thought has set in, opinions can be heard upon all sides not very flattering to the self-constituted leaders in the recent movement. Of course, outsiders cannot understand the feeling here, but when the citizens of New Orleans, who are only too well acquainted with the record of some of the personnel of those leaders see them at the head of anything, they are inclined to doubt or question the justness or real motives of such movement.[42]

It was an occasion which cried out for responsible journalism, for a calm, reasoned warning against the catastrophe of impassioned, reckless action. Passing judgment on the journals of a bygone era is easy enough in a day when the principle of law and order is more firmly established and when newspapers are financially secure and able to withstand the buffeting of the winds of disagreement. In the New Orleans of 1891 even the strongest daily was a fragile operation which could be wiped out by the displeasure of a few advertisers and not many subscribers. The people who led or joined the mob were more vociferous than the questioners reported by the *Mascot.*

The lynching caused a crisis in diplomatic relations between the United States and Italy. The government at Rome withdrew its envoy to Washington, and for a time some New Orleanians feared that the Italian navy, then the fourth strongest in the world, might bombard their city. Eventually an indemnity of $24,330 was paid to Italy by the government of the United States. Charges against the Sicilians who escaped the fury of the lynchers were dropped.[43]

Hearsey remained unreconstructed, so far as Sicilians and lynchings were concerned. In July, 1899, five Italians were killed by a mob in Tallulah, Louisiana, because one of them had wounded a local physician. In an editorial on July 26, 1899, the *States* commented: "A very pertinacious effort is being made to arouse a spirit of indignation over the lynching. . . . From our standpoint we can see no ground for indignation. The lynching was, in our opinion, an act of justice. . . . Judge Lynch has administered more substantial justice than all the criminal courts of the land combined." And the next day Hearsey commented again: "The intemperate and heedless abuse heaped upon the people of Tallulah by a considerable part of the Mississippi press because of the lynching of five bloody scoundrels is shocking. It shows one of the evil phases of modern journalism. Comment and criticism without due digestion of the facts."

Nearly nine decades later, the question of whether the accused Sicilians really killed Hennessey still has not been answered. They could have done it, but the prosecution did not prove in their trial that they were guilty. It is true that one man was convicted of attempting to bribe a tales juror. However, 1,375 prospective jurors were subpoenaed[44] and it strains credulity to suggest that all of these were fixed. A grand jury tried to find incriminating evidence against the twelve men who served and was forced to take cover in unsupported generalities while it was endeavoring mightily to justify the tragic denouement.[45] The ownership of the assassination weapons found at the scene was not established. Fingerprints, which now might have provided vital evidence, were not then used in criminal procedures. In an interview after the trial Jacob M. Seligman, foreman of the jury, said the jurors had doubt cast in their minds by the "extraordinary absence" of Captain O'Connor and officer Roe from the ranks of prosecution witnesses. Roe, it will be remembered, was at the scene when the shooting started, and O'Connor was the first to reach the wounded Hennessey. Seligman said the jury was instructed by the judge to give credence to the testimony of Italians, and he pointed out that the alibis offered were uncontradicted. Seligman told of doubts raised when jurors visited the shooting scene and found it difficult under the street light to identify people only thirty or forty feet away.[46] In addition, Seligman said anyone who wanted to kill Hennessey would have waited under the shed in front of the cobbler's shop because it was the only place of concealment along the superintendent's route.

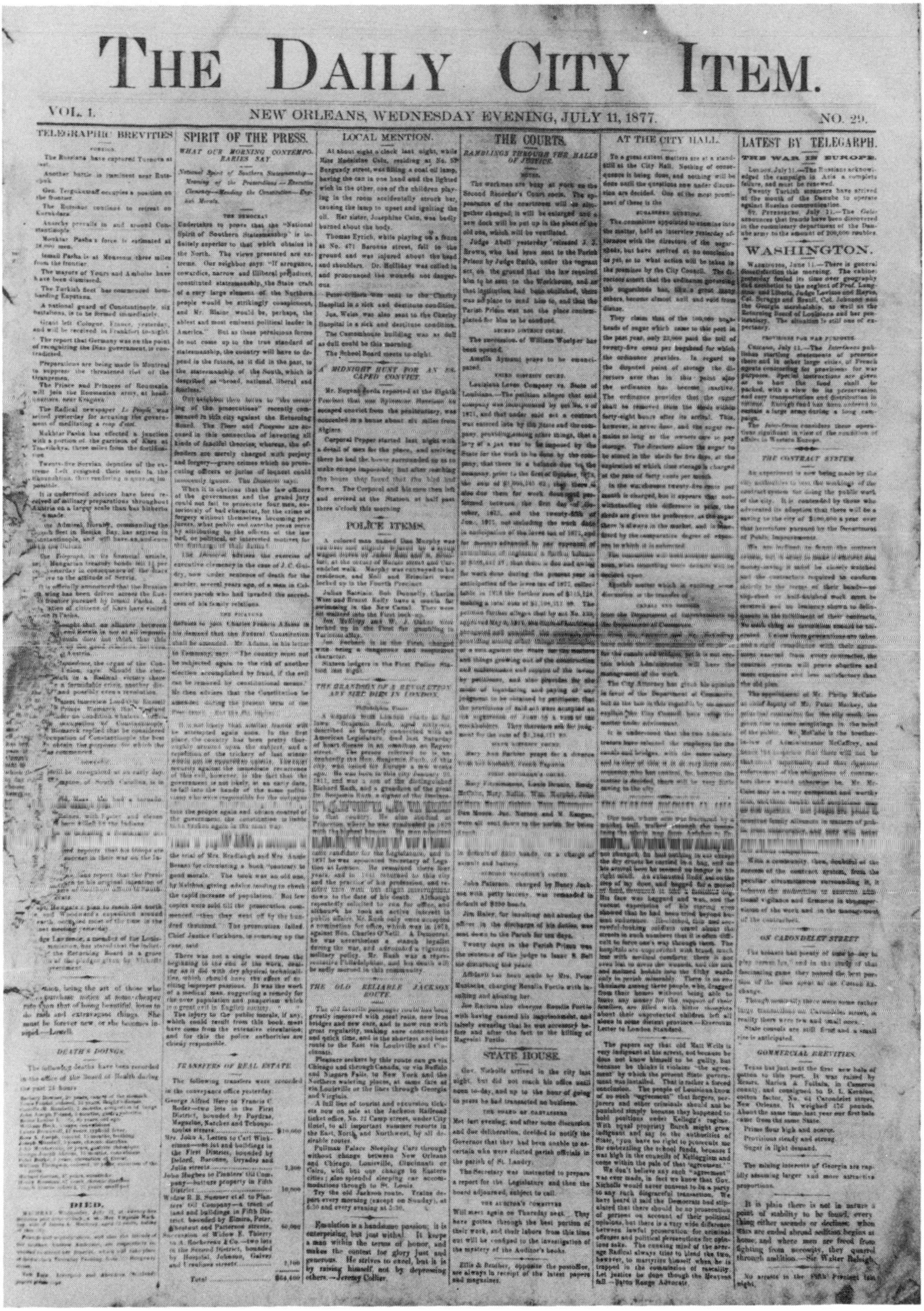

THE DAILY CITY ITEM.

VOL. 1. NEW ORLEANS, WEDNESDAY EVENING, JULY 11, 1877. NO. 29.

TELEGRAPHIC BREVITIES

SPIRIT OF THE PRESS.

LOCAL MENTION.

THE COURTS.

AT THE CITY HALL.

LATEST BY TELEGRAPH.

WASHINGTON.

POLICE ITEMS.

STATE HOUSE.

DIED.

This dull, cluttered front page of one of the first issues of the *Item*, July 11, 1877, is perhaps the earliest available for reproduction. No copies of the first edition, on June 11, 1877, have been found.

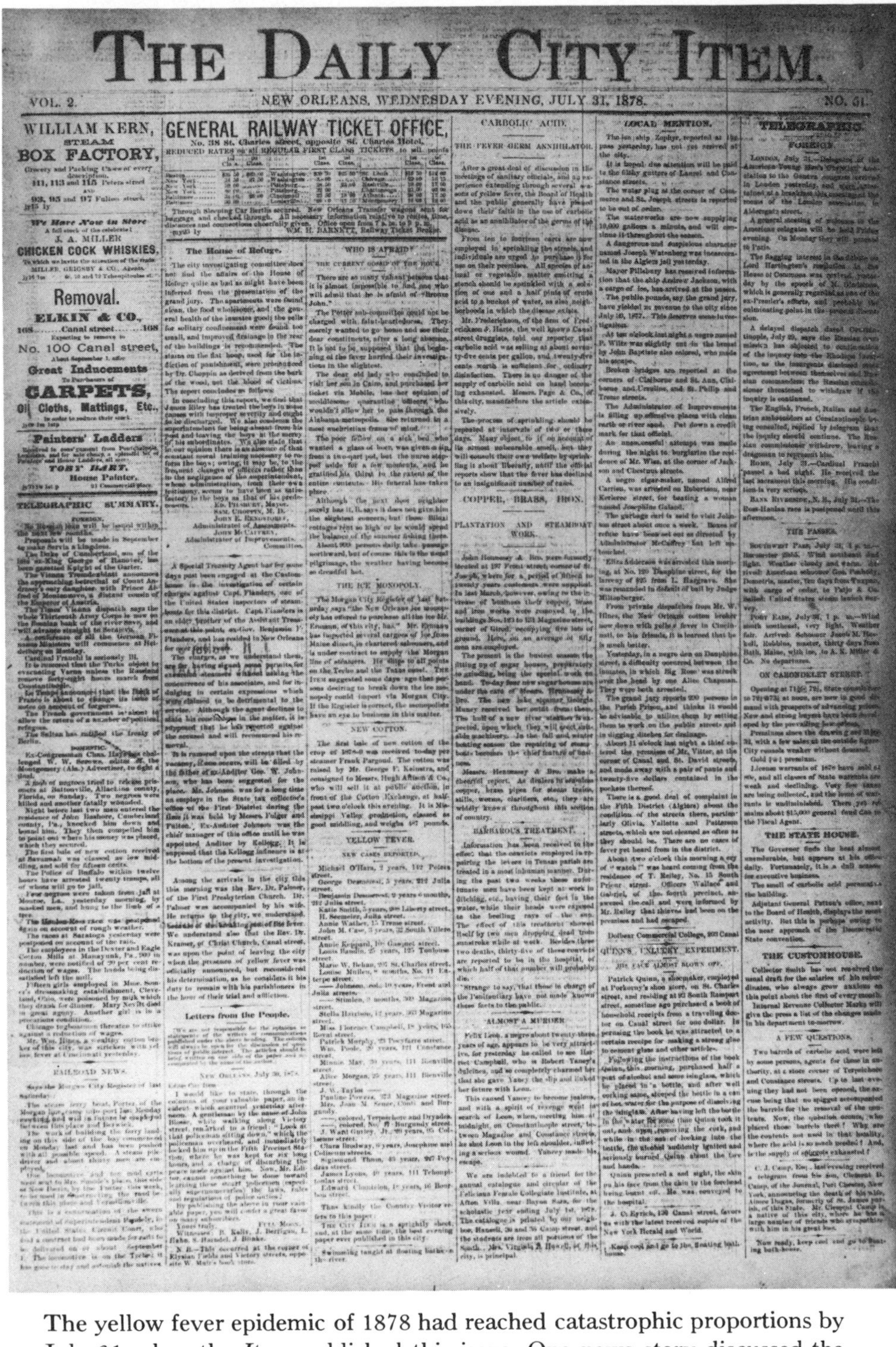

THE DAILY CITY ITEM.

VOL. 2. NEW ORLEANS, WEDNESDAY EVENING, JULY 31, 1878. NO. 51.

WILLIAM KERN, STEAM BOX FACTORY,

GENERAL RAILWAY TICKET OFFICE, No. 38 St. Charles street, opposite St. Charles Hotel.

CHICKEN COCK WHISKIES

Removal. ELKIN & CO.

No. 100 Canal street,

Great Inducements

CARPETS,

Oil Cloths, Mattings, Etc.,

Painters' Ladders

TOBY HART. House Painter.

TELEGRAPHIC SUMMARY.

The House of Refuge.

WHO IS AFRAID?

CARBOLIC ACID.

THE FEVER GERM ANNIHILATOR.

COPPER, BRASS, IRON.

PLANTATION AND STEAMBOAT WORK.

THE ICE MONOPOLY.

NEW COTTON.

YELLOW FEVER.

NEW CASES REPORTED.

BARBAROUS TREATMENT.

ALMOST A MURDER.

Letters from the People.

RAILROAD NEWS.

QUINN'S UNLUCKY EXPERIMENT.

LOCAL MENTION.

TELEGRAPHIC.

FOREIGN.

THE PASSES.

ON CARONDELET STREET.

THE STATE HOUSE.

THE CUSTOMHOUSE.

A FEW QUESTIONS.

The yellow fever epidemic of 1878 had reached catastrophic proportions by July 31 when the *Item* published this issue. One news story discussed the use of carbolic acid as a prophylactic measure, and another listed the latest victims. The *Item* beat all competitors with its coverage of the outbreak that claimed almost four thousand lives.

Lafcadio Hearn was paid ten dollars a week when he was hired by the *Item* in 1878. He later served as literary editor of the *Times-Democrat* before going to Japan and solidifying his standing as one of the most widely read authors of the time.

Peter Kiernan, once a reporter on the *Item*, later dabbled in the ownership of New Orleans newspapers. He was proprietor at one time or another of no fewer than six dailies. On at least one occasion he created a new paper by changing the name of the old one.

The *Item's* first home of its own was this structure at 39 Natchez Street to which the staff moved in January, 1878, from a printing company office at 112 Gravier Street. The rent for the Natchez Street building was $20 a month. Wooden cisterns stored rainwater for drinking purposes, although most newsmen of the period preferred to slake their thirst in nearby saloons.

George Washington Dupre shared the ownership of the *States* at one period with Henry J. Hearsey. He was a hot-tempered brawler, but as a member of a well-known family moved in high social circles. He was a White League captain in the Battle of September 14, 1874.

Henry J. Hearsey, who established the *States* on January 3, 1880, with an investment of $2,250, was a name-caller, a master of invective, and one of the most quoted southern editors of his day.

Dominick Call O'Malley, by his own count, went to his grave with the scars of fourteen bullet wounds. They were sustained in the gunfights in which he engaged as the most controversial figure in New Orleans over a period of twenty-five years. Many of his escapades occurred while he was proprietor of the *Item*.

The Daily States.

VOL. I. NEW ORLEANS, SATURDAY EVENING, JANUARY 3, 1880. NO. 1.

HOLIDAY NOTES.

The Season in New Orleans.

Christmas and New Year Came and Went.

General Jollification Along the Line.

CITY BREVITIES.

Crime and Casualty.

The following bacchanals sobered up in the First Precinct last night:

Agnes Filmore, Pat Burke, D. F. Costello, N. P. McKeon, Joe Walsh, Mollie Bell, H. Dixon, Frank Blake, Dan Harris, May Frisby, Mollie Shepherd, Emma Davidson, R. Granger, Louis Fido, Caroline Dickson and Eva Johnson.

Geo. Washington was locked up in the Third Precinct, charged with cutting one Geo. Holloway.

The lamp post corner Canal and Front was run into and demolished by a wagon.

Theo. Hassan has been indicted by the Grand Jury for complicity in the failure of the Citizens Savings Bank.

Takin' off the Kiver.

"Say, Mister, d'ye want to see some fun?" inquired a small but vigorous boy with a rasp in his voice and a bunch of crackers in his hand, hailing a STATES local on New Year's eve—"its going to be lively."

TELEGRAPH FLASHES.

Domestic.

NEW YORK, Jan. 2.—The Grocer's Bank of New York suspended; Stephen V. White of No. 17 Wall Street was appointed receiver.

In Washington, Judge Blatchford decided against the motion to remand in case of the Chicago, St. Louis and New Orleans Railroad vs. H. S. McComb and the Southern Railway Association.

Individual Mention.

Judge Henry L. Duffel, of Ascension parish, is in the city. The dockets of the courts over which he presides will be cleared, he thinks, before the newly elected Judges enter upon their official duties.

The advance agent of Miss Fanny Davenport, Mr. Marcus Mayer, has arrived preparatory to the opening of the engagement of that distinguished and charming actress, to commence to-morrow night at the Academy of Music.

THE TEHUANTEPEC ROUTE.

DISCUSSING THE INTEROCEANIC CANAL.

Januarianism.

In the bound volumes on file in the Louisiana State Museum Library is this faded and brittle, but still legible, page one of the first issue of the *States*, January 3, 1880. It was a two-page edition published on a Saturday. By Monday the paper had four pages.

Two years after it was launched in 1880, the *States* had prospered and taken over the entire building at 80 Camp Street in which it had its first quarters. The building, long since demolished, was in what is now the 400 block of Camp and was on Newspaper Row.

Newspaper Row—on the river side of Camp Street between Poydras and Gravier—is shown, *circa* 1890, in this photograph made by George Francois Mugnier, who captured the flavor of New Orleans with his primitive camera. The picture is provided through the courtesy of the Louisiana State Museum, which has a collection of Mugnier's works.

Frank Waters, shown in a *Mascot* drawing, was an *Item* reporter when he killed Joseph Baker, Third District assessor, on September 26, 1886, in a gun battle that developed when Baker took offense at a news story written by Waters. Nearly five years later, on March 18, 1891, Waters was fatally wounded in a pistol fight on Canal Street with Arthur Dunn.

Robert Ewing held sway in New Orleans for thirty-one years after he gained complete control of the *States* in 1900. His paper provided clout that helped in his political dealings as a member of the ruling Choctaw Club. He helped to elect Huey P. Long governor, then broke with the Kingfish.

The assassination of Police Chief David C. Hennessey on the night of October 15, 1890, is depicted in this drawing in the *Mascot*, a sprightly weekly scandal sheet. Hennessey was approaching his home on Girod Street when his assailants opened fire with sawed-off shotguns. He fought back with his pistol, but missed.

Always ready to ridicule the daily newspapers, the *Mascot* picked the *States* as the target of this cartoon based on an editorial in the *Picayune* in which C. Harrison Parker said the *States* existed on official "pap" from the state government. The *Mascot* said, "The youthful David got the best of the Philistines."

The *Mascot*'s artist captured the savagery with which eleven Sicilian immigrants were lynched on March 14, 1891, in the old parish prison at Marais and St. Ann streets. A jury had refused to convict the men accused of slaying Police Chief David C. Hennessey, and a mob took the law into its own hands.

A prelude to the assassination of Police Chief David C. Hennessey in 1890 and the lynching of eleven Sicilians in 1891 was the ambush of members of the Matranga faction of Italians on the night of May 1, 1890. Members of the Provenzano family were convicted of waylaying the Matrangas, but they won a new trial and freedom. The *Mascot* portrays the shooting at Esplanade and North Claiborne avenues.

The lively *Mascot* had some fun with this cartoon after George W. Dupre, coproprietor of the *States*, burst into the office of Dr. S. R. Olliphant, president of the State Board of Health, on June 6, 1891, and started a gunfight. Neither man was hit by the flying bullets. Olliphant had taken umbrage at a *States* editorial.

W. J. Leppert won an enviable reputation as a reporter for the *Times-Democrat* in the late 1800s, then became managing editor of the *Item.* When Robert Ewing of the *States* suggested a duel, Leppert offered to fight him with Roman candles.

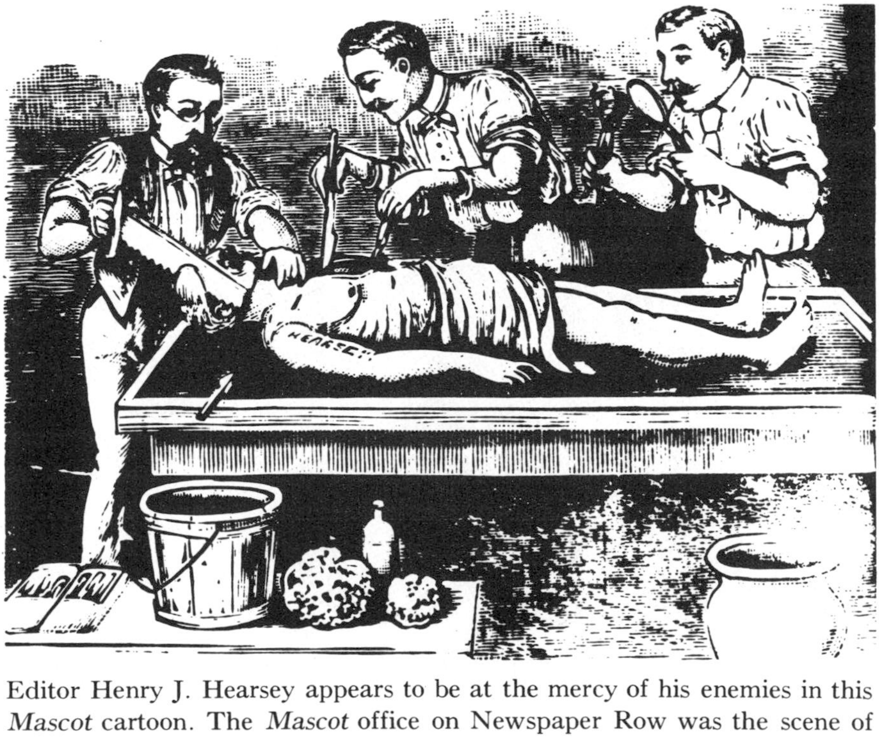

Editor Henry J. Hearsey appears to be at the mercy of his enemies in this *Mascot* cartoon. The *Mascot* office on Newspaper Row was the scene of two fatal shootings which occurred when irate readers came in to complain about articles in the irreverent weekly.

Newsboys were part of the New Orleans street scene from the time of the Civil War until the start of the second World War. A *States* artist shows some of their activities late in the nineteenth century.

Scenes in the building at 210-212 Camp Street to which the *Item* moved in 1908 after the failure of the *Morning World*, a short-lived paper founded by Joseph Mark Leveque, who was more successful with the weekly *Harlequin.* James M. Thomson was principal owner of the *Item* when the move was made.

ITEM

The four principal daily newspapers—*States*, *Picayune*, *Item*, and *Times-Democrat*—were the subject of this *Mascot* cartoon.

6

Canal Street Gun Battles

On October 29, 1874, the governor of Louisiana waged a gun battle on Canal Street with the man who was to become publisher of the *Times-Democrat.* Nobody was hurt.

On January 17, 1908, the New Orleans inspector of police invaded the office of the *Morning World* at 210-212 Camp Street and opened fire on the editor. He missed.

The incidents, although themselves bloodless, opened and closed the most violent third of a century ever experienced by New Orleans newspapermen.

Editors and reporters of the *States* and the *Item* wrote their share of chapters in the history of an era when the pistol and the pen both were journalistic tools.

Governor William Pitt Kellogg climbed into a horse-drawn cab at the Customhouse that day in 1874 a month and a half after the revolt of the White League threatened but failed to overturn his Carpetbag regime. He was driven out Canal Street. As the vehicle neared Rampart Street, Kellogg espied

Edward A. Burke, who was representing the Conservative State Central Committee in a dispute with the governor over the naturalization of several thousand potential voters. Burke was destined as managing editor of the *Democrat* to arrange in 1881 the merger of the *Times* and *Democrat*.

When Kellogg saw Burke standing on the sidewalk he grimaced and made a gesture of derision with his finger. Burke raised his hand, as though to hail the cab, and the driver brought it to a halt. Burke approached and extended his hand. The governor reached through the door to take it. Burke grasped his wrist and said: "Get out; I have something to say to you." Kellogg resisted. In the struggle Burke managed to get part-way into the cab and strike the governor with his fists. The cab started rolling, leaving Burke standing on the pavement. Kellogg aimed his pistol through the rear window and shot at Burke. The latter returned the fire, but the cab soon was out of range.[1]

Later in the same year Canal Street again was the scene of a fight between newsman and politician, this time with fatal results. Edwin L. Jewell, then one of the proprietors of the *Commercial Bulletin* and later alternately an editor of the *Item* and the *States*, had challenged former governor Henry Clay Warmoth to a duel. Warmoth accepted, and an encounter was scheduled to take place on Monday, December 28. Shortly before noon on Saturday, December 26, Warmoth was walking on Canal Street, between Royal and Bourbon streets. Without any prelude Daniel C. Byerly, coproprietor of the *Commercial Bulletin,* approached Warmoth and hit him on the head with his cane. The men clinched and fell to the banquette, with Byerly on top. Warmoth, who otherwise was unarmed, managed to get a hand into his pocket and take out his penknife. He stabbed Byerly several times in the stomach. When bystanders pulled Byerly off he was fainting. He was taken to a doctor's office on Dauphine Street, where he died at 10:30 P.M. Warmoth reminded that he had accepted Jewell's challenge, "and under all rules of the Code I thought I was out of danger from attack by Mr. Jewell's friends. I was very much surprised when Mr. Byerly, the friend of Mr. Jewell, made this assault."* Washington Marks, Jewell's second, said Byerly acted without Jewell's knowledge.[2]

It was Sunday, September 26, 1886. In the office of the *Item,* Reporter Frank R. Waters checked over the Sunday evening edition. In it was a news story he had written.

> Yesterday was policeman's day in the First Congressional District, and the so-called guardians of the peace held high revel at the polls in the Eighth Ward, where they manipulated the election in a manner which would make old time usurpers blush. About seven or eight in uniform, and as many dead-head specials stood by at the polls intimidating respectable citizens, and in every imaginable way impeded the success of the faction opposing the Mayor in this city. They were drunk and made no bones about telling of their connection with the famous special roll. The old residents of the Eighth Ward declare that yesterday's election eclipsed all ever held in that section, even when it was worth a man's life to go to the polls. It was predicted on all sides yesterday that Guillotte's** fight for gubernatorial honors will be made by his police force. The result of the display of partisanship on the part of the police force is a protest in the Eighth Ward, on the grounds above stated, that the contestants have a good case to go before the Convention cannot be gainsaid. The conduct of the policemen in the Eighth Ward yesterday was, to say the least, outrageous. They assumed to break up steps at the close of the poll, dictate to people which way to vote, and, in fact, run the machine entirely.

Waters finished his work and saw it was 1 P.M., time to go to his home at 85 Mandeville Street for dinner. He put on his coat, patting the pocket to be sure that his pistol, a cheap

* Warmoth was arrested and confined for five days in a parish prison cell which he shared with Sam Williams, a gambler who had been sentenced to hang for killing a woman. Warmoth was released after a coroner's jury ruled he acted in self-defense. The scheduled duel between Warmoth and Jewell was called off.

** Mayor J. Valsin Guillotte, who entertained gubernatorial aspirations.

American Bulldog, was in place. On the street outside he encountered Thomas Koops and Ben Theard. They talked about the election, and Koops announced his intention of filing a protest. The three walked to the residence of Jacob Vollrath, secretary of the Parish Democratic Committee, at 255 Bourbon Street, and Koops formally filed his action. The three men then went to Canal Street and boarded a streetcar.

Meanwhile, Chief of Police Zach Bachemin had stopped at the Fifth Station, on Elysian Fields Avenue at Dauphine Street, to await a train that would take him to Milneberg, where a rifle contest was scheduled. Seated in front of the station with the chief were Joseph Baker, city assessor for the Third District and the acknowledged political boss of the Eighth Ward; Baker's brother-in-law, Police Sergeant Patrick McGrath; and two or three other men. A copy of the *Item* bearing Waters' account of the election in Baker's bailiwick was brought to them. Members of the party arose and went into the saloon adjoining the station for a drink. Baker was fuming over the story.

Elysian Fields is wide, and the Rampart and Dauphine streetcars could be seen half a block away as they approached. Baker's brother-in-law looked out of a window and remarked: "Here comes Frank Waters now." The others turned to where he pointed and saw Waters on a car. Baker arose and walked out of the saloon and toward the corner with a copy of the *Item* in his hand.

When the car halted, Warren Easton, state superintendent of education, alighted and walked toward the corner where Baker stood. Baker called out Waters' name, and told him to get off, too. Following Waters from the car were Koops and Theard, and Tommy O'Brien, whom they had met. Waters walked toward Baker, who remained standing at the corner until Waters reached the sidewalk at a point which was out of the line of vision of those in the saloon. Bachemin told McGrath: "Go to the corner and don't let them go too far. Let them talk all they want."

Before McGrath could take more than a few steps, he heard a pistol shot followed by others in rapid succession. Then he saw Waters appear from around the corner, backing toward a lamp post. As Waters had approached Baker, the latter pointed to the newspaper which he held. Baker indicated the election story and asked: "Did you write that? "Well, Baker," replied the newsman, "I'm man enough to tell you yes." "You're a damned liar," shouted Baker. Easton later said Waters slapped Baker, but the other eyewitnesses did not agree with him. Baker drew his big Tranter and fired twice at five-foot range. How he missed, nobody can explain. Meanwhile, Waters unbuttoned his coat and got out his weapon. After Baker's second shot, Waters fired. Baker got off a third shot, as McGrath stepped from a door on the Dauphine side of the saloon and started toward Waters. The latter pointed his pistol at the sergeant. McGrath jumped back into the saloon, exclaiming: "Let up on that." "Make him let up," said Waters, motioning toward Baker who was attempting to fire again. "I'm a target," said Waters. "Give a man a chance to defend himself. I'll stay as long as he does." After others intervened and disarmed the antagonists, Baker told them, "I am shot." He was taken to Charity Hospital in an ambulance, and Waters was locked in the police station. Baker died on Tuesday as the result of a wound in the groin. He declined to make a deathbed statement.

The *Picayune* described Waters as a quiet, peaceable man who had not been in trouble before. "Baker's reputation for peace and quiet is also said to be good." In an editorial the paper said: "The affray, which resulted so tragically, took place in the very shadow of the police station, in the presence of the highest police authority in the city and of his assistants. They knew beforehand the causes which led to the conflict and watched it from its inception to its culmination without taking any steps to prevent it. It is also a fact that the attack made upon the journalist was in the interest of the Chief of Police and his faction."[3]

In another newspaper fight that titillated the town, not a shot was fired. The time was January 25, 1890; the place the crowded bar of the St. Charles Hotel at St. Charles and Common streets. George W. Dupre, one of the proprietors of the *States,* had been in an editorial dispute with John W. Fairfax, owner of the *Item.* Fairfax challenged Dupre to a duel. "Having in my career as a journalist and a member of the legislature had experience in the adaptation of the code for the eleventh hour apologies even so far as on the field itself, I did not propose to offer any further opportunity in that line," Dupre said in explaining why he did not accept Fairfax' challenge. "My purpose was and is, never to balk Fairfax or any other man who might feel aggrieved at any utterance of mine in redressing their wrong as their nature might prompt." Someone at the *Picayune*—Dupre blamed Major Nathaniel Burbank—could not decipher such rhetoric and ascribed other reasons for Dupre's failure to pick up Fairfax' gauntlet.

"If a man is a coward he must be consistent, and not claim to be brave when there is no danger," said one paragraph which was printed by the *Picayune.* "The other man who will not fight should not provoke a quarrel. He will become disliked and ridiculous," said another. And a third commented: "The fight that gets into print before it comes off is generally a failure, upon the reasonable theory that the watched pot never comes to a boil."

Dupre clipped the editorial notes, made sure his pistol was

loaded, and set out for the St. Charles bar where he knew he would likely run into Burbank. He did. While Dupre was at the bar drinking with Owen Roper and John Bruneau, Burbank walked in. Dupre drew his pistol. He stuck the editorial clippings between the fingers of the other hand. Then he strode up to Burbank and began slapping him on the face with the hand that held the clippings. "Take out your pistol," he ordered. "I am unarmed," replied Burbank, throwing up his hands to prove it. After the third slap, Chapman H. Hyams, Jr., a broker, led Dupre out of the saloon, and the incident ended.[4]

The adage you live by the sword and you die by the sword proved itself less than five years after Waters killed Baker, even though Waters was not the aggressor in that shoot-out.

It was March 18, 1891. Waters had left the *Item* and now was a writer for the *Mascot,* the weekly scandal sheet. Obviously upset by the lynching four days earlier of the eleven Sicilians accused of assassinating Superintendent of Police David C. Hennessey, Waters in the early evening, sat with several companions in the Gem Saloon on Royal Street, near Canal. He and the others drank three bottles of champagne while Waters denounced the prominent citizens who were in the vengeful mob. At 10:30 P.M., very drunk, he stood at the corner of Canal and Bourbon streets, not many feet from the spot where former governor Warmoth stabbed Byerly. Waters was talking with Scott Wells and others. Nearby, in a different group, was Arthur Dunn, an attorney who had served with the prosecution in the trial of the Sicilians. Dunn had been a close friend of Baker. Waters began making loud and derogatory remarks intended for Dunn's ears. After a few minutes Dunn left his companions and started across Canal Street to board a streetcar at the corner of Carondelet Street.

He had an overcoat over his left arm, and held his walking cane in his left hand. Dunn was halfway across the broad thoroughfare when Waters shouted the names of the lynch leaders, cursed them, and said he would whip any man who wanted to defend them. Suddenly the sound of a pistol shot was heard from the spot where Waters stood in front of Cluverius' Drug Store, 143 Canal Street. Dunn wheeled, yanked out his pistol, and fired. Dunn advanced toward Waters and both men emptied their weapons at each other. Waters walked into the drugstore, Dunn following. Dunn raised his pistol as though to strike Waters with it just as Waters reeled and fell in front of a counter. His empty gun lay near his hand. He died in a few moments as a result of two bullet wounds in the head. Dunn was hit in the chest and right thigh, neither wound proving serious. Waters' first shot missed Dunn. The bullet went through the trouser leg of Buddy Nienan, who was standing across the street at the corner of Carondelet, and lodged in the leg of T. J. McMahon, with whom Nienan was talking.[5]

"Oh, men of the Crescent City, by all that you hold dear, forbear," urged the *Mascot* in mourning Waters. "When the hot southern blood boils in rage at some imaginary or real offense and the demon rises in your breast urging you to appease that wrath by the blood of your fellow man, think of the dear ones at home, think of all the misery that will result from one moment's passion, forbear in the name of peace and in the fair name of the Crescent City."[6] But tempers did not cool easily, not on Newspaper Row.

Early in June the *States* printed an editorial on a slaughterhouse scandal. Dr. S. R. Olliphant, president of the State Board of Health, took offense and sent to the newspaper a letter demanding a retraction or, in the alternative, insisting on knowing the name of the author of the editorial. George W. Dupre sent word he had nothing to retract, and if Dr. Olliphant wanted the name of the editorial writer, he would give it to him. With this, Dupre handed his card to the messenger.

At 2 P.M. on June 6 Dr. Olliphant wrote a communication to Dupre stating, "You are so well known to be a coward, liar and traducer in this community, thus placing yourself beyond the pale of recognition by gentlemen, that I am barred from taking further notice of your personalities in said editorial." Dupre stormed out of the *States* office, vowing he would hold Olliphant personally responsible for the insult. He went to the Board of Health office at Carondelet and Perdido streets. Dr. Olliphant was reported to be out, and Dupre left word that he was looking for the physician. Dupre returned to the board headquarters at 3 P.M. and sent word into Olliphant's office that he was there. When there was no immediate response, Dupre burst into the inner office. There were conflicting accounts of what happened. Dupre said he found Olliphant standing beside his desk, pistol in hand. "Stand off," ordered Olliphant. "That's all right," Dupre said he replied. "That's what I came here for. Step back, and we will fire." Dupre related that he dropped his cane and hauled out his revolver. Shots were fired, and the two men clinched. When they were separated Dupre's cheek was bleeding. He was lowered to the floor, and Dr. Howard Olliphant, the duelist's brother, held his hand in the wound to stem the flow of blood until Dupre could be taken to a hospital.

Olliphant said Dupre advanced upon him with his cane upraised. He added that Dupre claimed to be unarmed. "I could have killed him at that time, but on the statement that he was unarmed I lowered my pistol." Olliphant stated that Dupre then produced a pistol and started shooting.

Dupre said that when he fired a fourth shot he was tackled

from behind. He insisted that a small man with a black mustache cut him in the cheek with a knife. Olliphant denied that others attacked Dupre. When the pistols were examined it was found that all of the chambers in Dupre's had been discharged. Olliphant got off one shot, and his weapon misfired four times. All of the bullets missed. For all the practice they had, New Orleanians in general and newsmen in particular were poor marksmen.[7]

On the afternoon of October 20, 1903, Bartley Brown, a reporter for the *Item,* called to his young brother: "Go home and tell mamma I've shot Judge Whitaker." He had, indeed, a few minutes earlier wounded Edward S. Whitaker as the latter sat at a desk in his law office in the Crescent Building, at the corner of Camp Street and Commercial Place, directly across the street from Newspaper Row. Brown had sought an interview with Whitaker, and once admitted to his office shot him in the stomach and left arm. Brown's mother knew what the message meant. The lecherous Whitaker had made advances to Sadie Brown, the reporter's good-looking sister, when she worked in the attorney's office. In the early days of the twentieth century the "unwritten law" still required that a woman be avenged in such cases. As the man of his household, Brown did what was expected of him.[8] It was one of the few times when Whitaker was the loser, as the reader will see.

Shortly after midnight on June 3, 1904, R. Lee Edwards, a reporter for the *States,* was ambushed as he entered the gate to his residence at 1737 Delachaise Street, near Baronne Street. Shots were fired from a clump of bushes across the street. Edwards had a narrow escape. One bullet penetrated a fence picket at his elbow, and another came even closer to his body. He wheeled and emptied his revolver in the direction from which the attack came. The would-be assassin fired once more, then disappeared. The newspapers did not speculate on the reason for the ambush.[9]

The last memorable occasion when bullets zipped on Newspaper Row was on the evening of January 17, 1908. The scene was the office of the *Morning World* at 210-212 Camp Street. Joseph Mark Leveque, editor, had been publishing critical articles about Edward Whitaker, then the inspector of police, calling him a "joke" who spent every afternoon at the racetrack instead of earning his $6,000-per-year salary. The *World* said Whitaker "did not have the courage to put a louse off the track." Whitaker, who was a hard-drinking and dissolute rounder but certainly no coward, moved in characteristic fashion. About 7:30 P.M. he stormed into the *World* building, accompanied by half a dozen of the hand-picked officers who made up his personal strong-arm squad. The others covered the newspaper employees with drawn pistols, while Whitaker went barging up to Leveque's second-story office. He waited outside until Margery Dare, women's department editor, concluded a conference with Leveque and left. Then Whitaker strode up to Leveque and slapped the editor. Whitaker said he drew his pistol and fired when Leveque moved his hands as though to take a weapon from his desk. The first shot missed. Edward F. Roberts, copy editor, tackled Whitaker just in time to cause his second shot to go wild.[10] The affair ended Whitaker's police career.*

* On October 3, 1927, Douglas Acomb, cashier, was fatally wounded by a bandit who shot him as he entered the *States* building at Camp and St. Joseph streets, four blocks up Camp from old Newspaper Row. The robber took $5,844 which Acomb had withdrawn from a bank to make up the *States*'s payroll.

7

O'Malley's the Name

Dominick O'Malley.

— The buildings that lined Newspaper Row and echoed the crackle of his pistol and the guns of his enemies fall one by one to the onslaught of demolishers who clear the way for a new skyline.

— Three generations of newsmen have come and gone since his turbulent reign at the *Item.* No longer does the mention of the name bring a glint of disdain to the eyes of a veteran editor, or a half-smile of grudging admiration to the lips of a young reporter.

— Three quarters of a century have passed since he scornfully stood in the midst of a lynch mob on Canal Street and heard a rabble-rousing orator cry for his blood.

— In no journalism school, for good reason, is he mentioned along with Adolph Ochs, E. W. Scripps, or the other publishers and editors who set standards of conduct for the newspaper business.

Dominick O'Malley.

— The syllables roll off the tongue and reverberate in the ear.

The note was dated October 22, 1890, and was signed by Edgar H. Farrar, chairman. It was addressed to D. C. O'Malley, corner Carondelet and Common streets.

Sir: The Committee of Fifty demand that you drop all connection instanter with the Italian vendetta cases, either personally or through your employees. They demand further that you keep away from the Parish Prison, the Criminal District Court and the recorder's courts while these cases are on trial or under investigation. That you cease all communication with members of the Italian colony. That you cease in person or through your employees, to follow or communicate with witnesses in the matter of the assassination of D. C. Hennessey. The committee does not deny those accused a right to employ proper agency, but they do not intend to allow a man of your known criminal record and unscrupulous methods to be an instrument for harm to the public at their hands. By order of the committee.[1]

The recipient was publishing a daily advertisement on the front page of the *Item*[2] soliciting business for O'Malley's Agency and Protective Police, 22 Carondelet Street, Telephone 735. "Civil and criminal matters carefully investigated and faithfully reported," the advertisement promised. "Uniformed officers furnished day or night on reasonable terms. Missing witnesses found; absent witnesses located; their general reputation investigated; and all matters connected with legitimate detective business properly attended to. None but experienced operatives connected with this agency. Every employee of this agency is bonded to it for the faithful performance of his duties."

Members of the committee set up by the city government to supervise the investigation of the Hennessey assassination, and other New Orleanians as well, felt that the agency's advertisement omitted references to some of O'Malley's more controversial activities. He had the reputation of a man who could be hired to bribe or intimidate witnesses and to fix juries. And already his police record was one of the longest in the city.[3] Farrar and other members of the committee either were naive in thinking they could frighten O'Malley, or the note was a ploy to put him on the defensive. In either case, it did not work. Back on the same day came his reply:

> Your extraordinary communication of this date has been received. In response I can but say that I propose to conduct the business of my office without instructions from you or the committee which you pretend to represent. Being unable to discover whence you derive any authority to "demand" that I should obey your behest with respect to the character of my employment, I shall continue to reserve to myself the right to think and act without regard to your wishes. Later I shall have occasion to "demand" at your hands the evidence upon which you have ventured to write of my "known" criminal record and unscrupulous methods.[4]

Afterwards, O'Malley said the committee's note convinced him "that they had made up their minds to convict some one whether the evidence warranted it or not. I at once set to work and investigated the statements made by Matranga and others, and being satisfied of their innocence, took an active part in the defense."[5] A grand jury later seemed to think he was self-deprecating when he said only that he took an "active part" in the defense. In a report on May 5, 1891, the jury said: "With his skill as acquired by years of experience, the most cunningly devised schemes were planned and executed for defeating the legitimate course of justice, the chief aim and object being to place unworthy men upon the jury in the trial of the nine accused. Without his assistance and corrupting influences we believe the verdict would have been radically different, and as a natural consequence the tragic occurrences of the 14th of March last never would have been recorded." The jury charged that the omniscient O'Malley arranged to have the engineer on duty at the Electric Light Company's generating station dim the street light at Basin and Girod streets on the night the trial jury visited the murder scene. The jury's reasoning was that he wanted to cast doubt on the credibility of state witnesses who were so positive in their identification of the men who were on trial. In support of its accusation, the jury quoted Thomas C. Collins a spy who was planted in O'Malley's office by Mayor Shakspeare.[6] The grand jury also reported that O'Malley was seen at the home of Jacob M. Seligman, trial jury foreman, on the day of the lynching. This hint of duplicity was pursued no further.

The selection of O'Malley as the villain by a group of citizens who wanted to justify the lynching was not surprising. The role did not displease O'Malley. He enjoyed being in the limelight, and headlines which pictured him as a master fixer did not hurt the business of his detective agency. Only one charge was brought by officials, most of whom would have enjoyed sending the detective to the penitentiary. He was indicted along with Thomas McCrystol for attempting to bribe tales juror Thomas J. McCabe. District Attorney Luzenberg later dismissed the charge. He said there was no evidence against O'Malley except a statement by McCrystol, who now refused to talk.[7] McCrystol was convicted and served a jail sentence.

Where was O'Malley on the morning of March 14, 1891, while leaders at the Clay Statue rally were inciting their fellow citizens to take the law into their own hands and exact their vengeance for the killing of Hennessey? Where was he while Walter D. Denegre was shouting that he should be lynched along with the Sicilians? "They (the jury) were bribed, and bribed by whom? By that scoundrel, D. C. O'Malley, than whom a more infamous scoundrel never lived. The Committee of Fifty have already notified him to leave town without avail. More forcible action is now called for. Let everyone here now follow us with the intention of doing his full duty." Those were Denegre's words.[8] Where was O'Malley? He was standing right there, in the middle of the mob. The full story of his audacity begins the night before. With friends, he said, he was promenading the streets at nine o'clock.[9]

I was informed of what was to occur the following morning and warned to get off the streets. I learned the number of the cab and the name of the driver who hauled the rifles from Mr. A. Baldwin's hardware store to the corner of Bienville and Royal Streets. I was threatened with death if I did not get off the streets, but instead of doing this I proceeded down to where the guns and the executioners were. They saw me and discussed the fact of my presence. I then discovered that I was being shadowed by Wash Tracy, an employee of the Boylan Agency, and a nephew of Col. Boylan. I passed him and laughed at him, but was not molested by anyone.

I proceeded to the *Times-Democrat* office and informed them of what was going on and asked advice as to whether I ought to communicate with the sheriff in order to save the unfortunate prisoners or not. I received no reply. I then returned to the streets to learn, if possible, the plans of the committee, and if there was any indication of measures being taken to prevent the contemplated outbreak.

I was kept well posted about everything the Committee of Fifty did, but not by the party they supposed. My information was derived indirectly from Mr. Walter Denegre, and my method was to send some parties with whom he was acquainted to him, instructing them to villify me and call me all kinds of names. This would generally open his mouth, and he would divulge a great deal of information, which was repeated to me, and proved of considerable benefit.

O'Malley said he learned of the announcement of the mass meeting at Clay Statue "and was aware of its purport." He went home and to bed, but was aroused by friends who begged him to leave the city with his wife. The O'Malleys spent the rest of the night at a friend's home.

In the morning I escorted my wife home and proceeded to do what I could to save the lives of those whom I earnestly believed should not suffer. I soon became convinced, however, that all my efforts to save their lives would be futile, and believing that my own life was in jeopardy, I commenced to make preparations to defend it to the last extremity. It was now about 8:45 in the morning. I had six double-barreled breech-loading shotguns, two rifles and 250 rounds of ammunition in my office. I looked over these and found that two of the shotguns were 12-gauge, so I went to Rhodes' gun store and purchased fifty rounds of 12-gauge shells, loaded with buckshot, to fit them, thus making in all 300 rounds.

I returned to my office and prepared for any attack. Eight staunch and true friends, men upon whom I knew I could depend, were in the office with me. After making all arrangements I proceeded to the first recorder's court, where I was to be tried on the charge of carrying concealed weapons. I had the case postponed, whereupon I obtained the consent of two of my friends to accompany me to the meeting at Clay Statue. I went there and listened to the harangues of the speakers, heard them calling me some choice pet names and saying what they would do to me if they had me. Their actions impressed me as being similar to that of what I had read of the Oklahoma boomers.

I did not conceal myself, but stood in the crowd. No one appeared to notice my presence for a time. Then several who were standing near me remarked: "If they want him so bad, there he is," and pointed to me, but no one appeared disposed to interfere with me. There appeared to me to be too much talk and I began to think that the crowd would not carry out their threats into execution, nor that they were disposed to kill unarmed men. Some of the crowd started down Royal Street to where the arms were, and others went out Canal Street towards Bourbon. I returned to the office and found it crowded with friends, who insisted on my going home. I did so, and that is the only step that I regret having taken. I felt confident of maintaining the defense of my office, and not for one moment did I fear the result of an encounter. I proceeded to the stable to have my horse harnessed to my buggy, but found that my buggy had not been washed. I walked out Gravier Street to St. Charles, took the car and went home. I found that my wife had gone out in search of me and as I subsequently learned reached my office a few minutes after I had left.

I started downtown again and was shadowed by a Boylan emissary who boarded the car with me. He appeared to be endeavoring to let every one on the car know what he was doing. I left the car at the corner of Carondelet and Erato Streets, Boylan's man following. I walked out to St. Charles Street and boarded a Carrollton car. So did the shadow. I got out at Felicity Street. So did he. I took a Jackson Street car, and the "shadow" had to run a block and a half to catch the car. As he entered I remarked: "I'll make you earn your money today," and laughed at him

He passed through the car and went out on the platform, where he spoke to Officer Tom Marshall, who was out there. He was badly winded and could hardly speak. At the corner of Prytania and Jackson Streets I alighted and saw Marshall and the "shadow" get off at the next corner. I walked down to Josephine Street as I was satisfied that my pursuer had had enough of the chase and was glad to let go.

I walked out to Magazine Street, and then down to St. Mary and out to Constance Street, where I entered the home of a friend of mine and sent for a carriage. I rode downtown in search of my wife and soon found her. She was comfortably situated and safe, so I went to find quarters for myself.

For nearly three weeks O'Malley disappeared, at least from the eyes of law enforcement officials. Newspapers carried reports that he had been seen in various southern cities, and there was a flurry of excitement on March 20 when a reporter in Memphis interviewed a man whom he identified as O'Malley and who was quoted at length about the case.[10] It developed that Louis S. "Tim" Allingham of Algiers could not resist the temptation to hoodwink the reporter. Finally, on April 3, O'Malley suddenly appeared at the court clerk's office and posted bond to appear on the jury-bribing charge. O'Malley said he had not been more than four blocks from the criminal court except when he went out every night in a cab to eat at a restaurant. He said he did not disguise himself but was recognized only once, in a restaurant on Rampart Street.[11] He would have surrendered earlier, O'Malley averred, had he known there was a charge against him.

Major Henry J. Hearsey must have had enough of bloodshed for the time being. "However just the resentment of the people may have been against this man," said a *States* editorial, "and we believe it was entirely just, he is now in the hands of the law, and he must be accorded a fair trial; not a hair of his head must be touched save by the hands of the law."[12] The editor might not have been so magnaminous if he could have foreseen O'Malley's entrance into the newspaper world, some three years later, as owner of the *Item*.

Who was this figure who made the city's power structure so nervous? Who was the man who seemed always to land in the middle of the action? What were the characteristics that made his name show up in the headlines for longer than a quarter of a century? The details must be read for O'Malley to become believable. The legend has to be built, brick by brick, for generalities do not do the man justice.

By his own count, O'Malley went to his grave with fourteen bullet wounds in his body.[13] He came out on the short end of the score, because his own pistol did not hit its mark that many times. And, for all his scrapes, he never killed a man.

But for the fast footwork of a police officer, John Teen, O'Malley's colorful career in New Orleans might have been cut off early. He had a brush with disaster on June 23, 1881, in an encounter with Mike Hennessey, David's swashbuckling cousin. His long-standing feud with the Hennesseys may have developed out of the incident. O'Malley and Teen were walking up St. Charles Street between Canal and Common streets. They met Hennessey and Captain C. C. Cain, keeper of the parish prison. Teen asked Cain if the latter had a cigar for him. No, said Cain, who then turned to Hennessey and wanted to know whether the police aid had spoken to O'Malley. Hennessey replied no, then walked up to O'Malley and demanded to know whether he had spoken. O'Malley said he had, whereupon Hennessey drew his pistol and started to draw a bead on O'Malley. Teen leaped across the banquette just in time to interfere with Hennessey's aim. Cain smacked Teen on the chin because the officer had interfered. Hennessey drew a ten-dollar fine for disturbing the police. At his trial a man named Shephard testified that O'Malley asked whether Jack Lee could be employed for $500 to assassinate Hennessey. And George Samuels swore that O'Malley offered him $500 to kill Hennessey.[14]

On the night of January 6, 1882, O'Malley had two pistol shots fired at him in a struggle in which he had only his fists to defend himself against two attackers. O'Malley was standing in Congo Square when Cain approached him from the direction of the nearby parish prison. Cain asked O'Malley to join him for a drink. "I said I didn't drink," O'Malley related. How about a cigar? O'Malley said he did not smoke. Well, a lemonade then? O'Malley thought he had better accept and they went into a barroom at North Rampart and St. Peter Streets. Theodore Stewart joined them. Cain revealed why he was so persistent in his invitations. He asked whether O'Malley, as a private detective, were involved in investigating a charge of misconduct against the prison keeper. O'Malley's answer was evasive, and Cain made a motion to draw his pistol. Stewart caught hold of the revolver, and a struggle ensued in which a window pane was broken. O'Malley walked out of the bar, and Cain followed, saying, "I'll lick the *** anyway." O'Malley told Cain and Stewart there were two against one, and he was unarmed. Cain hit O'Malley with his fist, cutting his eye. O'Malley loosed a blow that knocked Cain into the gutter. Stewart fired twice at O'Malley, missing him both times.[15]

O'Malley was not so lucky the next time. He got into a gun battle which the adversaries insisted resulted from an argument over a ten-cent bet on a game of tenpins in the Little Zazarac Saloon, 19 Baronne Street. On the night of May 21, 1883, O'Malley was playing a game with Richard Stockton and J. F. Borges. Stockton accused O'Malley of beating him out of a dime with a scratch shot. "Well, don't bet any more," O'Malley retorted. The game broke up and Stockton and Borges walked out, accompanied by O. E. Livaudais. When O'Malley left the saloon a short time later he found the men waiting for him in front of Schwaner's Pawn Shop. Pat Hennessey, an eyewitness, said Borges started shooting at O'Malley, and the others followed suit. O'Malley was hit three times before he could get out his pistol. He managed to fire one ineffectual shot, then was wounded in the right arm between the elbow and shoulder. "My weapon fell from my hand and when I attempted to pick it up my arm was numb," O'Malley recounted. Livaudais rushed Stockton and wrestled with him. "You damned murderer, you can't assassinate that man," Livaudais shouted, trying unsuccessfully to snatch Stockton's pistol. The shot broke O'Malley's right arm and left the fingers of his hand partially paralyzed. He also received a wound in the right thigh and two in the right leg.[16] He was becoming established as a page-one personality.

Newspaper Row was thrown into a state of excitement on September 9, 1895, when William B. Stansbury of the *Times-Democrat* accosted O'Malley, now proprietor of the *Item,* on Camp Street in the car tracks in front of the *Picayune* office. Stanbury fired twice at point-blank range, yet missed. Stansbury was irate over a news story in the *Item* which reflected on his integrity.

"Who is responsible for that article in yesterday's paper?" Stansbury demanded.

"I am," responded O'Malley.

"You'll have to retract what you said."

"I don't intend to retract anything."

Stansbury produced his pistol and fired. "I told him I was unarmed and said no one but a cur would shoot a man who had no weapon," O'Malley told newsmen. "My hands were at my side." Stansbury fired again, and O'Malley threw up the tails of his coat to show there was no gun in his hip pocket. A police officer disarmed Stansbury. Later Stansbury said it was O'Malley's custom to carry a revolver, and he believed when he started shooting that the publisher was armed. "I have no desire to praise O'Malley, but I must say he was game. He did not flinch a step. I can only say that bad marksmanship caused me to miss."[17]

The most humiliating incident of O'Malley's life, but one which demonstrated that he never panicked under fire, occurred in Baton Rouge on May 14, 1896. The scene, on Lafayette Street near Grouchy's Restaurant, would have provided the climax for a Wild West movie. O'Malley's antagonist was Louis Claire, a New Orleans gambler and political hanger-on who had killed Police Commissioner Patrick Mealey in a drunken brawl in William Johnson's saloon, 21 St. Charles Street, during a New Year's celebration at 1:30 A.M. on January 1, 1888.[18] O'Malley was on his way to Grouchy's for breakfast. He was reading a letter as he walked along Lafayette Street and was taken by surprise when Claire suddenly appeared and struck him from the side, knocking him to the ground. As O'Malley fell, his pistol dropped from his pocket. Claire kicked it into the street, and stood over the prostrate publisher, gun in hand. Claire's pistol was accidentally discharged, but the bullet went wild. Claire cursed O'Malley, and kicked him. Dr. George McD. Brumby of the United States Land Office was credited with saving O'Malley's life. He saw the latter's plight was desperate. Brumby sprang upon a bench, covered Claire with a pistol, and demanded fair play. Brumby did not recognize either O'Malley or Claire when he intervened. There was a bruise over O'Malley's right eye as he managed to get to his feet. Claire jumped out into the street and dared O'Malley to retrieve his pistol and fight. O'Malley refused, pointing out that Claire had allies with him and a battle would be one-sided. Instead, O'Malley suggested, why didn't each select two friends and retire to a secluded site and battle it out. Claire insisted on fighting on the spot. He walked to the streetcar track and laid his weapon down. He cursed and abused O'Malley and suggested that both go for their pistols at the same time. O'Malley repeated that he would fight Claire, but in some other location. Claire stooped into the gutter, scooped up some mud, and threw it into O'Malley's face. Finally, a policeman intervened, and Claire and O'Malley were led away in different directions. Claire continued drinking heavily. Pistol in hand, he walked up and down in front of the rooming house where O'Malley was staying until finally police locked him up in the interest of peace.[19]

In the 1890s O'Malley would have had to go into seclusion or else move out of New Orleans if he wanted to avoid fights. The *Item's* editorials and stories frequently hit home, and those who were the targets wanted to take it out on the proprietor. On January 14, 1897, J. B. Chisolm, a builder, boarded a Canal streetcar on which O'Malley was a passenger. While the car was running between Dryades and Baronne streets Chisolm cursed O'Malley and invited him to get off and fight. O'Malley blandly replied that he was not ready for fisticuffs just then. Chisolm became more abusive and several women and children rushed to get out of the car. The commotion attracted a policeman, who arrested Chisolm. The result was a $25 fine against Chisolm, who said O'Malley exasperated him by continually sneering at him. Two months later Sheriff Ike Broussard of Lafayette Parish encountered O'Malley at Canal and Royal Streets and attempted to attack him because of news stories impugning the sheriff's honesty. Broussard swung a fist. When O'Malley threw back his head to avoid the blow his hat fell off.[20]

For some reason O'Malley left his pistol behind on the afternoon of August 14, 1897, when he set out on an errand in the company of his young attorney friend, Richard B. Otero.* Had he been armed, the course of New Orleans police and journalistic history might have been different.

* There were repercussions twenty-five years later. Otero, an unsuccessful candidate for criminal court judge, sued the *States* for $172,000 on September 20, 1924, because of editorials which recalled that he had been an associate of O'Malley, described as "one of the most malefic influences about our criminal courts." Otero lost the suit.

The two men visited an office on Carondelet Street and were walking through Commercial Place enroute to the *Item*. Near the Camp Street entrance to Commercial Place they encountered Edward Stanley Whitaker, the former recorder's court judge who was under attack from O'Malley's newspaper. All accounts agree that no word was spoken. "I saw Mr. Whitaker coming toward us," Otero related. "He had an umbrella in his hand. When about seven or eight feet away he quickened his pace. I saw Mr. Whitaker clench his fist and raise his right hand as though to strike a blow. Mr. O'Malley drew back and raised his cane which he carried in his left hand. The cane struck Mr. Whitaker on the right arm. Just then Mr. Whitaker turned with his face toward Camp Street and, shoving his umbrella more securely under his left arm, he ran his right hand into his hip pocket. What transpired after that I do not know, except that there seemed to be something wrong in the movement of Mr. Whitaker's right hand — I reckon it was his pistol had hitched in his pocket." In a dive for safety, Otero smashed the glass door of a barbershop, cutting his arm. Had O'Malley been armed, he would have had time to draw his pistol and start shooting while Whitaker tugged at his weapon. Whitaker finally extricated his pistol, aimed at O'Malley's head and pulled the trigger. O'Malley was moving toward the Commercial Place entrance to the Crescent Building when the gun fired. Whitaker followed his foe to the doorway and got off another shot. O'Malley disappeared into the building, Whitaker following. A moment later Whitaker reappeared, the smoking pistol clutched in his hand.

The clock in the *Picayune* office directly across Camp Street showed 5:03 on that Saturday afternoon when the first shot was fired. A reporter sprinted to where Whitaker stood scanning the windows of the Crescent Building. "What's the matter, judge?" asked the reporter. "I shot O'Malley. Let him put his head out, the scoundrel." The door to the building was slammed shut, and an unseen hand snapped the lock. "What caused the trouble, judge?" The reporter flinched as Whitaker gestured with the pistol.

"That man, O'Malley, has been running me down. I wanted to speak to him about those articles in his newspaper; to tell him they must stop, when he struck me with the cane he carried. Then I shot. If Otero tells what is so, he will say the same thing." Spectators were filling the one-block-long passageway between St. Charles and Camp streets from both ends. Whitaker, his face pale and his eyes glowing, paced up and down. Once he raised his pistol, and bystanders scrambled to get out of range. Finally, someone persuaded him to go to his office directly across Commercial Place from the Crescent Building, and a reporter found him there. "I'm glad you're here. Look where he struck me with the cane." Whitaker opened his shirt, pointed to a pink mark on his chest, and amplified his account. "After the second shot I rushed up the stairs part of the way, and in that time O'Malley was scrambling on his hands and knees on the steps. On the first landing he turned to me and cried: 'Mercy. Mercy.' Now the idea of a man wanting mercy from me after he has persistently lied about me. Well, I gave him mercy; I did not want to shoot him while he was prostrate, and so I turned and went into the alley. I did not know then that I had hit him. In going into the alley I meant to give him time to recover and get a weapon and come back to meet me, but he did not." There is only Whitaker's word that O'Malley begged to be spared.

It could be true. As early as 1882 the *Mascot* reported that when O'Malley was cornered by an enemy "he has always been able to give no provocation for violence. He has had his face slapped. He has been spat upon. His hat has been smashed over his eyes. But he never by word or deed gave cause for follow-up action by an enemy.[21] O'Malley knew when to fight, and when to grovel.

O'Malley said Whitaker came up to him in the alley. "He said nothing, nor did I speak to him. Whitaker pulled out a pistol, which caught in his hip pocket and seemed to nettle him. When he did pull out the pistol he levelled it at me and snapped the trigger, I should say two or three times. It was when he first snapped the weapon at me that I struck him with my stick. Whether I hit him or not I cannot say; it was all over in a moment. I got into the building, as I was unarmed, and some man said to me on the stairway: 'Come in here, Mr. O'Malley.' That is all I know of the shooting proper. No, it is impossible for me to tell if I was hit on the first fire or the second." O'Malley was wounded in the left shoulder, the bullet grazing his lung as it passed through his body. He insisted on being driven to his home in a cab, and was treated by Dr. Rudolph Matas.[22]

The incident had important repercussions eight years latter. Because of it, Whitaker acquired a reputation as a man who could hold his own with O'Malley. But that's another story. Meanwhile, on April 20, 1900, while cleaning out his files as the end of a term approached, District Attorney R. H. Marr dismissed the indictment which charged Whitaker with wounding and intent to murder.[23]

At 2:30 o'clock on the afternoon of October 10, 1899, editors and reporters of the evening papers were nearing their final edition deadlines. Morning paper employees were getting ready for the long night ahead. In the *Picayune* office, Dorothy Dix (Mrs. Elizabeth S. Meriwether), the nation's best-known advice-to-the-lovelorn columnist, was at work. She heard gunshots and hurried to a front window overlooking Camp Street in time to see the most celebrated pistol battle ever staged on Newspaper Row. In the *Item* office the city editor, T. O. Harris, and reporters Henry White, Carey Harris and William Struve also heard the sound of shooting. Inasmuch as O'Malley had walked out of the front door only a moment before, one of the men guessed that his boss was in another scrape. He reached for the telephone and called an ambulance.[24] His hunch was a good one.

In front of the *Picayune* job-printing shop, 330 Camp Street, O'Malley and C. Harrison Parker, former editor of the *Picayune,* were emptying their pistols at each other at point-blank range. The spot was within a hundred feet of the site where Whitaker had shot O'Malley, and only fifty feet or less from the place where Stansbury had fired at him. Eyewitnesses could not agree as to which man first pulled the trigger. Some said O'Malley, others Parker. Because the question never was cleared up, and the law could not decide who was the aggressor, charges against both were eventually dismissed.[25] Parker had been standing in front of a cigar store across the street talking with General E. H. Lombard. O'Malley had been in the *Item* office conferring with Charles E. "Parson" Davies, his partner in theatrical enterprises. Davies suggested they walk over to McCloskey's on St. Charles Street for coffee. About the time they emerged from the *Item,* Parker left General Lombard and started cross Camp to the *Picayune.* He had crossed the streetcar tracks and was walking on a board which served as a bridge over an excavation in the pavement. He came abreast of O'Malley, who was on the sidewalk. Both men must have gone for their guns at the same instant, and they started firing almost simultaneously. O'Malley ducked behind twin utility poles, but left his cover to keep shooting at Parker until his big Tranter was empty. Parker fired all six bullets from his .38 caliber Smith's improved pistol.

Fred Rohrbacher, a young newsboy, was across the street near the place where Parker and General Lombard had stood. He was hit twice by bullets from O'Malley's gun. One scraped the right side of his forehead, and the other nicked his left heel. Parker was wounded in the muscles of the right shoulder and in the right side. O'Malley was hit in the left side, the bullet lodging in the groin. When his pistol was empty, Parker stepped upon the sidewalk and entered the *Picayune* office. Davies said he was a step or two behind O'Malley when they left the *Item* enroute to the restaurant. He related that a man approached O'Malley and called out something. Davies said he understood only the word "now." Davies said the man reached into his pocket and started drawing a pistol. "It was so big I thought he'd never get it out." Davies added that the man aimed at O'Malley and shot twice. He saw O'Malley wince and clap his hand to his side. Then O'Malley produced his pistol and started shooting. Davies managed to halt a woman who started to walk between the antagonists. The battle lasted about thirty seconds. As soon as it was over a throng blocked the newspaper entrances. An ambulance summoned for Parker could not reach the front of the *Picayune* because of the crowd. Finally it was maneuvered through Bank Place, and Parker and the newsboy were taken out through a rear door. Parker was driven to the Sanitarium on Carondelet Street and Rohrbacher to Charity Hospital. Another ambulance transported O'Malley to Hotel Dieu. At first he was believed in critical condition, and Andrew Hero, Jr., a notary, was summoned to draw up his will. O'Malley soon rallied and Hero was dismissed. But he came back the next day, and at 10 A.M. O'Malley dictated a testament witnessed by Remy Klock, Dr. Max Levy and John Stumpf. It was the only will he ever made. It said, "I bequeath to my wife, Kate, all I possess.[26]

Two days before the shooting the *Item* in a cartoon had depicted Parker, then state tax collector for the First District, as a dog following at the heels of a politician.* The *Times-*

* Henry Grelle, the *Item*'s engraver and artist who drew the cartoon, was worried about the reception he would receive when he went to visit O'Malley in the hospital. O'Malley greeted him warmly, and handed him a slip of paper which was an order for a five dollar hat at Godchaux's store.

Democrat reporter jumped to a conclusion, as did many another New Orleanian, that the exchange of bullets was a result of the cartoon.[27] But the *Picayune* said Parker had not complained or indicated that he would take action.[28] Parker was well acquainted with the finer points of the dueling code.

It remained for Henry Hearsey, as usual, to become wrathful. In an editorial the *States* said: "Colonel Parker is our friend, and we shall not see him misrepresented. The report set abroad that he waylaid O'Malley is a scandalous lie. . . . We do not believe that Parker was the first aggressor. . . . We regret the whole matter. We have nothing against O'Malley. But it must be conceded that for several years he has had a life in this community that has excited the wonder of everyone at his escape from death on a number of occasions. Indeed, many persons had assumed that O'Malley had terrorized the community; and men with that reputation, be they desperadoes or cowards, must sooner or later come to grief."[29]

It took a long time but there was an eventual reconciliation between O'Malley and Parker. Not many of O'Malley's enemies ever relented, and O'Malley was no turn-the-other-cheek philosopher. In 1912 O'Malley had a conversation with William F. Millsap, secretary to Governor Luther Hall. He made a complimentary reference to Parker, who was about to be appointed president of the board of control of the state penitentiary. Millsap told Parker what O'Malley said. "Well, I haven't any grudge against O'Malley," commented Parker. "He hasn't spoken to me since we had that fight, but I don't hold anything against him." The next morning the two met in the rotunda of the Capitol. "How are you, Dominick?" asked Parker, putting out his hand. "Very good, Colonel," replied O'Malley, shaking hands. "How are you?" "Oh, I'm feeling well. My arm is all right." "So is my side," responded O'Malley.[30]

O'Malley was born in County Mayo, Ireland, on October

16, 1858. Through the years in New Orleans he was a private detective, proprietor of the *Item,* president of the American Fish, Game and Oyster Company during 1912-1914, and finally in 1916 editor and publisher of the New Orleans *American.* [31] He was married to Katherine Cooney of New Orleans.

James M. Thomson, later publisher of the *Item,* who first saw O'Malley in 1906, wrote that he was "a man of medium height, partly bald, with sandy grayish hair. He had light colored bluish-gray eyes, was stockily built and wore a mustache. His forehead was bald. . . . O'Malley spoke with a decided Irish brogue."[32] Chroniclers could not always find anything kind to say about the truculent, hard-driving man. However, his generosity has been commented upon,[33] and the various activities of his *Item* in providing cheap bread and coal for poor families and shoes for needy boys support this assessment. He was devoted to his Kate. He was no teetotaler, not in a day when the saloon was the hangout for most of the adult male population. O'Malley's favorite was the Redwitz Bar and Restaurant, 632-634 Common Street. He always looked over the customers as he entered in order to locate any enemies. Then he walked to the last table and sat with his back to the wall.[34] O'Malley's audacity was cool and calculating rather than reckless. "Insider," who wrote a series of reminiscences for the *Times-Picayune,* said he had seen O'Malley run from fights, "but I am sure he was no coward." The writer said O'Malley realized many New Orleanians were "aware of his peculiar traits and twists of character and they would not tolerate his taking human life unless in indisputable defense of his own; hence his running was stimulated by a shot of discretion with no trace of cowardice in it."[35]

An incident that enhanced his reputation for bravado occurred in 1888, while he was serving as volunteer investigator for the Committee of One Hundred, a group of citizens organized to combat lawlessness and gambling. His assignment was to locate establishments conducting banking games and to provide evidence against them. As a result of O'Malley's work, John Vanquelin was indicted for running a banking operation at 5 Canal Street. The gamblers directed their wrath against O'Malley, and Vanquelin was heard to threaten that he would kill the detective if he were charged. On the morning of February 8, O'Malley entered the criminal court building at Camp and Lafayette streets. He saw Vanquelin and several of the latter's friends standing in the corridor, discussing the indictment. O'Malley strode up to Vanquelin and remarked: "If you have anything to say about me go and see Mr. Browne of the Committee of One Hundred. Here is his card." He handed the gambler a card of Messrs. Singleton, Browne and Choate, attorneys. Vanquelin threw the card away and said: "Go away from me; I don't want to have anything to do with you." He made an insulting remark and O'Malley seized him by the coat collar. "You thief, come outside, I want to see you," said O'Malley. Vanquelin followed him to the Camp Street sidewalk. As O'Malley pulled out his pistol, Vanquelin grabbed him by the wrist. When he did so the weapon fired, the bullet passing through the left leg of the gambler's pants.[36]

O'Malley and his lawyer associate, Lionel Adams, created a stir at the corner of Common and Baronne streets on the morning of January 23, 1894, when they staged a tug-of-war with detectives over two suspected criminals. O'Malley and Adams had arranged the release of William Thompson and George Hall from fugitive charges and left recorder's court with them. Immediately after the four had gone the district attorney's staff called and asked that the suspects be retained. Two detectives were sent after them. Adams and O'Malley disputed the right of the officers to arrest the men, and tried to yank them from their grasp. The altercation attracted a big crowd. Police intervened and Adams and O'Malley lost the decision.[37] On one occasion O'Malley outwitted his learned legal ally. A group accused of illegal lottery operations visited O'Malley and agreed to pay a $5,000 fee which he asked for arranging dismissal of the charge. O'Malley persuaded Adams to become attorney in the case, offering $500. All O'Malley wanted Adams to do was to file a list of names with the statement that they would be called as witnesses for the defense. The list included the names of well-known citizens who were conducting another lottery. They sent a lawyer to see Adams, who told them O'Malley wanted them to swear that they did not know of any lotteries in New Orleans. A few days later the charge against O'Malley's clients was dropped. When Adams learned the size of O'Malley's fee, the two had a fistfight.[38]

O'Malley's father, Mike, died in a Cleveland almshouse on November 25, 1885, and Dominick himself well knew what it was like to be broke. He was determined to acquire enough money to assure security for Kate and himself, and he succeeded. By 1906 he could testify that he was worth more than $200,000 in stocks and bonds, plus real estate in Gravesend, New York, and in Kenner. He valued the Gravesend estate at $22,000 and said he had been offered $27,000 for his property in Kenner. O'Malley told a jury he then owned a one-third interest in the *Item* and held notes for $50,000 from the sale of his majority stock in the newspaper. "I have been in New Orleans for twenty-five years, and I have done business totaling several million dollars," he said. "I do not owe a cent to anyone." He recalled that he was penniless when he settled in New Orleans and first found work on the Mississippi River levee at one dollar a day.[39]

O'Malley said he never made big money in the private

detective business, although he was paid $5,000 for his work in the Hennessey assassination case. He reported that he subscribed $5,000 to the Boodle City Council investigation in 1894 and spent another $8,000 to aid the prosecution at the trials. As a partner of "Parson" Davies, well known over the country as a manager of champion prize fighters, O'Malley for a time operated the huge Crescent Billard Hall at Canal and St. Charles streets, in the building which now houses the Pickwick Club. Each had a one-half interest. O'Malley and Davies, along with J. D. Hopkins, leased the St. Charles Theater and the Academy of Music for $23,000 a year. They were making money with vaudeville and a stock company in the St. Charles, known locally as Old Drury, but were losing on the Academy of Music operation. On the night of June 4, 1399, the St. Charles — situated on St. Charles just below Poydras Street — was destroyed and the nearby Academy of Music slightly damaged by fires which police blamed on an arsonist. O'Malley indignantly denied that he had anything to do with the fires. He said he was the loser because of them.[40]

The fact that gambling was illegal did not deter O'Malley from trying his talents as an entrepreneur in some of the clubs which flourished in New Orleans. Along with Jack Curry he became interested in a gambling house at 18 Royal Street on February 20, 1892. O'Malley retained a one-sixth interest until 1899. During the month of the James J. Corbett-John L. Sullivan boxing match in New Orleans in 1892, the house cleared $16,000. In 1900, O'Malley had a one-fourth interest in the Hole in the Wall, 734 Canal Street. In June, 1900, O'Malley's return from this house was $833. In addition to his partnership in the legitimate billiards operation at the Crescent, O'Malley also owned 35 percent of the gambling room there.[41]

He made about $12,000 from this business, and his share was $4,194 when he and Curry pulled out in 1903.[42] Curry said he never forgot O'Malley's gesture of writing a check for $1,000 to help him on an occasion when he was broke. While O'Malley was sleuthing for the Committee of One Hundred in the 1886-1888 period his evidence led to the indictment of thirty-one gamblers in all. As usual, he was double-dealing and the crime-fighter role was only a pose. The *States* exposed his ploy, reporting that he had allowed one gambling house to operate unmolested in return for being given one-fourth ownership, while closing the establishment of a gambler who refused to be blackmailed.[43]

"D. C. O'Malley, who is at the head of the detective agency which bears his name, has long borne an unsavory reputation in this city, and on several occasions has been publicly denounced as a blackmailer and a man who could not be believed under oath," said the *States* on October 28, 1889. The newspaper quoted two anonymous gamblers who said O'Malley had accepted one-fourth ownership of a gambling house in 1888, while he was investigating vice for the Committee of One Hundred. They also said O'Malley brought about the closure of another house when the proprietor refused to cut him in. O'Malley called the gamblers to a confrontation in the presence of a *States* reporter. They met on the sidewalk in front of the St. Charles Hotel, the *States* reported on October 30, 1889.

One of the men — the *States* used only the name Willis — said: "I went to O'Malley and told him I was broke. I told him if he would allow me to run a game in my house I would give him 25 percent. He agreed and for three months he received his profits when there were any and met his losses equally with the other partners."

O'Malley asked: "Did I not lend you $100?"

"Yes, and I paid it back."

"Did I not lend you on another occasion $120?"

"Yes. You always helped me when I went to you, and I always returned the money."

"Wasn't the transaction you refer to in reference to the money you owed me?"

"Not at all. You were always accommodating to me, but this transaction about running a game in my house was another matter entirely, and I made the proposition to gain your protection."

"I'd lend you $1,000 tomorrow, and you know it."

"Yes, I believe you would. I told this gentleman (the reporter) we were on speaking terms. During the three months you were interested in the house you shared profits and losses alike with me."

The other gambler, identified as Stratta, put in:

"The last month we lost $114, and your name was on the books for it."

"Who put my name on the books?"

"I told the bookkeeper to put it there."

"I suppose if he had put me down for $1,400 that would have made it true that I owed it?"

"No, but you owed $114 and I had to put it in the books, so I told the bookkeeper to do so."

"Well, I would believe Vernell, but I deny that I owe you the money."

"Well, all right. I knew the money was due and I put it on the books. I asked Willis, will O'Malley pay his share of the loss and he said yes he would pay some time."

"Who sent for the books?"

"They told me they wanted them at the chief's office, and I took them there about a week ago."

O'Malley asked Willis: "Did Chief Hennessey ever ask about me in connection with your house?"

"Yes; he said, 'If I thought O'Malley was connected with

your house I would close it up in a minute.' "

Willis and Stratta said it was not they who told the *States* that O'Malley had closed the establishment of a gambler who refused to give the private detective a share.

Always on the lookout for an opportunity of making a dollar, O'Malley turned to the numbers racket after the Louisiana State Lottery Company was forced out of business. Attorney General W. J. Cunningham obtained an injunction prohibiting O'Malley, Louis A. Gourdain, and others from operating the Premium Club Lottery, which Cunningham described as "a fraudulent scheme to obtain money from the ignorant and unwary."[44]

Gourdain was a diminutive, dapper promoter who reigned for a period as king of the illegal lotteries in New Orleans. He was in and out of the Louisiana Retreat, an institution for mental patients, and his wife once brought interdiction proceedings. He left for one sojourn in New York, where he advertised in the newspapers an offer to keep anyone alive indefinitely for one-half of that person's fortune, no matter how large or small. "My secret is a simple one," he explained.

"The blood is not pumped by the heart. It circulates itself and works the heart, which is the safety valve to keep the blood from going too fast." It was Gourdain who provided some of the lighter though more exasperating moments in O'Malley's existence during the mid-1890s. Soon after O'Malley bought the *Item* he was boastful of his part in sending some members of the Boodle City Council to prison. Gourdain approached one of the convicted aldermen, L. O. Desforges, in the parish prison and offered in return for a $5,000 payment to get him released. Desforges charged Gourdain with obtaining money under false pretenses, testifying that the latter said he was acting on behalf of O'Malley and Adams. Adams and O'Malley denied in court that they had anything to do with Gourdain's scheme. But Gourdain was acquitted.[45]

Some of the humor was lost on O'Malley, because undoubtedly there were residents of New Orleans who believed Gourdain was telling the truth. Gourdain charged that O'Malley embezzled $6,580 from him and used the money to buy the *Item*. He contended that O'Malley was acting as his agent in acquiring stock from E. W. Talen, the editor, and others, and that he, not O'Malley, was the actual owner of the newspaper. In his testimony, Gourdain said he lost $284,000 in the failure of the Bank of North America. He asserted that O'Malley got into the bank, took the money, and buried it in his backyard. The testimony brought a roar of laughter in the courtroom. Talen appeared as a witness for Gourdain, but other testimony strongly backed O'Malley's claim to the *Item*, and the charge against O'Malley was dismissed.[46]

Lieutenant Governor Jared Y. Sanders, appearing as a lawyer at a trial, put into the court record in 1906 this observation: "I would connnect the man, O'Malley, with the boy, O'Malley, and connect him with every crime committed in this city for the past twenty-five year."[47] Sanders was carried away by his own rhetoric, although it is a fact that the police department could claim O'Malley as one of the most active recipients of its professional services. Not only was he arrested frequently; he also went to jail occasionally. Before moving to New Orleans he served a term in the Cleveland workhouse for pilfering iron.[48] "Whatever connection I may have had with that misdeed," O'Malley said, "you must remember that I was only seventeen years old then, and if men were constantly held responsible for the mistakes they made when they were boys there would be very few ministers."[49]

He started meddling in the affairs of the police department as soon as he lost his job as an informer for the internal revenue service and became a private detective. He had a run-in with ranking police officers in 1881. It started when he arrested Dr. Francis Tumblety, a wealthy Briton who came to New Orleans for Mardi Gras. Tumblety met Henry Goven on Canal Street and they had some drinks together. Later Goven went to police to report his pocketbook missing and accuse Tumblety of stealing it. Police gave Goven no satisfaction, and he engaged O'Malley, who as a special officer arrested Tumblety. When Tumblety's case came up Zach Bachemin, then a police captain, arrested O'Malley in the courtroom and charged him with being a dangerous and suspicious character, and with carrying concealed weapons. The dangerous-character charge was refused. When Bachemin arrested O'Malley he took the latter's private papers and did not turn them over to the police property clerk. He found a copy of a letter to the foreman of the grand jury, which said: "I deem it my duty as a citizen and as a special officer to call to your attention that barrel and gambling dens are still in full blast on Canal Street, between Front and Levee, in violation of the law, and of repeated orders of his honor, the mayor. I beg to tender my services, gratis, to furnish information sufficient to find an indictment against the proprietors, and to implicate high police officers."[50]

The accusation brought retaliation from Police Chief Thomas N. Boylan, who arrested O'Malley as a dangerous and suspicious character. The detective had to stay in jail all night before he could win his release. O'Malley was acquitted of Boylan's charge but was required to post a $250 bond to keep the peace[51] The *Mascot* charged that James "Charcoal Jimmy" Norton and O'Malley sought to blackmail "a sewing machine man named Cowart." Norton introduced Cowart, a married man, to some girls. When Cowart flirted with one of them, according to the *Mascot,* O'Malley tried to bleed him under threat of exposure. O'Malley was arrested but released because no money actually changed hands.[52] O'Malley lasted for nearly eight months as superintendent of the Merchants' District Telegraph Company and Detective Agency in 1884 and 1885 before the connection was sundered by suits and counter suits. The company charged that O'Malley was "negligent and disobedient in the performance of his duties, extravagant in the expenditure of money of the defendant, unfaithful and careless in keeping the accounts and books." He was accused of collecting money for services and failing to turn it over to his employer. O'Malley sued for nonpayment of his salary of $250 a month.[53]

Things seemed to happen when O'Malley was around. On Christmas night, 1885, he was on Canal Street, near Burgundy, when he saw a man running. With the help of Dave Heller, O'Malley stopped the fugitive, who turned out to be Mathew Heindel, who had stabbed his wife to death in the alleyway of a house of prostitution at 166 Customhouse Street. O'Malley turned Heindel over to police.[54]

The assassination of A. H. "Cap" Murphy in 1885 was a headline news story for weeks, and O'Malley couldn't resist the opportunity to jump into the action. He landed in the middle, as a special report of the grand jury will attest. The jury called his conduct reprehensible. After he succeeded in getting himself employed by the prosecution, the jury said, "he sought, as it appears from the testimony, to hire his services to the attorneys and friends of the accused, and proposed to communicate to them such information as he might have obtained by reason of his connection with the prosecution." In addition, the jury said, "he falsely pretended to the members of Fire Company No. 20, that the District Attorney, and counsel associated with him in the conduct of the prosecution, had been derelict and dishonest." The jury recommended that his special officer's commission be revoked. It was. But that did not end gumshoe O'Malley's activities in the case. He set up a trap which brought about the conviction of Dr. Samuel Dreifus for subornation of perjury. O'Malley hid behind a door in a bedroom of the residence of Mrs. Susan McMahon at 212 South Rampart Street, while A. C. Lindauer, a reporter for the *Picayune,* secreted himself under the bed. They heard a conversation among Dr. Dreifus, Mrs. McMahon, and the latter's sister, Mrs. Mary Smythe, in which it was revealed that Dreifus had coached the two women in false testimony in the trial of Murphy's slayers. It was at the Dreifus trial that Chief Boylan, David Hennessey, and newsmen Frank R. Waters and W. B. Stansbury said they wouldn't believe O'Malley under oath.[55]

It is difficult to get an accurate count on the number of times O'Malley was run in for carrying a concealed weapon, a not uncommon habit, and a necessary precaution for a man with so many enemies. Even after he bought the *Item* he was taken to parish prison on November 20, 1895, to serve a ten-day sentence on a concealed-weapon charge. O'Malley paid fines on more than one assault charge, but who knows how many times he was forced to defend himself with his fists?* There is cause for suspicion that as early as 1881 he was learning how to protect himself in the courts. He was indicted for perjury when his testimony in the trial of Edward Schleider differed from statements he made in an affidavit. Before he came up for trial in the United States Circuit Court the affidavit was stolen from court records, and the case had to be abandoned.[56]

He completed a short stay in parish prison for attempting to blackmail George W. Randolph in an interdiction proceeding.

* On the evening of March 18, 1893, O'Malley encountered Alex Carruthers, editor of the *Comet,* at Canal and St. Charles streets and punched him in the face because of an article Carruthers had written about O'Malley. They were separated by bystanders.

His activities as a private detective brought three or more charges of intimidating witnesses, including an indictment which said he prevented Rose Baxter from appearing at the trial of Thomas McCrystol, who was accused of the murder of H. W. Smith.[57] It was McCrystol who later refused to testify against O'Malley in the jury-tampering incident during the Hennessey slaying trial. During the Hennessey investigation O'Malley sued Henry J. Hearsey and George W. Dupre for $10,000, contending they libeled him by publishing in the *States* of October 25, 1890, the disclosure that he had served the workhouse sentence in Cleveland.[58] Whereupon the *States* got its lawyers busy and followed with an answer making other accusations. The *States* said O'Malley attempted to extort $500 from the father of John Oriole by offering to obtain dismissal or acquittal in a counterfeiting charge of which Oriole was cleared. The paper said O'Malley attempted to blackmail Cutter McMahon by falsely alleging that he robbed jewelry stores. The libel case was dismissed when O'Malley failed to put up bond to cover court costs. There was a period when Judge Alfred Roman would not allow O'Malley to enter his criminal district courtroom.[59] A federal indictment charged that O'Malley opened and destroyed a letter addressed to the prize fighter Jimmy Fleming. He was cleared by directed verdict because the letter was sent in care of O'Malley. Lieutenant Governor Sanders charged that in 1898 O'Malley bribed a jockey to pull a racehorse. The *Item* commented that Sanders offered no proof.[60]

George Denegre sued O'Malley for libel because the *Item* said he was unscrupulous and dishonest in connection with the operations of the New Orleans Railway Company.[61] Denegre testified that in 1879, "when I first came into contact with Mr. O'Malley, he made a proposition of blackmail to me which I indignantly refused." The irrepressible O'Malley stood up in court and said, "That is false." Judge Joshua G. Baker dismissed the action. Although he did not become a United States citizen until May 10, 1916, O'Malley for years had been voting in city, state, and national elections,[62] leaving himself liable to a prison sentence had anybody prosecuted him.

This was the man who in 1894 bought a three-fourths interest in the *Item* for a reported outlay of $2,704.[63] John W. Fairfax had sold the paper to four employees, Eric Talen, the editor; Charles Burkhardt, Talen's brother-in-law; and printers George Kern and John Lagroue. Each had a one-fourth interest. O'Malley approached them with an offer to pay dollar-for-dollar on their investment. Burkhardt, Kern, and Lagroue accepted. Talen held on as editor for a few weeks until he and O'Malley had a falling out, and he also sold,[64] making O'Malley the sole owner as of July 21, 1894.[65] O'Malley later said the *Item* was on the verge of folding, and he offered to take it over because he had friends on the reportorial staff. "The circulation was 720," he recalled, "with at least 400 deadheads."[66]

The rough-and-tumble, uneducated, thirty-five-year-old Irishman was an unlikely prospect as a publisher. But the advantages offered by newspaper ownership to a promoter of his wide-ranging interests were too obvious to be overlooked. Besides, O'Malley had taken the city to his heart. He felt at home in the New Orleans of his day. He knew how New Orleanians thought, how to stimulate their interest, how to put out the kind of daily many would buy and read. He had a way with words, a knack for expression, as his statements and interviews demonstrate. More important, he enlisted some gifted writers to give the *Item* pungency and readability. One of his early moves was to arrange for his associate, the lawyer Lionel Adams, to write editorials.[67] Adams, who won distinction in the courtroom both as prosecutor and defense counsel, had been allied with O'Malley even before the Hennessey trial in which his brilliance was an important factor in the verdict New Orleanians were so unwilling to accept. Adams had the polish and literary skill lacked by O'Malley. Later Joseph H. Hodgson and Walter M. Smalley, editorial writers, and Willis J. Carter, reporter, could capture readers with their ability to express O'Malley's policies, and could help him at least hold his own in word jousts with his newspaper enemies.[68]

With O'Malley in control, the *Item* opened a campaign against disreputable beer parlors and dancehalls which were giving a bad name to a section of Royal Street near Canal. The *Item* would announce that the Eden Theater would have its usual Monday night dance. Reporter Billy Struve would stand inside the door and spot the men who entered. On Tuesday the paper would print a list of the revelers. The publicity helped to drive the places out of business.[69] Edward Laroque Tinker said O'Malley's motives were not strictly journalistic. His detective agency had been retained by interests which wanted to rid Royal Street of two of the establishments, and O'Malley found a way to let his newspaper do the job for the agency.[70]

An eye-gouging, groin-kicking street brawler, O'Malley took into the newspaper business the same instinct for destroying an opponent. He went after his foes with a ferocity uncommon even in the not-so-genteel journalism of his day. New Orleans witnessed a display of his technique in 1894, immediately after he took over the *Item,* in a campaign against the Boodle Council.

In early July of that year the *Item* resembled the conventional newspaper of the day. Most of page one was covered by advertisements; headlines wordy and ambiguous, were printed in small type. There was some representation of national and international news, along with the police reports, political, and City Hall happenings which, along with editorials, made up the bulk of the nonadvertising content. By the end of July, O'Malley's hand was evident.[71] Advertisements all but disappeared from page one. The reader who looked for Washington or London news was unlikely to find any, since the staff was concentrating its energies on local scandals, exposes, and sensations. Headlines were as bold as one-column type would permit.

And what headlines they were! O'Malley's copy readers perfected a style in which three or four words in big, black, capital letters were interspersed with decks of smaller type. The eye would be caught by the big words which read alone promised a juicy disclosure or excoriated an O'Malley foe. But when the entire headline, small type as well as bold, was read in sequence the meaning would be entirely different. Some of the headlines show how blatantly misleading they could be:[72]

THE JURY

That Will Try John T. Callahan Will Hear Indisputable Evidence

To Prove That Mr. Widney Paid Him Money For Certain Privileges--There

IS

Other Strong Evidence Against Him--Should He Not Be Convicted?

The People of New Orleans Will Want to Know How the Jury Was

FIXED,

THE WORST

Has Not Been Told About Louis Octave Desforges.

His Rascalities are Unparalleled in the Annals of Crime.--A

MAN IN

His Grave, Sent There By Desforges, Now Comes to Accuse Him

Of a Crime. Poor Pete McGinn Said His Murderer Was a Fire Bug. Such a Man Should Be Driven From

NEW ORLEANS,

FRIENDS

Of John T. Callahan Fill Section B, Criminal District Court,

To Listen to the Selection of a Jury to Try Him---A Jury

CANNOT

Be Obtained Without Considerable Difficulty as the Counsel on Both Sides.

Are Exercising Great Caution in the Selection of Jurors. Cal ahan's Lawyers Doing Everything In Their Power to

HELP HIM,

DESFORGES

Indicted for Bribery and Intimidating a Witness.

There are Many Persons who will Not Forget That He was Said to be a

MURDERER,

And That He Defeated Justice by Bribing the Jury That Tried Him.

He will Now Have an Opportunity of Securing Another Jury to Prove to the World that He Is No

THIEF.

O'Malley had another device which he used to taunt the councilmen and other members of the City Hall faction, and to hold them up to public ridicule. Almost every day during the summer of 1894. The *Item* published accounts of imaginary meetings of the Crescent Democratic Club, with liberal quotations to suggest that O'Malley had planted a spy in the inner circles. He laid the groundwork for the series when he learned that Alderman Desforges had paid a midnight visit to the home of District Attorney Charles A. Butler, 333 North Claiborne Avenue, in behalf of the erring aldermen. The *Item* quoted a participant in one of the ghostly club meetings as saying: "I think that scoundrel O'Malley is ubiquitous and is watching every man that is crooked. Nine different men told me they looked out of their windows at 12 o'clock last night, and all declare they saw O'Malley in the street on the lookout for another midnight visit. Strange that all the men live in different parts of town and they all saw O'Malley at exactly the same time. And you know, gentlemen, there is not a man in this club who could tell a lie."[73]

O'Malley liked to advertise his own considerable role, and one of the phantom club stories started in this manner: "'I told you fellows four months ago that you could never expect to carry such a thing through unless that d—d fellow O'Malley was out of town or with you people.' Such were the words used by the Secretary to the Chief of Police George Vandervoort at the Crescent Democratic Club last night while 'de gang' were speaking of the Numa Dudoussat bribery case and the manner in which O'Malley had discovered that certain parties were on the jury who were relatives of the Councilman." [74] The *Item* used one of its special headlines to say:

DEAD

The Members of the Club of Clubs Broken-Hearted.

The Popular Verdict in the Callahan Case Killed Them.

ANDTHEY

Recognize the Fact That Hoodlum Methods Will no Longer Be Tolerated.

The Law-Abiding Citizens Will No Longer Put Up With Ring Rule --The Boodlers Will All Go Up the River and They

KNOW IT.[75]

In the midst of the trials the *Times-Democrat* reported that O'Malley had pleaded guilty at Crown Point, Indiana, and paid a $1,000 fine because the Columbian Athletic Club, of which he was president, had staged illegal boxing matches at Roby, Indiana.[76] True, said the *Item,* but O'Malley was in New Orleans at the time the fine was levied. "It is a well-settled fact, in the public mind, that I originated this investigation of the City Council," O'Malley was quoted as saying.[77] "That being a fact, to some, my absence during the Callahan trial would look strange and possibly they would misconstrue my motives in being in Indiana when my business required my presence here. To be candid, I pay but little attention to what anybody thinks or says about my motives in anything." At any rate, he said, he wired his attorneys in Crown Point to plead guilty for him, and forwarded $1,000, the amount of the maximum fine, by express. "I believe the public will appreciate my sacrifice," he commented, "but if they do not, it will not have the effect of keeping me awake at nights." O'Malley's involvement in Indiana came when he left New Orleans for a period after the Sicilian lynching.

O'Malley's proudest hour in the developing scandals came on August 20, 1894. He learned that Numa Dudoussat, city councilman representing the Seventh District, had asked a one-hundred-dollar bribe of Charles Sherman, who wanted a permit for operating a bar in his grocery store at Bayou Road and Treme Street. O'Malley instructed Sherman to have Dudoussat come to the store for the payoff. He told the grocer to place a barrel in a hallway where it could be seen from upstairs.

The conniving publisher gave up the opportunity to score a journalistic exclusive for his paper. He telephone H. J. Seiferth, city editor of the *Picayune,* and — without tipping off the nature of the assignment — invited him to have two reporters come at 6 A.M. the next day to Clay Statue, at St. Charles and Canal streets. He told Aubrey Murray, city editor of the *Item,* to join them and also arranged for Police Sergeant J. C. Aucoin to be there.

C. W. Kindrick and William P. Ball, *Picayune* reporters, appeared. O'Malley led the other four men aboard an Esplanade streetcar and then to Sherman's grocery. Sherman took the group to the head of the stairs. Through a hole in a tacked-up sack, they had a clear view of the barrel below. O'Malley gave Sherman ten marked ten-dollar bills after the newsmen recorded the serial numbers.

"He's coming. He's right outside." Sherman whispered the words at 7:45 A.M., then hurried downstairs and entered the store to greet Dudoussat. He escorted the councilman into the hall and counted out the ten bills, placing them on the barrelhead. Two fluttered to the floor, and Sherman retrieved them. Dudoussat hesitated for a moment, then stuffed the money into a coat pocket — or so a jury was to rule later.

Sherman invited Dudoussat to have a drink, then tiptoed up the stairs while the councilman walked into the store. "He's got it," Sherman murmured to the five concealed eyewitnesses. The grocer took Dudoussat into a rear room where he had set up a bar in anticipation of obtaining a permit over the objection of neighbors. O'Malley and the others went out onto Treme Street and strode into the room where Dudoussat was about to lift his glass. His first intimation that he was in trouble came when he saw O'Malley. "Well, this is rich," the startled official remarked. "You have set this trap for me, have you?"

Police found the marked money in Dudoussat's pocket. He insisted that O'Malley had planted the bills there. But the jury that tried him on a bribery charge did not believe him. The verdict on December 5, 1894, was guilty, with a recommendation to the court for mercy.

The *Picayune* took full advantage of its opportunity with an account that filled page one on the morning of August 30, along with a drawing that showed Sherman and Dudoussat facing each other over the barrel.

O'Malley's prominence in the Boodler case apparently nettled the other newspapers, as well, perhaps, as some of the citizens who were active in the exposure. The *Times-Democrat* said the investigation was the work of the executive committee of the Citizens Protective Association, naming George W. Young, president, and J. J. McLoughlin, Henry P. Dart and Bernard McCloskey. "It has been rumored, and is generally supposed, that the two indictments against Councilmen Callahan and Dudoussat were based on information received from D. C. O'Malley," the newspaper added, "but as a matter of fact neither of them were based on information from him, although he has given information which was laid before the grand jury in other cases which have not yet been acted upon."[78] The *Picayune* said its reporter was told that only three members of the protective association directed its activities, and all were lawyers.[79]

A few hours after Councilman John T. Callahan was convicted, O'Malley went to Wenger's Theater, Burgundy and Customhouse streets, to talk with Henry Wenger, Sr., about a report that the latter had paid money in connection with a pending ordinance. Larry Coleman, a friend of Callahan's, was at the bar. He began abusing O'Malley, who at first replied good naturedly. "I came to the conclusion no matter how I might endeavor I was in for a fight and the first blow was half the battle," O'Malley related. "There were two blows hit. I hit Coleman and he hit the floor. He had a very nice countenance before the contest. Afterwards, his eye was all swollen and bleeding and the bosom of his shirt was crimson."[80]

As the year progressed the *Item* reported the indictments of

Aldermen W. J. Kane, John T. Callahan and Numa Dudoussat for bribery; the indictment of Kane and Alderman Francis B. Thriffley for taking a $200 bribe; the conviction of Callahan; the indictment of Alderman L. O. Desforges for bribery; the indictment of Thriffley and Aldermen Thomas Haley and Peter B. Caufield for seeking bribes; the conviction of Dudoussat; and the mistrial in the cases of Kane and Thriffley. [81]

Whether his own machinations had shown him the possibilities, as the Sicilian lynching grand jury suspected, or whether he was merely cynical about the operations of the courts, O'Malley was preoccupied with the juries impaneled for the Boodler trials. As early as August, the *Item* was offering a $500 reward for information leading to jury fixers. Under the headline, "All Hope Centered Here," the newspaper published the names of the prospective jurors on the criminal court panel for August. It repeated the procedure for subsequent trials. Names of the jurors who convicted Callahan and Dudoussat were printed as a sort of honor roll to encourage jurors in future trials. [82]

"Outrage," headlined the *Item* when a mistrial was declared because the jury could not agree in the Kane-Thriffley case. The paper said jurors M. L. Costley, Samuel Wolf, E. V. Reiss and F. C. Hoffman held out for acquittal. For days the *Item* devoted an entire column on page one to listing the business and residence addresses of the four men. There were only four paragraphs in the column, the great amount of white space calling attention to the few words. [83]

It was not long before the *Item,* under O'Malley's direction, began to prosper. Whatever his faults, the Irishman was not a penny-pinching, corner-cutting businessman. He went first class. In October, 1894, the newspaper bought a new press, and in the same month it moved from its dingy quarters on

Natchez Street, for which the rent was $240 a year, to 72 Camp Street, near the *Picayune,* where O'Malley paid $2,000 a year. The *Item* made arrangements with a bakery for poor families to buy a thirty-five-ounce loaf of bread for a nickel, and with a coal company for the poor to obtain a barrel of coal for thirty-five cents. O'Malley footed the bill for free shoes for boys who otherwise might not have been able to go to school.[84]

Circulation and advertising revenues leaped. By 1899 the newspaper claimed the largest circulation in the city, morning or evening. It boasted that its circulation increases in a year exceeded the total of any two other papers in town. And it said its increase in mail circulation also was greater than that recorded by any other New Orleans journal. With a typical gambler's gesture, O'Malley offered to bet $1,000 that he could prove each of the three statements.[85]

8

Dominick's Downfall

After several days of hibernating, presumably devoted either to incubation or the accumulation of a 'jag,' the *States* was able yesterday to sit up and take notice. Whenever "Col." Ewing can get away from the onerous duty of securing credit for enough white paper to get his daily windjammer on the street, he feels so jubilant that he begins to cerebrate in the same old way and then there is always something doing; and it is always the same. The "colonel" is not what one would call versatile, and he believes in sticking to the beaten path, as he realizes his limitations and takes no chances of getting beyond his depth. As soon as he takes one drink he imagines he sees O'Malley, and these images increase in geometric progression with the drinks he absorbs until about twelfth drink time in the morning he sees O'Malleys floating in the air and all he has to do is to reach up and pick them out of the atmosphere. By the time his paper goes to press, the click of the machinery sings "O'Malley, O'Malley, O'Malley," and it is to this soothing refrain that he drops off into a troubled sleep, but his stertorious breathing shows that the Nemesis is still at his side.[1]

The opposing commanders in a newspaper war that preempted the front pages in the first decade of the twentieth century were Robert Ewing of the *States* and Dominick O'Malley of the *Item.*

Nineteen hundred four was Dominick O'Malley's year. His *Item* was edging up to the 20,000 mark in circulation, and was seriously challenging the city's other dailies both in the number of copies distributed and in advertising linage.[2] Politically, O'Malley was riding high. He used his influence with Governor Newton C. Blanchard to humble the *States, Picayune,* and *Times-Democrat* — then known as the united Democratic press — in a showdown over the nomination of Chandler C. Luzenberg for a full term as district attorney. O'Malley, who wanted to demonstrate he had clout in the courts as well as in the police department, was determined to get Luzenberg out of the office. The other papers wanted Luzenberg retained. "Shall O'Malley Rule?" demanded the *States* in an editorial.

> A few days ago the New Orleans *Item* announced in emphatic terms and with an air of authority that Mr. Luzenberg's name would not be presented to the convention to assemble in the city tomorrow. This defiant challenge was insolently hurled in the teeth of a united Democratic press and the universal sentiment of the people of New Orleans and it was followed up day by day with articles of the most libellous character reflecting upon the character and official integrity of Mr. Luzenberg, every single one of which charges was instantly met and refuted by that gentleman. . . . The remarkable spectacle is presented that O'Malley is leading the fight for the defeat, if not the destruction of Chandler C. Luzenberg, and the Governor of the State is aiding in the work. . . . Let no man be deceived. The situation is full of the gravest peril. The very atmosphere is surcharged with the fierce spirit of revolt and the people demand that the leaders shall not basely abdicate their functions, betray the confidence reposed in them and run up the white flag to O'Malley. Gentlemen of New Orleans, the question is up to you.[3]

The *States* estimated that 10,000 persons attended a mass meeting at Liberty Place, at the foot of Canal Street, to hear speakers denounce Governor Blanchard. As John C. Wickliffe opened up his castigation of the governor, somebody shouted from the crowd: "How about O'Malley?" "Gentlemen," responded Wickliffe, "I'm hunting bear tonight; I've got no time to skin a skunk."[4] O'Malley prevailed. Governor Blanchard put pressure on ward leaders, and J. Porter Parker was nominated for district attorney on the ticket headed by Martin Behrman, the successful candidate for mayor. Luzenberg filed a $30,000 libel suit against O'Malley and the *Item,* a suit which he was destined to lose in the lower court but through which he won a $5,000 judgment in an appeal to the state supreme court.[5]

In May, 1905, as he began his lengthy occupation of the mayor's chair, Behrman called a meeting in editor Page M. Baker's office at the *Times-Democrat.* Present, besides Baker and Behrman, were Thomas G. Rapier, manager of the *Picayune;* Robert Ewing, owner of the *States,* and Peter Kiernan, publisher of the *Daily News.* Conspicuously absent was O'Malley. He had not been unintentionally overlooked. Behrman asked for the get-together because he wanted to line up newspaper support for his decision to oust John Journee and replace him with a new police inspector.[6] Everyone present knew the mayor's reason for wanting to make the move: Under Journee's administration, O'Malley was pulling the strings, manipulating police like puppets.

Out of the meeting developed a newspaper war, complete with spies and infiltrators, with charges and countercharges of assassination plots, with lawsuits and countersuits, with exchanges of invective which taxed the vocabularies of editorial and news writers on both sides. Before it was over, O'Malley went to prison. Coincidentally, but not as a result of the machinations of his enemies, he also lost his dictatorial control over the *Item.* It was only a matter of time afterward, before he sold his minority interest in the newspaper and went into a more peaceful field, the fish business.

At the meeting, Behrman and Ewing took seats close together. Baker paced the floor, while Rapier sat at a distance. Kiernan, who made no secret of his own ambition to be police inspector, took an active part in the discussion. "That damned fellow has done it again," complained Behrman, referring to a derogatory article in the *Item.* He said he wanted to make Edward Stanley Whitaker inspector. Behrman conceded that Whitaker was disreputable, but said it would take that kind of man to do the job, and "He is the only one who can handle O'Malley." Ewing agreed that someone was needed to keep O'Malley under control, and supported the appointment of Whitaker. Baker and Rapier did not join in the denunciation of O'Malley but were agreeable to Behrman's suggestion. Kiernan spoke out against O'Malley, but also denounced Whitaker because of the man's record and his temperament. There was unanimous agreement that Journee had to be ousted. The *Item* later contended that Ewing, Baker, and Rapier joined with Behrman in the selection of Whitaker "for no other reason than to place a premium on assassination." Kiernan said he did not know whether the meeting was a conspiracy, but he himself certainly was not present as a conspirator. All who participated, he said, were taxpayers interested in the welfare of the community, and the city's future was dependent on having an effective police inspector. Ironically, the *Item* had supported Behrman in the recent municipal election, while the *Times-Democrat* had led the opposition to him. Behrman recalled in court testimony[7] that O'Malley had been friendly during the political campaign, but the mayor now saw that it was for the purpose of trying to retain influence in the police department. Behrman said O'Malley ran the department while Journee was the inspector.

The appointment of Whitaker created an explosive situation because his trigger finger was fully as nervous as O'Malley's, and nobody would have been surprised had the bullets started flying. O'Malley recalled the incident in 1897 in which he was shot by Whitaker. "While walking through Commercial Alley one afternoon, unarmed, in company with Judge Otero, with an alpaca coat on my arm, I was shot from behind by Whitaker," he wrote.[8] "This, no doubt, convinced Col. Page M. Baker, Maj. Thomas G. Rapier and Col. Robert Ewing that personally I would be afraid of Whitaker, and this is the sole reason why he occupies the position of inspector today." But, added O'Malley, "I believe I do know Whitaker, as I do a great many others. He loves to live, he realizes that when he meets me in a combat where I am armed and in a position to defend myself that he has no better chance than I have." Long afterward, Edward Laroque Tinker wrote: "A friend pointed out to Whitaker that O'Malley was his salary insurance and he'd be fired once O'Malley was killed."[9]

There may have been an element of business jealousy in the decision of the united Democratic press editors to gang up on Behrman's side. The *Item* still was claiming the largest circulation and was continuing to gain in advertising linage. O'Malley charged that the morning papers had a combination which worked against the advertisers. He said Samuel Geoghegan of the D. H. Holmes Company, Ltd., S. J. Schwartz of Maison Blanche and S. G. Kreeger of Kreeger's "called me to their aid in breaking this combination, which I succeeded in doing, though the rate today is higher in proportion to circulation than in any other city in the United States." O'Malley made a public offer to subscribe $25,000 toward the establishment of a new morning paper to break the "monopoly."[10]

It was Ewing, however, who drew most of the *Item*'s fire. O'Malley's paper called the *States* a "pensioner on the State," and said, "It received from the treasury of this commonwealth hundreds of thousands of dollars. Printing bills which would be considered fair compensation at eighteen or nineteen thousand dollars were passed by the legislature at sixty and seventy thousand dollars. No one had nerve enough, for it was considered a crime and almost ostracism to have the *States* opposed to anyone, to expose this robbery, and for these reasons, few, if any, could assume the responsibility of showing up this robbery of the *States*."[11]

Behrman and the united Democratic press were determined to purge the police department of O'Malley's influence. Otherwise, they never would have accepted Whitaker, whose only apparent recommendations were his audacity and his hatred of the *Item* publisher. Whitaker served with distinction as a captain in the Spanish-American War. In New Orleans he never was known to back down from a fight. Once, in 1883, he ran into Pen Poincy, who had offended him, at Carondelet and Common streets. Whitaker went after Poincy with his walking stick. Poincy whipped out two pistols, whereupon Whitaker reached for his ever-present weapon. Poincy fled into a cigar store and hid behind a pillar. Whitaker stood outside, cursing Poincy and daring him to come out. Finally Whitaker handed his pistol to a friend and walked off. In 1892 Whitaker was a successful candidate for judge of the first recorder's court. O'Malley said he advanced the money for Whitaker's qualifying fee and supported his candidacy, then learned later that the judge was levying exorbitant fines and pocketing the money. Whitaker was indicted for embezzlement of public funds, was tried three times without a verdict being reached. After the second trial, the *Times-Democrat* criticized him for having the effrontery to return to the bench while the charge still was pending against him. After the third trial the *Times-Democrat* said Whitaker made a "repulsive spectacle" in trying to serve while the case was unresolved. At last, in 1899, District Attorney R. H. Marr dismissed the charges. O'Malley related that Whitaker raped or seduced "unfortunate girls."[12]

Since, as Tenth Ward leader and a Choctaw Club member, Ewing was a close political associate of Behrman's, the *States* spearheaded the campaign to win public acceptance of Whitaker's appointment. The *States* and the *Item*—who could have guessed that someday it would be the *States-Item* — waged a wordy battle of insult that kept the city entertained for two months. On May 25, 1905, the *States* tipped its readers to impending events by printing an editorial which said the criminal element — O'Malley was not mentioned by name — would not allow Whitaker to become inspector if it could be prevented. On June 2 both papers announced the firing of Journee and the appointment of Whitaker.

O'Malley tried to operate a newspaper using the same tactics that worked for his detective agency. The result was that while his editorial writers could win the page-one skirmishes with deadly verbal sharpshooting, O'Malley lost the war. He missed out on the only chance to rally public opinion to his side when his trickery was exposed. In the editorial dueling, *Item* writers used an epee, *States* writers a bludgeon. The *Item* seized upon the favorable lower court result in the Luzenberg libel suit as an opportunity to jab away at Ewing, who had appeared as a witness for the district attorney.

Under cross examination Mr. Ewing admitted frequenting gambling resorts and being "under the influence." "Tight" was the metaphor used by the witness, but many incline to the impression that good, plain "drunk" more amply fills the bill. Drunk or sober, this witness could not divest himself from his responsibilities as tax collector, and as stated before, the custodian of enormous sums of money that belongs to the State. But, anyway, he admitted that he frequented 18 Royal Street, "Behan's Place," coquetted with the Goddess of Chance, frequently won and lost large sums of money, and when he lost, if he didn't have the ready cash on hand wherewith to liquidate his debts, he gave "bits of paper," I O U's in plain English. And this all took place, mark you, while this same Ewing was a sworn officer of the law, a State tax collector, and the custodian of enormous sums of money reposed in Ewing's charge.[13]

There was more to come. In an editorial the *Item* said: "There is no possibility that Robert Ewing drunk is any better man than Robert Ewing sober. He is a vain, crafty, selfish man, of obese conditions, puffed up with his importance or imagined importance. . . . He cheated the late Peter Farrell, then leader of the Tenth Ward, by the agencies of fraud and forgery."[14] Ewing was not the only target of still another blast:

> It seems to be the theory of the inspector and his ally, the U. D. P., that O'Malley is either directly or indirectly responsible for everything that has happened in New Orleans for the last quarter of a century. Murder, the boll weevil, arson, the low cost of cotton, highway robbery, the kissing bug, high water and the renaissance of the hoop skirt are all laid at his door. . . . Coming down to more modern times and to matters of greater local interest, it might be found that it was he who jollied Whitaker into embezzling the money of this city while he was recorder, and for which he was indicted by a grand jury; he may have induced Page M. Baker to "draw a small weapon" and commit a deadly and cowardly assault on Edgar H. Farrar; it might not cause surprise if it were learned that it was he who aided Thomas G. Rapier to wreck the Bank of Commerce, and escape prosecution on a mere technicality; that it was none other than O'Malley who induced Mayor Behrman to commit a long series of acts of which he was in mortal terror lest they be exposed during the recent municipal campaign, and it may be shown that he induced the Right Honorable Robert Ewing to pay his gambling debts in due bills instead of cash, and then pushed him off the water wagon.[15]

And a shot which must have hit home:

> Oh, how the lamented Major Hearsey would shake with disgust and indignation were he to see to what straits, intellectual and financial, the object of his care and devotion has been reduced! Leaving behind a newspaper, lofty in tone, logical in reasoning, classical in its language, financially solid, steered by him for many a year with cleanliness and ability, he yielded the helm to other hands, who, in the space of a few years, have succeeded in destroying his great work, cutting its circulation to nothing; no more reasoning, but vituperation; plenty of body, but no brain.[16]

But O'Malley's shady, even illegal activities left him wide open to the bolts of the persistent, if somewhat less imaginative writers who worked for Ewing, and day after day, on page one and on the editorial page, the *States* attacked. One of O'Malley's ploys had been to import two notorious pickpockets and burglars from Chicago — Seeden and Burke were their names although they used various aliases — and turn them loose in New Orleans. Their instructions were to establish an arrangement to share their loot with police detectives, giving the *Item* a sensational exposé and establishing O'Malley as a watchdog in the public interest. The *Item* spent $1,112 to bring in the pair. They participated in burglaries, but apparently never could establish the right police connections because the *Item* failed to capitalize on its plot. The *States* righteously pointed out that "none of the booty secured by the burglars in thirty or more robberies has ever been returned so far as can be learned."[17]

"Under the inefficient police service which has prevailed here for many years," said the *States* in a news story, "O'Malley has had practically a free hand in protecting the varied lawless interests of which he has been the promoter and from which he has derived graft of cash and precious stones. He has filled the department with his emissaries and since Hennessey's death he has been almost uniformly free from molestation."[18]

The imported burglar episode was only a prelude to a plot which O'Malley must have thought of as his masterpiece, at least until he found himself under arrest and also in the red-faced position of reading a full account in the *States* of how the *Item* had published faked news stories. It would be difficult in a search of the annals of the newspaper business in the United States to find a parallel to the Slocum-Gerken affair.

Harry Slocum and S. Ed Gerken were police reporters for the *Times-Democrat.* Slocum had worked in New York until about 1900, when he migrated to Chicago to escape payment of alimony. He lasted in Chicago for about three years until he had to flee to avoid arrest for attempting to blackmail barkeeps and brothel operators. In Kansas City, where he remained for a year, he was known as "Coke" because he used cocaine. He drifted to Dallas and Fort Worth before going to Beaumont, where he worked for the *Enterprise*. He was hired by the *Times-Democrat* as a copy reader and then was made a night police reporter. The background of Gerken, day police reporter, is obscure. He appeared in the headlines only for a day or two, then vanished from view. When Slocum and Gerken made a surreptitious visit to O'Malley's home and offered to sell him some information, he saw an opportunity to obtain ammunition for his fight against Whitaker, and at the same time embarrass the *Times-Democrat*. He paid fifty dollars for the information offered and arranged another meeting. His plan was to make it appear that he had planted Slocum on the *Times-Democrat* staff and was using him as an undercover agent to expose police corruption in the Storyville red-light district while Slocum was covering police news for the rival paper. The *Item* fabricated a news story about the hiring of Slocum, even printing the texts of phony telegrams and letters which the newspaper said were exchanged between O'Malley in New Orleans and Slocum in Chicago. O'Malley made his scheme a little too elaborate, because the telegrams and letters bore dates in March and the *States* later could prove Slocum was in Beaumont at the time. Slocum also spoiled the timing by going on a spree and getting fired from the *Times-Democrat* by the city editor, D. D. Moore. O'Malley tried to salvage something from the wreckage of his plan. On June 6 the *Item* published a page-one account of Slocum's "investigation" in the tenderloin district. Slocum reported that Ike Miller was the kingpin of the district and Sam Felix was his partner. The paper said every woman in the district had to pay protection money.[19]

With exposure inevitable, Gerken resigned from the *Times-Democrat.* The *Item* on June 8 published Gerken's letter to D. D. Moore. "According to reports that are in circulation a police inspector was elected by three of the papers of this city with the avowed intention of running another newspaperman out of business. How true this is the men connected with the affair know," the letter said. It actually was handwritten by O'Malley.[20] On June 9 the *Item,* without the flicker of a smile, published a letter from Gerken, who blandly asked how the newspaper managed to obtain a copy of a communication from himself to his city editor.

By then Inspector Whitaker had police in search of Slocum and on June 13 they found him. He made a self-serving affidavit which nonetheless throws some light on the shenanigans in progress and also shows that Whitaker and his newspaper confederates were grasping any opportunity they could find for harassing O'Malley.[21] Slocum blamed an "unnatural craving for drink" for getting himself involved. He told of going with Gerken to meet O'Malley at the Cosmo Club, where they were given $150 for the use of their names in the Storyville expose. Then, he said, O'Malley told him he could make a considerable amount of money by helping in another plan. "The scheme was gradually unfolded to me that it was imperative to put a cessation to the reign of Judge Whitaker as inspector of the police department. I was told by Mr. O'Malley that Judge Whitaker was his bitter personal enemy, and that it would be necessary for Mr. O'Malley to obtain a firm grasp on departmental affairs. I knew that I would not lack the necessary money to establish myself in business in some town where I was unknown, provided the intimated plans were carried through. While no direct statement was made to me, yet I was firmly convinced of the fact that Judge Whitaker's life might possibly be placed in jeopardy. So much was I impressed with this fact that, in a consultation with a trusted friend, lasting for nearly a day, we went over the matter together, and I confessed to the fact that while I might have acted unscrupulously in ever allowing myself to be mixed up in a case of this kind, yet I was not an assassin, and I was loath to have anything further to do with the case."

Slocum related that O'Malley gave him money:

"(He) asked me to return at 4 o'clock to the *Item* office, when an engagement would be made for 10 o'clock tonight. He said I did not need my revolver at that time and took it in charge, remarking that he would give it to me when I returned. He made an engagement for 10 o'clock tonight and told me that something was likely to come off. He was armed at the time and used an epithet in referring to the inspector, Mr. Whitaker. There were two men with him at the time, and I was led to believe that something desperate was contemplated. While I cannot swear that an attack was about to be made on the inspector, still by intuition I believe such was to be the case, as he was particularly anxious to ascertain the inspector's movements at night.

The *States* seized upon the Slocum affidavit, and in an editorial entitled "Conspiracy to Assassinate" the newspaper said:

Whatever may be thought of the man Slocum, the former tool of O'Malley, who was arrested last night, there can be little doubt in the mind of any reflecting person of the truth of his confession that a conspiracy had been formed by O'Malley to assassinate, or cause the assassination of Inspector Whitaker last night. . . . There can be no doubt of the fact that affairs are drifting rapidly into a condition similar to that which immediately preceded the assassination of the late Chief of Police Hennessey, and that unless it shall be dealt with, with an iron hand, this community will be horrified by a crime similar to that one. . . . At the time that Hennessey was assassinated, it will be remembered, he was engaged in investigating a system of lawlessness in which O'Malley was interested, and the trail he had struck was leading straight to the door of this most unspeakable crook and criminal.[22]

At 8:15 A.M. on June 16 O'Malley was arrested at the corner of Poydras and South Rampart streets, taken to the first precinct police station, and charged with conspiracy to commit murder. Until release bond of $2,750 was posted an hour later by Peter Gallagher, O'Malley was held behind bars. "This discrimination is hardly surprising," said the *Item's* account, "when it is recalled that Whitaker has some use for colored prostitutes and the like, while he has no use, for obvious reasons, for anyone connected with the newspaper that has exposed his outlandish past criminal record and his nefarious connection with the present conspiracy."[23]

Slocum's vague affidavit was the only basis for the charge, and predictably a grand jury soon refused to return an indictment against O'Malley.[24]

But in the *Item* story of the arrest, O'Malley was quoted in a statement that resulted in his downfall. What he said was: "When the public learns that this man Martin Behrman has been saved by my instrumentality from indictment, prosecution and a possible penitentiary sentence, I rather fancy that the public will appreciate some of the circumstances governing the incident this morning." The next day, June 17, O'Malley found police officers waiting for him when he boarded a Canal streetcar at 8 A.M. at the Cortez Street stop. O'Malley took a seat beside Judge A. M. Aucoin of the Second City Criminal Court. An officer tapped him on the shoulder and told him he was under arrest. The police detail wanted to take O'Malley off the streetcar and subject him to the humiliation of a ride to the precinct station in a police wagon. But he balked, and stayed on the car until the stop nearest the First Precinct station was reached. Officers then accompanied him on a walk to the jail, where he was charged with criminal libel of Mayor Behrman.[25]

The basis for his statement about Behrman never was clearly developed publicly. At the trial O'Malley testified only that in 1901 Behrman approached him and said he did not want his name used in connection with a ferry franchise. When he ran for mayor in 1904, O'Malley said, Behrman again came to him and asked that his name not be printed in connection with the franchise matter.[26]

On Monday, June 19, O'Malley walked into the First Precinct station. "I want to surrender, for I suppose the detectives are making a search for me. They are probably waiting for me at the office," he said, explaining that his home on the uptown, river corner of Canal and South Pierce streets had been surrounded by police both the night before and that morning.[27]

The *States* was gleeful. "The Fall of Dominick" was the title of an editorial:

> An ancient legend tells us that on a certain occasion Humpty Dumpty had such a fall that all the king's horses and all the king's men were unable to set him up again, but we are constrained to believe that the tumble suffered by Humpty Dumpty was a mere trifle compared to D. C. O'Malley's sudden and crashing drop from ruler of our police force to daily jail-goer. Only a few moons ago Dominick dominated the police completely and with unctious servility they crawled into his presence to receive their instructions for the day and the night, but now when they call it is for the purpose of galloping him grimly to the donjon keep. . . . From a police ruler to a police dodger is a terrible descent for Dominick, but he has taken the grand slide, and now has in his heart great fear of the men who only a short time ago came at his beck and call. He has heard, perhaps, the story of Actaeon, who was devoured by his own dogs, and not desiring to suffer a similar fate, takes a swift back trot when a bluecoated animal with silver buttons looms up before his vision. Police dodging in warm weather is not an engaging pastime, and we believe it will be admitted even by Dominick that a bird in a gilded cage is a more inviting spectacle than a crook in a grated cell, and furthermore, that the bird feels more comfortable than the crook.[28]

O'Malley was convicted of libeling Behrman, and on August 14, 1905, was fined $500 and sentenced to serve eight months in the parish prison. An appeal to the Louisiana Supreme Court failed, and on February 2, 1906, shortly after 2 P.M.

O'Malley left the *Item* office and leisurely proceeded to the parish prison at Tulane Avenue and South Saratoga Street, where he surrendered himself.[29]

He was no ordinary prisoner. He had spacious quarters above the entrance. With him he brought an icebox, and he had all of his food sent in because, he said, he feared his enemies would poison him. He also brought along some books and one of those new-fangled phonographs.[30] He even kept his two bulldogs with him.

The O'Malley era — a remarkable episode in any account of bygone years in New Orleans — ended not long after the restless publisher chafed in prison. Charles M. Palmer, the majority owner who had let O'Malley have his own way at the *Item,* sold his interest to James M. Thomson. O'Malley later sent word to Thomson that he was ready to sell his minority interest, which the latter bought.[31]

After divorcing himself from the *Item,* O'Malley invested in the American Fish, Game and Oyster Company, and served as president of the firm. "Why did you go into the fish business?" he was asked. "Because I've never been in it before," he replied.[32] He reentered the newspaper business briefly as publisher of the New Orleans *American,* a morning paper operated by union printers between 1914 and 1917. But the thunder and lightning were missing.

Whitaker served the purpose for which Behrman and the united Democratic press wanted him. He still was running the police department after O'Malley lost his power base and was in eclipse. It was only a matter of time before the reckless inspector would put the mayor into an embarrassing position. This occurred when Whitaker invaded the *World* office and shot at the editor, Joseph M. Leveque. Behrman suspended Whitaker and the inspector resigned. On January 5, 1912, Whitaker died at Presbyterian Hospital. He was under police guard because he had been sentenced to ten years' imprisonment for sex crimes against small girls.[33]

O'Malley outlived his enemy by eight years. His last public appearance was made on September 14, 1920, when he went to a precinct near his Canal Street home to vote against his enemy Behrman. "I will live long enough to see Behrman go down," he said. He was right. Behrman lost the election to Andrew McShane.

The clocks at Touro Infirmary were pointing toward the midnight hour on November 26, 1920, when O'Malley died despite the treatment of his long-time physician, Dr. Rudolph Matas.[34] He was buried in Greenwood Cemetery. The will which he had dictated in 1899, the day after his gun battle with C. Harrison Parker, still was in effect. A nephew of Mrs. O'Malley, James Cooney, certified that the O'Malleys were childless.[35]

"Everybody knew him or of him," said the *Item* in a valedictory on November 28, 1920.

> Almost everybody had definite opinions concerning him. A great many feared him. Many hated him. Some admired him. And a few loved him. For Dominic *(sic)* in his prime was an active citizen, after his own lights, wherever he happened to tread. . . . It is unfortunate, we feel, looking back down the years, that his activity should not have been consistently turned altogether into constructive channels. For O'Malley had abilities. We knew him well enough to have but small opinion of some of the talents for which he developed the largest repute, and to recognize other qualifications for which he was not commonly known at all.
>
> Be that as it may, however, it requires unusual personality for a boy without schooling, friends, or even acquaintances, an alien in so large a city as this, to impress himself so vividly on its whole people as this man did. . . . Dominic was temperamentally an irregular. Any established order would present details that roused his gorge to disagreement. He could not be a regular very long in the cultivation of anything — even his own diversions, which he often changed. Had he been more stable, and cultivated, consistently, the substantial interests of the city — as at times he served them in "heats" as he might say himself — he would have been a

great and powerful figure. As it was he was neither great nor powerful except in the eyes of those whose horizon is limited by the circle of the police department and the criminal courts.[36]

Clay Statue long since has been moved from the corner of Canal and St. Charles streets to Lafayette Square. Little is left to remind New Orleanians of the intersection which in 1891 was the focal point of the streetcar system.

But a ghost remains — the image of a young detective who stands there, a sneer on his lips, in the midst of an inflamed mob which was being exhorted to lynch him.

For bravado, for recklessness, for flaunting fate, for sheer guts, was there ever an act in a city's long history to match this performance by Dominick Call O'Malley?

9

Swift Legs and Shrill Voices

The newsboy of New Orleans has always been regarded, and is, a privileged character and an independent citizen. By common consent he is allowed to do as he pleases, and he never fails to exercise his privilege. He knows the community cannot get along without him, therefore whenever he feels disposed he uses the sidewalk as a track for a footrace, and butts the most pompous and plethoric bank president in the stomach with impunity.

When he desires to exercise his lunge he shocks nervous people by screaming like a steam whistle, and should a policeman remonstrate with him, he thrusts his hands into his trowser *(sic)* pockets and says with charming nonchalance, "Say, Cully, what's de matter wid yer," and leaves the policeman to answer the question at his leisure.

The *States* on November 8, 1885, was paying its respects to the swift-legged, shrill-voiced, street-wise urchins who until the early 1940s were a vivid part of the business district scene.

New Orleans newspapers and successive generations of waifs and other underprivileged boys needed each other in the long years between the Civil War and World War II. The evening dailies, particularly, since they depended on street sales, each had to have a corps of vendors who could fan out rapidly to peddle the late editions. Since the sales price was two or three cents, and never over five, except for Sunday issues, vendors' profits were meager. Yet the opportunity to pick up a pittance was a blessing for lads who were homeless or neglected. The adventure to be found on the streets attracted others.

In reconstruction days, the *States* reported,[1] "When the ragged and hardy little fellows had no roof to shelter them, it was their custom of cold winter nights to seek the press rooms of the daily papers, and there sleep in the nooks and corners, huddled together as thick as kittens in a rag basket." But in 1869 the Society of St. Vincent de Paul and the Sisters of Mercy from the convent of St. Alphonsus joined forces to open a newsboys' home on Franklin Street between Poydras and Lafayette. A bed was offered for five cents a night, if a boy had the money, but he did not get turned away if he lacked the nickel. By 1879 the home had been moved to a three-story brick building at 20 Bank Place, across from the rear entrance to the *Picayune.* There boys could obtain for five cents a breakfast of bread, cold meat, and coffee; for ten cents a dinner of beef, potatoes, hot soup, and coffee; and for five cents a supper menu similar to the dinner offerings. A bed was to be had for five cents, but the sisters welcomed only boys who had no other home. On the second floor were schoolrooms and a chapel. Sister Mary Philomene, who ran the school at which attendance was mandatory, said of her charges: "They are good boys and you have no idea how rapidly they learn. Their senses seem to be sharpened by the lives they live."[2] For one period, fund-raising festivals were held annually at the Fair Grounds. The Society of St. Vincent de Paul finally gave up maintenance of a home in 1917.[3] As recently as 1929 some boys slept in *Item* circulation trucks.

The boys ranged in age from eight years, and sometimes even younger, to the late teens. While Newspaper Row still was the focal point of publishing activity, the youngsters amused themselves between editions in the area. The fun took different forms.

> Despite the fact that Natchez Alley is a narrow thoroughfare, the newsboys use it as a ball ground, and many games are played there under difficulties which would discourage stouter hearts. A match game between the "Doherty's" and the "Mulcahey's" is an occasion dreaded by the business community, for the reason that the reckless character of the contest inspires more or less terror among those who are compelled to pass through the alley. It often happens that the thoughtful man of business, while hastening by and pondering over the pork market, is suddenly aroused from his reflections by a ball hitting him in the eye, and a small boy darting between his legs and causing him to sit down on the sidewalk with a crash sufficiently severe to cause his suspenders to explode like a couple of dynamite cartridges.
>
> The man of business naturally gets very angry, and swears and dances around, and declares he will have the police put a stop to the nuisance, but the game proceeds as though nothing had happened; and the disgusted citizen is compelled to seek shelter in a doorway, and wait for an opportunity to escape without further injury.[4]

Police interference held no terrors for the boys. On October 2, 1903, Patrolman Harry Dodson was walking his beat on Camp Street when he heard suspicious sounds emanating from Bank Place. Dodson turned onto Natchez Alley and tiptoed to the entrance of Bank. Peering around the corner he saw a group of boys intent on one of their frequent nickel dice games. The patrolman noted that the players had spotted him, and he knew he could never run them down. Therefore, he twirled his billy club and sent it flying toward the boys. As soon as the club landed, one of the lads grabbed it, and all scurried away. "So far as Dodson knows they are still scampering," reported the *States*. "What he does know, though, is that he is clubless."

On December 3, 1895, one of the morning papers produced an extra and notified the vendors that they would have to be responsible for all of the copies taken out; none of the unsold papers would be redeemed. The regular boys refused to accept the arrangement, and outsiders were substituted. Reported the *States:*

> There are few people in this world who will as readily resent being imposed on as the average newsboy. So when the boys who did not belong to their contingent appeared with the extras the "strikers" promptly took possession of them, tore them up or stamped on them, or else threw them in the gutter, and whenever it was necessary to scrap in order to assert their rights, they were fully equal to the emergency. If the assistance of the patrol wagon had not been called it is doubtful whether enough extras would have been circulated to stock an ordinary reading room.
>
> There were lots of black eyes and torn clothes, and bloody noses belonging to New Orleans boys this afternoon, but it is safe to say that the little newsboys who were defending what they believed to be their prerogative, have not many of them.[5]

A year earlier the Southern News Company proposed a plan to sell newspapers on streetcars, thus eliminating the newsboys. The *Item* successfully opposed the arrangement and was visited by a group of fifty vendors who offered their thanks.[6] Existence could be perilous on the streets even before automobiles became a threat. Newsboys risked arms and legs by leaping onto precarious perches on the outside of moving streetcars. On January 13, 1885, a nine-year-old vendor, George W. I. Martin, was killed on Canal Street near Burgundy when he ran in front of a dummy, one of the small steam locomotives that pulled streetcars. The *Picayunes's* account proves that reporters were as anxious then to coax a tear from readers' eyes as they are today. When the mangled body was picked up, said the morning paper, "a bundle of newspapers fell from his arm."[7]

For a period in the late 1890s newsboys provided a daily

footrace that attracted spectators to the corner of Canal and Camp streets and along Camp to Newspaper Row. It was an outgrowth of the intense competition for circulation between the *States* and *Item*. The Crescent City Jockey Club was conducting winter horseracing at the Fair Grounds. Each afternoon at three o'clock the racing secretary handed out the entries for the following day, information of prime interest to bettors at the track. The newspaper that could get to the Fair Grounds first with an edition containing the entries would sell about two hundred copies before the other appeared. It was a prize worth running for.

The *States* and *Item* each had a boy stationed at the track, and they were given the entry list at the same time. The material had to be delivered to the newspaper plants to be printed. As soon as they had the lists in hand, the two boys began the race by speeding out of the Fair Grounds gate to the streetcar stop. If a car had just departed for Canal Street, the contestants dashed after it. Otherwise, still even, they waited for the next car. While the vehicle was braking to a stop at Canal Street, both boys leaped off and sprinted to Canal and Camp streets. There they were met by a relay of two fresh lads, who resumed the race for two and a half blocks to the newspaper entrances, cheered on by the onlookers. Waiting messengers snatched the lists out of their hands and headed for the composing rooms. As soon as the editions rolled off the presses, the return chase to the Fair Grounds began.[8] Long since, transmission of typed material by telephone has replaced the newsboy express.

The newsboys were by no means friendless. Their chief benefactors were Mr. and Mrs. Ben Beekman, who operated a clothing store at 330 St. Charles Street. In 1901 they began the custom of furnishing complete outfits — suits, shirts, underwear, shoes, and caps — on Christmas Day to the small-fry vendors. They started by outfitting one hundred boys. Mrs. Beekman died in 1917, and her husband continued the practice. By 1935 he was playing Santa Claus to about two hundred boys each year. By that time there were more adult vendors than there were boys, and Beekman began giving Christmas clothing to one hundred needy children picked by a committee. There were tears in the eyes of the philanthropist when on Christmas Day, 1917, he was presented a watch inscribed: "To Ben Beekman From the Newspapers and Newsboys of New Orleans." He died on October 4, 1946.[9]

By 1941 the newsboys had vanished from the streets. Men took over the busy intersections, and hundreds of boxes were spread about the metropolitan area. A customer could pick up a paper and was on his honor to leave a coin in payment. In recent years coin-operated vending machines have replaced almost all of the boxes. It still is an honor system because anyone who drops in ten cents to open the box can take as many papers as he wants. But the editions don't get soaked by the frequent New Orleans showers.

Circulation suffers, of course, because no inanimate contrivance can stimulate sales in the style of the hustling, yelling vendor. But stricter school attendance laws and social welfare programs that provide for young boys have helped remove the ragamuffin newsboy, probably forever.

John Walker Ross, who served the *States* in capacities ranging from proofreader to editor, wrote the editorial of July 4, 1917, that resulted in a libel suit filed by the publisher and editor of the *Item*. The suit was withdrawn after a trial that made big headlines.

James M. Thomson, who acquired control of the *Item* in 1907, is shown with his wife, Genevieve, the daughter of Champ Clark, long-time speaker of the United States House of Representatives. The *Item* used its news, editorial, and advertising columns in an unsuccessful campaign to elect Mrs. Thomson to Congress.

In the late 1920s and early thirties, the *States* was published in the Fairbanks Building, 900 Camp Street, corner of St. Joseph, for which Robert Ewing paid $250,000. The paper was housed here when it was bought by the Times-Picayune Publishing Company.

James Evans Crown, a peripatetic newsman who finally settled in New Orleans about the time of World War I, worked for a period on the *Item*, then moved over to become city editor, managing editor, and editor of the *States*.

When Governor Huey P. Long and Robert Ewing, owner of the *States*, had a political falling-out in 1929, *Item* Cartoonist John C. Chase adapted a famous cartoon by Sir John Tenniel, published in *Punch* when Kaiser William II fired Prince Otto Bismarck. Ewing is going down the gangplank while Long watches.

Election night in 1934 in the newsroom of the *Item* at 722 Union Street. James M. Thomson, the publisher, is standing at center, with his hand showing in front of his coat, as though he is holding a cigarette. Beside Thomson is Richard W. Leche, a Huey P. Long lieutenant, who later became governor.

Ralph Nicholson, at right, owner of the *Item* from 1941 until 1949, says goodbye to Marshall Ballard, editor from 1907 until his retirement on January 7, 1947. The *Item* enjoyed its most prosperous days under Nicholson's direction.

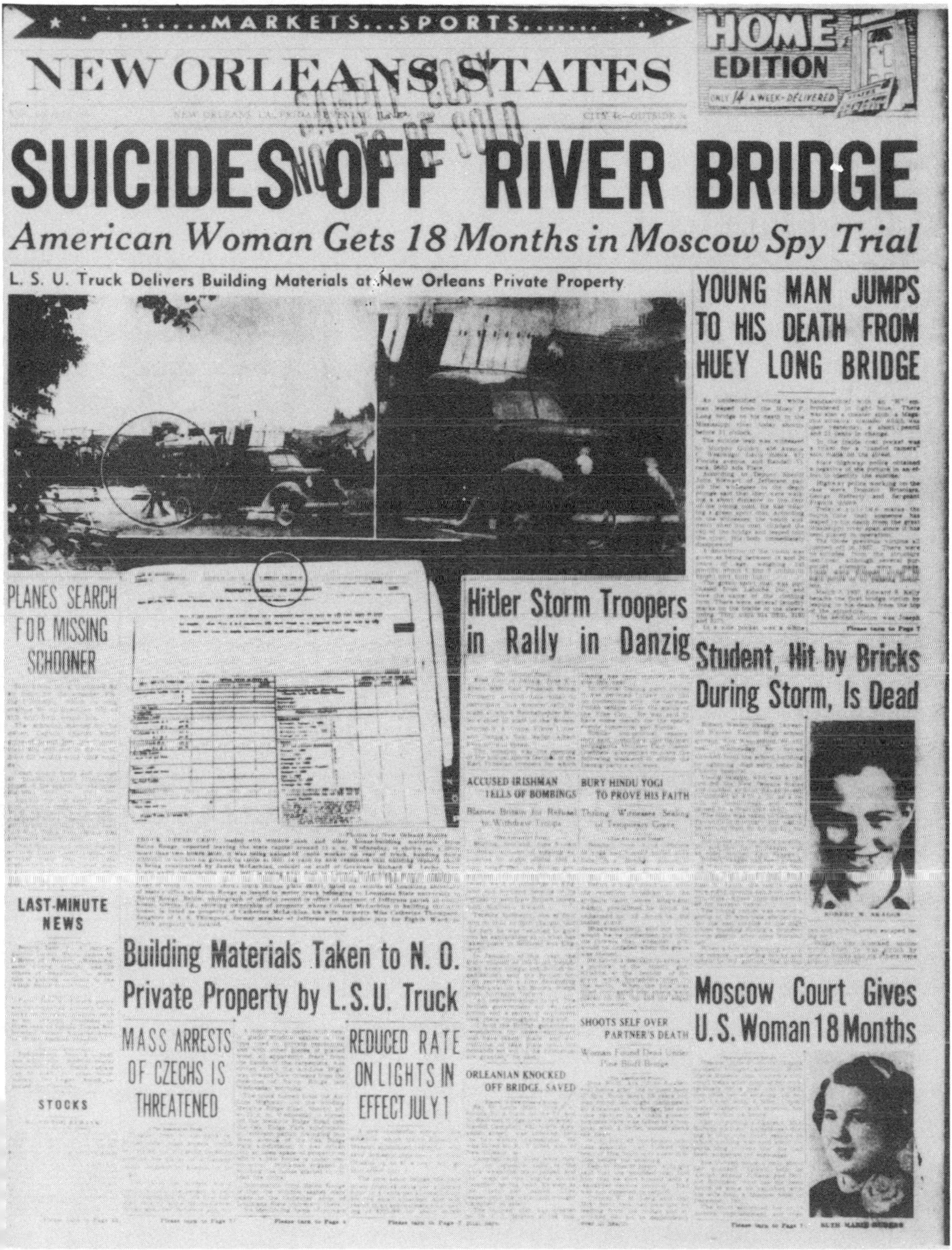

MARKETS...SPORTS

NEW ORLEANS STATES

HOME EDITION

SUICIDES OFF RIVER BRIDGE

American Woman Gets 18 Months in Moscow Spy Trial

L. S. U. Truck Delivers Building Materials at New Orleans Private Property

YOUNG MAN JUMPS TO HIS DEATH FROM HUEY LONG BRIDGE

PLANES SEARCH FOR MISSING SCHOONER

Hitler Storm Troopers in Rally in Danzig

Student, Hit by Bricks During Storm, Is Dead

ACCUSED IRISHMAN TELLS OF BOMBINGS

BURY HINDU YOGI TO PROVE HIS FAITH

LAST-MINUTE NEWS

Building Materials Taken to N. O. Private Property by L.S.U. Truck

MASS ARRESTS OF CZECHS IS THREATENED

REDUCED RATE ON LIGHTS IN EFFECT JULY 1

ORLEANIAN KNOCKED OFF BRIDGE, SAVED

SHOOTS SELF OVER PARTNER'S DEATH

Moscow Court Gives U.S. Woman 18 Months

STOCKS

The front page of the *States* on June 9, 1939, containing the news story and photographs that broke the Louisiana Scandals. Reporter Meigs O. Frost and photographer Wilfred L. d'Aquin obtained the damning material with the aid of Raymond F. Hufft, later Louisiana adjutant general. They documented the delivery of window sashes fabricated at Louisiana State University to a private residence under construction in Metairie.

Clayton Fritchey, at right, the editor, checks over the makeup of an *Item* page while managing editor James A. Wobbe looks on. After leaving the newspaper, Fritchey became an aide to President Harry S. Truman.

Frank C. Allen was the first newsman with a *Times-Picayune* background to take over direction of the *States*'s news and editorial activities after acquisition of the paper by the *Times-Picayune*.

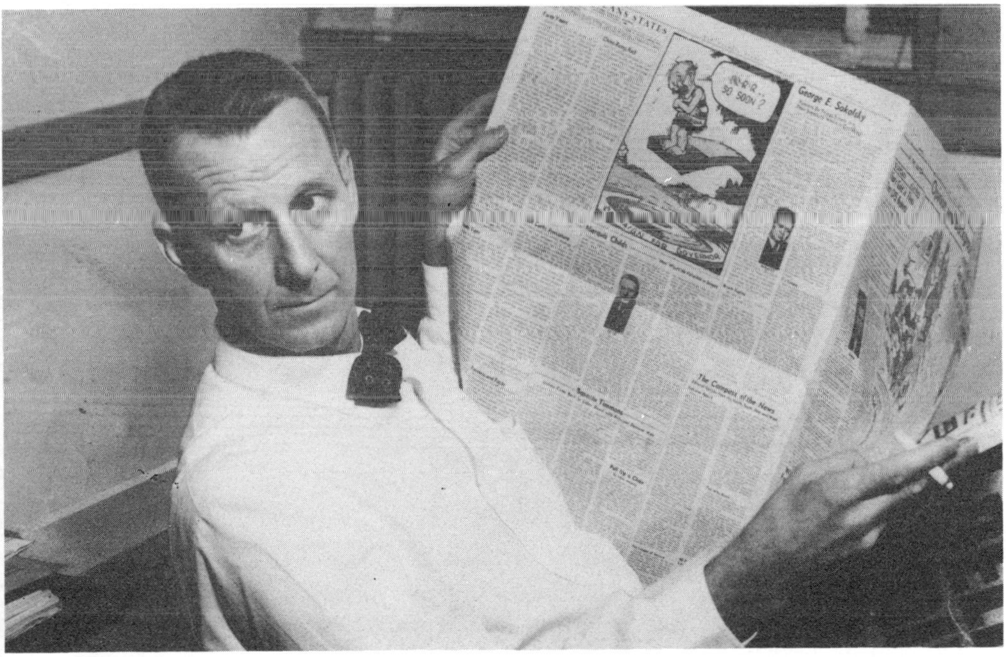

William H. Fitzpatrick won a Pulitzer Prize as editor of the *States* for a series of editorials in 1950 attacking the Genocide Convention and Covenant on Human Rights. He came back from service in World War II in time to direct the paper's editorial campaign which helped unseat the Old Regular city administration in 1946.

The biggest headline ever published in the *Item* announced the surrender of the Japanese on August 20, 1945. The rival *States* used the same word in a headline fully as large. Holding the paper is Gus White, pressman.

This by-no-means-imposing building at 722 Union Street was the home of the *Item* from 1920 until the paper was merged with the *States* in 1958. The front page and other key pages were displayed in glass-covered bulletin boards where passersby could get a sampling of the day's news.

Eleanor Nicholson Corbin, the daughter of Mr. and Mrs. Yorke P. Nicholson, attempted to block the election of John F. Tims, Jr., as a member of the voting trustees of the Times-Picayune Publishing Company. Before her marriage she was a writer for the morning paper.

Members of the Board of Directors of the Times-Picayune Publishing Company, most of whom figured in the rift in 1963 over sale of the company to S. I. Newhouse, are shown at a meeting in 1953 or 1954. From left are Chapman H. Hyams II, Jerry K. Nicholson, John F. Tims, Jr., Ira B. Harkey, J. Cornelius Rathborne, Alvin H. Howard, Ashton Phelps, and Carl M. Corbin.

George Chaplin, at left, editor of the *Item* during its final years, and David Stern III, at right, owner from 1949 until 1958, are shown in 1952 with City Councilman A. Brown Moore. Moore is the son of the late D. D. Moore, long-time manager of the *Times-Picayune*.

Mrs. Yorke P. Nicholson was a principal figure in the breakup of the voting trust, a development that opened the way for the sale of the Times-Picayune Publishing Company by interests which had held control since 1914.

Leonard K. Nicholson served as president and chairman of the board of the Times-Picayune Publishing Company until his death in 1952. He was the son of Eliza Poitevent Nicholson, the first woman ever to control a New Orleans newspaper, the *Picayune*.

Jerry K. Nicholson fought a losing battle against the sale of the Times-Pica yune Publishing Company to S. I. Newhouse. He said he came within one percent of lining up enough stock to block the transaction

Carl McArn Corbin, the husband of Eleanor Nicholson, was editor of the *States-Item* and a member of the board of directors of the Times-Picayune Publishing Company at the time of the sale in 1963. He was invited by S. I. Newhouse to continue his duties and remained for two years.

Ashton Phelps, publisher, delivers the address at the dedication exercises for the new Times-Picayune Publishing Corporation building on March 18, 1968, when he announced that the *States-Item* would go its own way editorially. Seated behind him are, from left, United States Representative Hale Boggs (holding a box in his lap), S. I. Newhouse, John F. Tims, Jr., and Governor John J. McKeithen.

THE STATES-ITEM

Vol. 99—No. 265 | Wednesday, April 14, 1976 | New Orleans, La. | 10 Cents

Employes to end 1-day walkout

Water rate hike OK expected

The New Orleans Sewerage and Water Board was expected to approve a 28 per cent rate hike today as some 1,400 board employes prepared to end a one-day walkout.

The employes walked off their jobs yesterday morning, protesting the City Council's refusal last week to approve a 45 per cent hike in water rates.

But last night at City Hall, they voted to return to their job sites only on a standby basis until the S&WB votes on the rate hike and until they receive written assurances that no reprisals will be taken against them for the walkout. The board was to meet this morning.

The board has authority to raise water rates 28 per cent without further approval by the council or other city officials.

THE 28 PER CENT would give board employes 5 per cent anniversary or seniority pay raises, along with tenure awards of $2 a month for those with three or more years of continuous service.

The employes will probably receive the raises and awards May 3 if the board approves the hike at its special meeting today.

Board employes also wanted a general 5 per cent cost-of-living raise that would have been financed by the 45 per cent rate boost.

But J. F. "Red" Allen, a spokesman for the non-union employes, advised them at last night's meeting to accept the anniversary and tenure raises now, since it could take months for the City Council and the Civil Service Commission to approve a cost-of-living pay hike.

ALLEN ALSO acknowledged that the wage increase the workers were demanding would anount to 5 per cent more than employes in other city departments are getting. He said it was hoped that such a raise would have been the first step toward advancing the pay scale of all city employes, particularly those at lower pay grades.

S&WB General Supt. Joseph Sullivan said about 500 of the board's 1,600 civil service classified workers make about $125 a week or less.

City officials said about one-third of some 8,000 other classified employes in other city departments make around the same figure.

The S&WB depends on its rate revenues to finance pay increases. Other city employes' raises are budgeted through the city's general revenue fund.

THERE WERE NO problems reported yesterday with the city's water system after the walkout. Supervisory and management personnel manned the stations where workers walked off, and no difficulties were anticipated unless there was a major breakdown.

Allen emphasized that the employes' demand for the cost-of-living raise has not been abandoned, but deferred pending further negotiations.

A sizable number of S&WB employes last night were against reporting to work unless they were assured of the cost-of-living raise also. However, after Allen informed them how long it could take for such a raise to materialize, possibly months, the majority voted to return to their jobs.

Killer paroled; conflict charged

By ALLAN KATZ
and PATRICIA GORMIN

Convicted murderer Frank N. Chisesi Jr. goes free on parole today after nearly 16 years in confinement amidst a furore over charges that his parole may have been politically manipulated.

A Parole Board spokesman in Baton Rouge confirmed that Chisesi, 31, son of a New Orleans meat packer, will be released from the state prison at DeQuincy where he has been since his conviction for the 1959 slaying in Plaquemines Parish of schoolmate Rhett Blanke. Chisesi was 15 at the time of the slaying.

Plaquemines Parish Dist. Atty. Leander Perez Jr. says that the defense counsel who represented Chisesi April 7 before the state Parole Board, Camille Gravel, who is also executive counsel to Gov. Edwin W. Edwards, "might well be guilty of a very possible conflict of interest."

Gravel says the charge by Perez "is a lie and distortion," allegedy growing out of "a vow by Mr. Perez that Frank Chisesi would never be released regardless of the circumstances and a personal animosity by Mr. Perez for me that comes from our frequently being on different political sides."

GRAVEL CONCEDES that the furore is "embarrassing" for Gov. Edwin W. Edwards, who appointed Gravel, the members of the state Parole Board and the members of the state Pardon Board that recommended a commutation of sentence for Chisesi which the governor also approved.

Blanke's body was found near Violet on Dec. 9, 1959. He was shot twice and stabbed 17 times. Arrested two days later in Trenton, N. J., Chisesi spent three years in a state mental institution before being brought to trial in 1963. Described by psychiatrists testifying at his trial as a "psychopath" and "sociopath" who "evidenced an omnipotent or God-like feeling," he entered a plea of not guilty by reason of insanity. A jury found him guilty and he was sentenced to life imprisonment. Testimony at the trial indicated Chisesi invited Blanke, who had annoyed him in school, to go hunting with tbe intention of killing him.

Chisesi is described as having been a model prisoner at DeQuincy, demonstrating a 137 IQ in tests, working in the prison library and as editor of the prison paper. Psychiatrists told the parole and pardon boards that Chisesi is no longer dangerous.

On April 7, Gravel personally represented Chisesi at a key hearing before the Parole Board at DeQuincy. At previous hearings before the Pardon Board, which commuted Chisesi's sentence from life imprisonment to 30 years, the defendant was represented by Gravel's law partners.

AFTER THE SUCCESSFUL Parole

Turn to Page A-5, Column 1

Streets:

Do you realize the street name marker has mysteriously disappeared from its lakeside post at the Seventh and St. Charles neutral ground? S'il vous plait, give us a sign to let us know you're still alive and in business.

A. Latas

Charles Hopkins, a suspect in a shooting spree that left one person dead and five wounded at Baltimore's temporary City Hall, is carried to a waiting ambulance. Hopkins, who was wounded in the incident, is in critical condition. (UPI Telephoto.)

Chief booted out by Slidell voters

By SUSAN FINCH
States-Item staff writer

SLIDELL. Longtime Slidell Police Chief Edward C. Schilleci was booted out of office here yesterday as nearly 49 per cent of Slidell's 11,100 registered voters turned out for the first recall election im the city's history.

Schilleci, who is appealing 1975 federal court convictions of wiretapping, eavesdropping and perjury and who faces trial next month on a state charge of malfeasance in office, lost his bid to stay in office by a margin of almost 2 to 1. The unofficial tally, said St. Tammany Parish Registrar of Voters Gary Faciane, was 3,549 votes for Schilleci's recall and 1,881 against.

Schilleci was acquitted of state charges of contract fraud.

In all the city's nine precincts, votes for the recall outnumbered those against it. This was the case even in older Slidell, where it had been widely believed that Schilleci would carry the day.

A DRIVE to garner enough voter signatures to warrant calling yesterday's election was begun in December by the Slidell Federation of Homeowners, after Schilleci refused requests to step down voluntarily until court matters pending against him were settled.

Schilleci, appearing somewhat subdued after learning the election results, said he was strongly considering throwing his hat into the ring when the city's mayor and council set a date for voters to choose someone to serve out the remainder of his four-year term (it ends in 1978). Last week, the chief had predicted voters would keep him in office and pledged to run for re-election again in two years.

Schilleci said last night that though he "felt like" he would win yesterday, he wasn't really surprised at the election outcome. He said he had been up against "great odds," including what he called biased news reporting and "high-pressure tactics."

THE CHIEF is not yet officially out of office. Results of yesterday's election must be certified within 10 to 20 days by the secretary of state, who then must notify the governor that the recall is effective. Once that is done, the governor must issue a proclamation that the office is vacant, and the way will then be open for the City Council to appoint an interim successor for Schilleci.

According to law, the council must hold a special election to fill the vacancy at the same time it holds any election slated within three to six months of the vacancy. If no other election is scheduled during that period, the special balloting may be set anytime within six months after the vacancy occurs.

Despite his recall, Schilleci is eligible to run in the special election the council will set, legal sources say. And, says Schilleci's attorney, Robert Thorne, the chief may run for re-election even if his federal court convictions are upheld.

THORNE REASONS that although the

Turn to Page A-5, Column 1

Weather

Partly cloudy with slight chance of showers through tomorrow. Highs today, tomorrow in low 80s. Low in mid-60s. Probability of rain 20 per cent today, tomorrow. Relative humidity at 6 a.m. 100 per cent. Records: High, 87 in 1936, low, 46 in 1909. (Map, details on Page A-18.)

Rows of posts and rows of men: ditch-diggers at work in the fields of Angola

Angola: A case study in futility and failure

By JIM AMOSS

It was mid-morning and we were driving through Angola's well-manicured fields, a reporter, a security guard and an inmate.

In the distance to our left we could see a clump of men, set off sharply against the deep green of the pasture. We approached and the clump lengthened into a row of convicts, hacking away rhythmically at the loamy soil as they dug a drainage ditch. Posted around them like listless satellites were five mounted prison guards. A horseless sixth stood closer to the workers.

From time to time, a prisoner would pause, wipe his face or stand at ease astride the ditch, then return to the brigade. The guards appeared to be doing nothing. They did not move. They did not talk to one another. They simply stared blankly at the column of workers.

I asked our guard-escort why it was necessary to employ six apparently idle men to watch over a mere three dozen densely grouped prisoners.

"Those three dozen men combined got about 3,000 years to serve. That answer your question?"

It could have answered a number of questions that occur to a visitor to the Louisiana State Penitentiary. Why are these men so violent to one another? Why all the stabbings, beatings and rapes? Why were there 18 murders last year among a population of about 4,000? Why don't more of the inmates try to improve themselves? Why has rehabilitation failed so utterly here?

As we drove away from the well watched ditch diggers, the inmate next to me gave his answer.

"Those man have nothing to look forward to," he said. "And when a man's got nothing to look forward to, he's dangerous. He's dangerous, even if he himself doesn't know it."

FUTILITY EXACTS a high toll at Angola. The state prison system provides little incentive for prisoners to engage in meaningful work and is unable to discriminate between those who do and those who don't. It hardly matters whether a man actively seeks to change for the better or simply spends his term lounging around "on the walk."

So long as he remains on the good side of the guards and doesn't collect too many "write-ups" for prison rule violations, he can expect to survive his imprisonment without the inconvenience of soul searching, character reform or the need to find a new line of work.

You can't force a man to rehabilitate himself, according to one of the first precepts of penology. But you can often coax him into it. Prisoners and prison officials generally agree that the goal of most prisoners is to get out of prison as soon as possible, sooner than the judge said. If rehabilitation is possible, this hope of an early release is often the only incentive for it. But what happens when there are no incentives, when release is abrupt and arbitrary?

Part of the answer is to be found in Angola's recidivism rate of 55 to 60 per cent.

ABOUT 100 MILES downriver, at the Jackson Barracks Work Release Center in New Orleans, recidivism runs at about five per cent. Even allowing for the fact that work release inmates constitute a select group of relative short-termers (only eight of the center's 122 inmates are serving long sentences or life terms), the difference is dramatic and points up the failure of Angola.

At the Jackson Barracks center, entering inmates begin with a "maintenance" program, during which they work within the confines of the barracks. Six months before his release date, the inmate enters the work release stage, taking a job on the outside, earning regular wages and returning to the barracks each evening. The 1,500 inmates who have passed through the program since 1969 have earned a total of $2.8 million and have paid the state $484,198 in taxes and $525,525 in room and board expenses.

Work release prisoners are allowed 48-hour passes home. According to Col. Franklin E. Woodruff, the head of the center, there have been few escapes and about half a dozen crimes committed by Jackson Barracks inmates over the past five years "and that's a big half dozen."

Those who improve far offset those

Turn to Page A-2, Column 1

The *States-Item* of 1976 had taken on a new look, sharply contrasting with the dull, gray appearance of the early editions produced by Mark F. Bigney or Henry J. Hearsey. This issue of April 14 is typical of the layouts favored by editor Walter G. Cowan.

Ashton Phelps, at left, who was to free the *States-Item* from editorial domination by the *Times-Picayune*, is shown with John F. Tims, Jr., center, president of the Times-Picayune Publishing Company, and S. I. Newhouse on June 5, 1963, the day on which Newhouse acquired ownership of the company.

The $16-million plant at 3800 Howard Avenue, in which the *States-Item* and the *Times Picayune* are produced, was dedicated on February 17, 1968. At the ceremonies publisher Ashton Phelps announced the editorial divorce of the two papers.

Charles A. Ferguson, seated, the associate editor of the *States-Item*, and Walter G. Cowan, the editor, pose in the newsroom. They gave the paper a new look and a new editorial and news direction upon their appointments in 1969.

10

Robert Ewing: The Last of the Swashbucklers

"When Robert Ewing puts on the four-league boots of that splendid and gallant man and tremendously sincere editor, the late Major Hearsey, he prepares laughter for the most high gods!

"Big boots breed bunions on bad feet."[1] Joseph Mark Leveque's words, written for the weekly *Harlequin* in 1906, proved to be prophetic.

Days of decline lay ahead for the *States*.

Robert Ewing was the link between the swashbucklers who prowled Newspaper Row in the dying years of the nineteenth century, pistols cocked and fists clenched, and modern editors and publishers who fight their battles with the printed word or court action.

There is no record to show that Ewing ever drew a weapon either in anger or self-defense after the row in City Hall in 1895 over city printing. He did get involved in two or three physical encounters, the last in 1913. After that, in keeping with the more sedate customs which evolved, the transformation was complete, and Ewing's only exchanges were verbal or legal.

As early as the New Year period of 1903 there was an editorial skirmish between Ewing and W. J. Leppert, managing editor of the *Item,* which demonstrated that the New Orleans newspaper environment was becoming effete. They exchanged insults that a decade or two earlier would have required them to shoot it out or else be scorned by their hotheaded colleagues. The *States* boasted that it had given the *Item* a kick in the pants during a dispute over a streetcar franchise.[2] Leppert replied with a personal attack on Ewing that filled two columns on the editorial page. Wrote Leppert:

> There was a time, Robert — and that was when you were known as "Buck," and before you became popular with yourself — that the *Daily States* stood for respectability. That was when the late lamented Major Hearsey had control and before it was the daily bulletin of a self-seeking politician, masquerading as a philanthropist, a publisher and a gentleman. We have no recollection of an occasion that Major Hearsey did aught but as his honorable conscience dictated. You remember Major Hearsey, Brother Ewing, and you must remember Capt. J. Pinckney Smith — of course, you do.
>
> You remember how they took you up when you were a poor telegraph operator and how you repaid their kindness to a stranger in our city by wresting the *Daily States* from them both. Is the memory pleasing to you, Brother Ewing, or does the recollection ever trouble your heavy sleep? Is it not odd that within so short a time after they nursed you that they were quietly elbowed out of position and then passed away? Yes, you dear, delightful ambitious man, it is odd, and the story is still fresh in the memories of some. . . .
>
> We have no desire to be a martyr to the cause of amusement, and suggest that if you insist on being accorded the rights of a gentleman and can convince the public of your title, we will, despite religious views to the contrary, fight you a duel. We will name blue, pink and white roman candles at 100 yards, the winner to take 75 per centum of the gate receipts. At that distance it will be difficult for us to recognize the difference between you and a gentleman.[3]

And after those fighting words, what happened? On January 4, 1903, both the *States* and the *Item* published Notes to the Public. Leppert's name was signed to a communication to Ewing, which said: "Sir — In reply to your communication of January 2nd, 1903, in regard to the editorial in the *New Orleans Item* dated January 1, 1903, entitled 'Genius or Gentleman,' I beg to say I withdraw same. Very respectfully." And Ewing wrote to Leppert: "Your letter of January 3, 1903, received. I beg to say that in the articles published in the *Daily States* there was no intention of reflecting on you personally; and I now disclaim any such intent. Very respectfully." Times were changing.

One last joust with Ewing's old enemy Dominick O'Malley in 1906 was described at length in the *Harlequin* and denied in a perfunctory way in the *States*. "Bobby Has 'Made Friends' With O'Malley," said the headline in Joseph M. Leveque's impudent weekly. "Now what do you think of that?" asked Leveque. "Dominick O'Malley and Bobby Ewing have kissed and made up. No longer does the *States* allude to that jailbird. The cessation was singularly contemporaneous with O'Malley's release from jail. It is possible for the good and peace of the town that peace articles have been entered into." Leveque related that shortly before O'Malley began his prison sentence for libeling Mayor Martin Behrman, the publisher encountered Ewing. He said O'Malley called Ewing a "jobbing —— — - ———," knocked him down, and announced that he was going to thrash the *States*'s owner every time he met him on the streets. While O'Malley was safely locked up, the *Harlequin* noted, the *States* called him a jailbird every day, and "now that O'Malley is out they've made friends." "I tell you what, that Boss of New Orleans is a man of shrewdness and courage," said Leveque. The *States* called Leveque a willful and malicious liar. "This indignant demurrer has set a considerable portion of amused New Orleans wondering!" replied Leveque. Leveque offered to meet either Ewing or *States* editor W. C. Chevis and settle the matter with their fists, and there it apparently ended.[4]

While the *States* made a general denial of Leveque's version of the Ewing-O'Malley incident, the main facts of a contretemps a few weeks earlier involving Ewing and Leveque were not disputed. The *Harlequin* printed a report that Ewing sought a $15,000 bribe from L. M. Berg, president of the New Orleans Terminal Railroad, in return for the support of the *States* of proposed city ordinances favoring the Frisco railroad. Ewing replied with a card in the *States,* calling Leveque a base and malicious liar. Leveque strode into Ewing's office and attempted to hand him a letter in which he proposed that either he or Ewing begin court action to determine who was lying. Ewing refused to accept the letter. Leveque slapped his face. James Grady, one of Ewing's assistants, sprang to his aid and knocked Leveque across the room.[5] On April 26 Leveque published a card in the *Harlequin* in which he said: "On January 5, 1906, Mr. E. H. Farrar, attorney for the Frisco road, informed me that Mr. Robert Ewing had attempted to obtain from Mr. Farrar's clients fifteen thousand dollars ($15,000), the consideration of which would be Mr. Ewing's support of the Frisco ordinance. After I had repeated Mr. Farrar's statement in the public print, Mr. Farrar denied that he had made it. Hence I am unable to substantiate the charges that I published against Mr. Ewing, Mr. Farrar being my only source of information, and therefore I retract them. In view of the foregoing, I regret extremely having precipitated this unfortunate affair, with its unhappy incidents in Mr. Ewing's office, as it now appears my utterances were based on irresponsible information." Below this the *Harlequin* printed a card signed by Edgar Howard Farrar: "Having been permitted by the courtesy of the publisher to see the above card of J. M. Leveque before its insertion, I desire to announce to the public that Mr. Leveque's statement is absolutely and unqualifiedly false." In an article accompanying the card, Leveque recited the circumstances under which he said Farrar made the accusation against Ewing. He staked his reputation as a reporter on the assertion that he had quoted Farrar accurately. And thus concluded another controversy in which the dueling code could have been invoked, but wasn't.

With evident glee, the *Item* printed on page one on January 15, 1913, the last published account of a fist fight in which Ewing reportedly was involved. "Although it was supposed to have been kept a profound secret," said the paper, "the story got out somehow Wednesday morning, and has since gained currency, that a fierce altercation, a regular old-fashioned rough and tumble fight, took place during the late hours Tuesday evening in the editorial sanctum of the *Daily States*. The belligerents, rumor hath it, were Colonel Robert Ewing, publisher of the *Daily States*, and Mr. Norman Walker, of the editorial sanctum of the *Times-Democrat*." Since editorial fisticuffs by now were deemed undignified, Ewing was upset because a meeting of publishers convened in New Orleans a few days later and the *Item* printed on page one a cartoon showing him and Walker wearing boxing gloves.

Ewing was born at Mobile, Alabama, on September 27, 1859. He was the son of an immigrant from Scotland, James Lindsay Ewing, a graduate of the University of Edinburgh, who became a cotton merchant in Mobile, and Martha Ann Hunter Ewing, a member of the Toulmin family which was prominent in Alabama. His elder brother, John, served as United States minister to Honduras from 1913 until 1918. The Civil War brought financial ruin to Ewing's father, who died in 1866. At the age of twelve years Robert withdrew from school and became a runner in an uncle's bank. At thirteen he got a job as messenger with the Western Union Telegraph Company. He learned telegraphy, and by the age of seventeen was a competent operator handling Associated Press news dispatches. In 1879, at nineteen, Ewing, as an employee of Jay Gould, helped to establish the American Union Telegraph Company. He became manager of the Mobile office, and two years later moved to New Orleans to head American Union's operations there. When Western Union took over American, Ewing remained in its service as an Associated Press operator. He was a member of the seven-man national executive committee of the Order of Telegraphers which directed an unsuccessful strike against Western Union in 1883. Blacklisted by Western Union, he worked outside the telegraph field in Texas and St. Louis before returning to New Orleans in 1885 as manager of a telegraph office of the Baltimore and Ohio Company. When the company was absorbed by Western Union, Ewing was out of a job again. This time he abandoned commercial telegraphy for good, and broke into the newspaper business as manager of the *Morning Chronicle,* a small daily operated by the proprietors of the *States.* It wasn't long before he got his first taste of politics. In 1888 the *States* backed the Young Men's Democratic Association in a reform campaign which swept the city administration out of office. Ewing was an active campaigner, and as a reward was appointed city electrician and superintendent of the fire and police telegraph alarm systems. His political faction lost out in 1892, and he joined the *States* as telegraph editor. He was put in charge of circulation in 1893, became assistant business manager in 1895, business manager in 1898, and proprietor in 1900 upon the death of Major Hearsey.[6]

On August 15, 1908, Ewing bought the Shreveport *Times*

for $55,000 at a sheriff's sale. He founded the Monroe *Morning World* on October 20, 1929, and bought the Monroe *News-Star* on December 1, 1930.[7]

Ewing could be called publisher-politician or politician-publisher; in his way of doing business the two vocations were inseparable. The only question was which, if either, of the pursuits claimed his primary interest. Probably he looked upon his newspaper properties as a means of making money and also as an indispensable adjunct to his political activities. The newspapers, especially the *States,* gave him a big political club. At the same time, his political connections could help swing public benefices for his newspapers.

He became a Regular Democrat in 1896 and was a member of the 1898 Constitutional Convention, the one remembered for adopting the artful grandfather clause as a means of disfranchising Negroes. His racial feelings were every bit as unreasoning and violent as those of Major Hearsey. By 1899 he owned a substantial interest in the *States* and began to turn the newspaper into a personal political instrument even before the death of Hearsey, whose pen was a political weapon but who never would have thought of using it in furtherance of his own selfish ambitions, if he had any. Politics, for Hearsey, was a matter of beliefs and principle. For Ewing, politics meant power.

In 1899 Ewing was a candidate for Tenth Ward leader, and for the first time the *States* used its political muscle for the personal gain of one of its owners. By now, Ewing either could dictate policy or had acquired enough influence to sway Hearsey. Ewing turned on his former political friend and mentor, Peter Farrell, in setting out to displace the latter as Tenth Ward leader. On June 29, 1899, the *States* announced the opening of Ewing's campaign headquarters at 2016 Magazine Street. On August 3 *States* readers got a sampling of the new policy when the paper devoted three columns on page one to coverage of a Ewing rally at Camp and St. Andrew streets. There also was an editorial running longer than a column. It was not the only time during the campaign when the *States* gave prominence to Ewing's candidacy for the minor office. Ewing won the election, and on September 9 an editorial writer, who must have thought readers had short memories, commented: "The *States* took no part in the fight; the victory was won by Mr. Ewing's own indomitable energy and keen political sagacity."

Thus Ewing became a member of the Choctaw Club, the close-knit cadre of ward bosses that for years exerted power in city government. He was influential during most of the first four terms of Mayor Martin Behrman, then broke with the latter in advance of the 1920 election in which Behrman was unseated by reformer Andrew McShane. Ewing complained that Behrman was subjecting the city to one-man rule. Ewing also opposed Behrman in the latter's successful comeback campaign four years later.

The only paid political job held by Ewing, from 1900 to 1908, was that of state tax collector for the Fourth Municipal District. On May 29, 1904, the *Item* reported the *States* had lost its state printing contract to the Baton Rouge *Times*. The *Item* said Ewing had been paid $370,000 from the state treasury in his capacity as state printer and state tax collector.

The publisher's political activities extended into the national scene. He achieved influence in Washington such as few New Orleanians have matched. He was an ally of Democratic party leader William Jennings Bryan, and served as one of Bryan's national campaign managers before the presidential election of 1908. In the 1912 Democratic national convention at Baltimore, Ewing was one of seven floor leaders for Woodrow Wilson. It was the convention in which Champ Clark of Missouri, speaker of the House of Representatives, was the front-runner for the presidential nomination. The rule requiring a two-thirds' majority kept Clark from winning on the first ballot, and subsequently Bryan, Ewing, and other Wilson strategists managed to take the prize away from the speaker and give it to Wilson. Ewing was bitter because Clark in 1911 had favored San Francisco over New Orleans as the site of the Panama Exposition. There also was an element of local business rivalry involved. Clark was the father-in-law of James M. Thompson, publisher of he *Item,* whose wife was Genevieve Clark. Ewing was western campaign manager for Wilson. During Wilson's two terms Ewing was a frequent visitor to the White House. Reports that he could have had a cabinet post if he wanted it are believable. He was elected Democratic national committeeman from Louisiana in 1908, 1912, 1916, and 1928.

In 1908 Ewing used the *States* to collect campaign funds for Bryan. Every day the newspaper published the names of contributors and otherwise solicited money for a partisan cause. It may never have occurred to the colonel to question the propriety of involving his newspaper as an agent in a party function. Other newspapers did the same thing, and as late as 1932 Publisher Thomson had the *Item* pass the hat for Franklin D. Roosevelt's first presidential bid.

For the first seven years of Ewing's control, the *States* managed to compete on fairly even terms with the *Item.* But in 1908 the *Item* jumped into a circulation lead of about nine thousand, and established a dominance in the evening field which continued as long as the *States* was a Ewing paper. By 1919 Thomson was scorning the *States* as a rival, and was pitting the *Item* against the *Times-Picayune* instead. The *Item*'s success was not a triumph of journalistic excellence. In content and presentation it was the *Item* — tweedledum, and the *States* — tweedledee. Both papers splashed the front page with black headlines aimed at street sales. Both played up local news, most of it provided by police and City Hall reporters. Both put a premium on local human interest stories. Sports coverage claimed a generous share of each paper's space. The State Capitol was not neglected.

Yet the *States*'s fortunes waned while Ewing's political career waxed. In addition to sitting in the inner councils of the Choctaw Club, which ran the city, he also promoted his candidates in one statewide election after another. He hoped to become a kingmaker by backing Huey P. Long for governor, as will be seen in another chapter. He was a figure to be reckoned with. With the exception of Behrman, Ewing may have been the name most heard in New Orleans during the first quarter of this century. He was an imperious, loudmouthed boss who was known on occasion to summon the mayor to his office at the *States* when he wanted to throw his weight around: Ewing's unblushing use of the *States* as a political mouthpiece to build up his friends and tear down his enemies was a tactic that would prove costly. The price was the sacrifice of public confidence, and the sinking of the paper to a subordinate place in circulation and advertising. It was an example that James M. Thomson should have observed.

Ewing died unexpectedly on April 27, 1931, at his home at 6020 St. Charles Avenue. He had returned the day before from New York, where he had had a mild heart attack. His will directed that his estate be divided into seven equal shares, one each for his five sons, his daughter, and his second wife, Grace Nolan Mackay of Kansas City, to whom he was married in 1917.

The *States* remained in the hands of his heirs for scarcely two years. The respected and influential newspaper built up by Major Hearsey had sunk to the point where its circulation was barely two-thirds of the *Item*'s. The economic troubles of the 1930s foredoomed the Ewing interest in the *States.* The bank crisis of 1933 was the finishing blow. The *States* owed $160,000 to the Canal Bank and Trust Company of New Orleans and a like amount to the Commercial Bank and Trust Company of Shreveport.[8] Advertising and circulation revenue was not sufficient to cover the payroll and the paper was reduced to the necessity of paying off its employees partly in cash and partly in scrip. The scrip was issued by food stores in payment for advertising, and could be exchanged for groceries. Philip Guarisco, later chief photographer, recalls that his salary was $15 a week. He received $7.50 in cash and the rest in scrip good at Great Atlantic and Pacific Tea Company stores. Some employees received part of their wages in tokens good for rides on streetcars.[9] The *Item* also resorted to scrip, but the *Times-Picayune* met every payroll with cash.

In late June, 1933, John F. Tims Jr., business manager of The Times-Picayune Publishing Company, accompanied Leonard K. Nicholson, president, on a trip to Chattanooga where they attended a convention of the Southern Newspaper Publishers Association. With them on the train out of New Orleans was James L. Ewing, eldest son of Robert and publisher of the *States.* Ewing visited Tims's drawing room and confided that something would have to be done about the *States.* "Where do you suppose I was last Sunday?" Ewing asked, then answered his own question: "I was at Huey Long's home and Arthur Newmyer (associate publisher of the *Item*) was there."

Also present at the convention was John D. Ewing, publisher of the *Shreveport Times.* As trustee of the Robert Ewing estate, John Ewing also exerted influence in the affairs of the *States.* During the stay in Chattanooga, Tims recalled, John

Ewing "had some words" with James. "I don't know what the brother threatened to do," Tims said. When they started back to New Orleans, Nicholson and Tims found that John Ewing was on the train. Ewing asked Tims to go with him into the smoking compartment. Tims by now knew the subject that Ewing wanted to discuss in private. Ewing mentioned the debt of $320,000 which the embattled *States* had no prospect of repaying. He told Tims that Thomson and Newmyer of the *Item* and Claude G. Rives, a vice-president of the Whitney National Bank, had visited him in Shreveport and proposed that the *States* be sold to the *Item* for $700,000. The *Item* would put up $320,000 to clear the debt to the two banks, and issue $380,000 worth of common stock in the Item Company to the Ewing heirs. Ewing wanted cash instead of stock. And the thought of surrendering the *States* to the long-time competitor galled him.

"He asked me if we were interested," Tims related.[10] "And I told him that I would discuss the matter with Mr. Leonard Nicholson, which I did the next day." Ewing mentioned to Tims that he was going to be at his home at Pass Christian for a long Fourth of July weekend but would be in the *States* office on Wednesday, July 5, if the Times-Picayune Publishing Company wanted to make an offer. "I reported that to Mr. Nicholson, discussed it with Mr. Yorke Nicholson, his brother, who was — or rather with Mr. Alvin Howard, who was first vice-president; Mr. Yorke Nicholson, who was second vice-president, and Mr. Esmond Phelps," Tims said. "Mr. Nicholson told me to go to see Mr. Ewing on the fifth of July and offer him $525,000 cash, which I did, and he accepted it immediately. I said, 'this is going pretty fast. I've never been in a deal this big. You had better let me go back and confirm this.' So he said he was having lunch that day with Colonel John P. Sullivan at the St. Charles Hotel, and inasmuch as

Mr. Nicholson and Mr. Phelps and Mr. Howard and I usually had lunch there, to come over the tell him if it was okay." Tims returned to the *Times-Picayune* and confirmed the arrangements, then went back to see Ewing and told him the offer was good. The final negotiations were concluded with the signing of a purchase agreement on Monday, July 17. The *Times-Picayune* bought the *States*'s circulation list, its advertising and feature contracts, its Associated Press franchise and its goodwill agreement. The building at 900 Camp Street for which Robert Ewing paid $250,000 in 1923, and all the equipment remained the property of the Ewing estate.

At 4:30 o'clock on that Monday, Ewing called employees into a meeting and in a voice that broke with emotion announced the end of his family's ownership of the *States.* On Tuesday, July 18, at 7 A.M. most members of the *States* news staff reported, as instructed, to the building of the Times-Picayune Publishing Company at Camp and North streets, four blocks down Camp from the old office. The staff was guided to a section of the newsroom which had been set aside for the *States,* and went to work immediately. On that starting day in new quarters the editors and reporters managed to produce the first edition three minutes ahead of schedule. Walter Valois acted as city editor in the absence of James Evans Crown, who was recuperating from surgery at Touro Infirmary. Key men in the advertising and mechanical departments kept their jobs.[11]

For thirty-five years, ten months and sixteen days, the *States* lost its independence. The Times-Picayune Publishing Company had been planning to establish an afternoon paper of its own when the opportunity came to acquire an existing publication. The *States* — and after the merger of the rival papers in 1958, the *States-Item* — became de facto an afternoon

Times-Picayune. Management's position was spelled out in an antitrust suit in 1952: the *Times-Picayune* and the *States* were really morning and evening editions of the same newspaper. Since all of the top officials of the company had long-time loyalties to the *Times-Picayune,* and since the morning paper had by far the more circulation and advertising, nobody could seriously question which partner ruled. To the public the papers presented a united front. Editorial stands and political endorsements of the *Times-Picayune* invariably were echoed by the *States* or later the *States-Item.*

It is true that the evening paper managed to retain some of its identity. The makeup and the emphasis on news coverage were different, largely because of circulation strategy. Traditionally, the *Times-Picayune* had delivered at least three-quarters of its circulation to subscribers who want papers on their doorsteps every morning. These are editions which have been sold before they come off the presses; there is no need for catching the eye of a prospective reader with a headline that will titillate him and make him dig into his pocket. On the other hand, the *States, Item,* and *States-Item* depended on street sales for nearly one-half of their circulation. Every edition has had to be designed to attract buyers from among the throngs out shopping during the daytime or pouring from office buildings and heading homeward in the late afternoon. Every weekday for a hundred years the problem has been the same for evening paper newsmen. Dig up a story with intrinsic interest to New Orleanians or one that can be given a twist to whet the curiosity. Display it in bold type, and, as in the past forty years, illustrate it with attention-grabbing pictures. Send it out on the streets to sell. Under the *Times-Picayune* ownership, the *States,* until the merger of the evening papers, had to compete with the *Item* for street sales. Editions were produced almost simultaneously; competition was frantic. A sensational headline could mean a swing of hundreds of papers. If things were dull on press association wires or if the usual sources of local news were dry, it was the responsibility of the editors to find something to offer. For twenty-five years evening journalism in New Orleans belonged to the "this is a stick-up" school. A $49.39 armed robbery was seized upon, milked for every detail by hustling legmen, composed in lurid prose by rewritemen, and blazoned across the top of page one in the fervent hope that the rival had nothing more exciting to offer.

Men who worked for the *States* in the early thirties passed down a legend of a newsless day when the city editor, Jim Crown, became desperate for a headline. It was the heyday of Huey P. Long, and suddenly Crown had an inspiration. "Long Ill, Suicides," screamed the biggest type the *States* could muster. The avid paper buyer finally found, near the bottom of the page, a three- or four-paragraph story relating how some obscure Orleanian, hopeless after a lengthy illness, took his own life. It wasn't Huey at all. Nobody has been able to find the headline in the old volumes, but then many editions are missing from the files. The incident could have occurred. Whether or not it did, it illustrates the tactics of the times. It wasn't that editors and publishers were insensitive to the incongruity of using the resources of metropolitan newspapers to produce a jazzed-up police blotter. Occasionally they rebelled, but after a few days the complaints of circulation managers and vendors no longer could be ignored.

Company executives did nothing to squelch competition between the news staffs of the *States* and the *Times-Picayune*. There were personal rivalries at the editor level, and *States* reporters were prodded to bring in news beats. The afternoon paper staff, with a red-headed-stepchild, second-class-citizen complex, exulted over triumphs, suffered over setbacks. Reporters of the *Times-Picayune* took advantage of opportunities, but they felt less compulsion to prove themselves.

In the early days after the purchase, holdovers from the Ewing regime directed the news and editorial operations of the *States,* even though they steered the course set by the corporate office. Captain John Walker Ross, who had been publisher of the *States* for a period after the death of Robert Ewing, made the transition as editor. Ross, who was born in Gretna on February 22, 1868, dated from the early Major Hearsey times. He was hired as a proofreader but soon caught the attention of city editor Theodore D. Wharton with West Bank notes which he supplied on his own initiative. He was made a reporter. Ross established a reputation for his coverage of prize fights. He went to Richburg, Mississippi, on July 8, 1889, to report on the John L. Sullivan-Jake Kilrain bout, which was held at the whistlestop rendezvous in order to circumvent the Louisiana ban against boxing. Ross persuaded the engineer of a special train which took a delegation of spectators from New Orleans, to uncouple the engine and speed him back to the city to report Sullivan's victory, which came after two hours and sixteen minute of fighting. Ross was flabbergasted upon passing the *Picayune* office that night to see the result posted on a bulletin board. Instead of the beat he expected, he had been scooped by his fellow *States* reporter, J. C. Aby. Because secrecy was necessary, no telegraph wires had been stretched to the ringside. The first word was passed out by a railroad telegrapher during a gossip period. A railroad operator in New Orleans tipped off Aby, who wired the results throughout the country, even beating the special correspondents sent by big city papers. Aby's word filtered back to the *Picayune.*[12]

A civic banquet was held on June 6, 1935, to mark the fiftieth anniversary of Ross's joining the *States.* One of the speakers remarked: "Gentlemen, Captain Ross has worked fifty years on one newspaper and the man who sits beside him worked on fifty newspapers in one year." His reference was to James Evans Crown, the second-in-command on the *States* news staff. Of course the orator was exaggerating, but the vagabond Crown indeed had put in stints on the Washington *Times,* New York *Evening World,* New York *Journal,* Richmond *News,* New York *Commercial,* Norfolk *Dispatch,* Atlanta *Constitution,* Memphis *News,* St. Louis *Post-Dispatch,* Chicago *Examiner,* Chicago *Inter-Ocean,* Chicago *Chronicle,* Chicago *Tribune,* Denver *Republican,* New York *Morning World,* and the *Item* before he settled down on the *States.*[13]

He belonged on the newspaper for which Major Hearsey and Robert Ewing established a hard-drinking heritage. He was a steady horse player, a fifty cent and one dollar bettor who kept copy boys running to the nearest bookmaker. The son of a preacher, he once bet a New Orleans clergyman he could outdo him from the pulpit. And he did, with a sermon on "Don't Sell God Short" that had the congregation in tears. Members of his staff who has gone to the church to heckle him found themselves singled out before the parishioners as sinners who needed salvation. In all his years of newspapering, he never learned to use a typewriter. He delighted in dictating his editorials in declamatory style, stealing a glance at listening staff members for a sign of appreciation when he made a point. Crown succeeded to the top position upon the death of Ross on September 30, 1937. He was managing editor, then editor until he died of a heart attack on January 10, 1945. The passing of Crown removed the final important link with the *States's* past. City Editor F. Edward Hebert already had left to become a congressman. The men who would call the tune in the years immediately ahead all had *Times-Picayune* backgrounds. Inevitably, the *States* fitted more snugly into the *Times-Picayune* mold.

The Gray Lady of North Street — the *Times-Picayune* of the thirties — was respectable, authoritative, disciplined, independent, prim, and, when aroused, fearless. Other adjectives are equally valid: long-winded, prosaic, humorless, pompous, opinionated, conservative, and sometimes condescending. The *Times-Picayune* had sounded the rallying cry for opponents of Huey Long and for the reform forces which took over the State Capitol in the aftermath of the Louisiana Scandals. The paper was preoccupied with politics, and played for keeps. Friends were friends; enemies were enemies; and the news columns reflected the difference, although the standards of integrity which enabled the paper to come out on top were never lowered. Long berated the "lying press," but readers knew they could believe the accounts printed in the *Times-Picayune.*

Hard news hogged the pages. Legislative sessions, City Council meetings, and murder trials received voluminous and detailed coverage. A dressing down awaited the reporter who mixed interpretation with facts. Sacred cows — the newspaper term for sacrosanct figures about whom no adverse word may be printed — didn't exist. The biggest advertiser could expect to find his name in print if he were arrested for swindling. Taboos did apply. Even the word *radio* was sparingly used when broadcasting stations were becoming competitors for the advertising dollar. Readers got little help in understanding the social, economic, and environmental changes that affected their lives. The *States* soon was reflecting the strengths, as well as the weaknesses, of the *Times-Picayune.* The sins of the Ewing era were behind.

When Crown died the climactic period of World War II was approaching. His designated successor, William H. Fitzpatrick, was serving as a naval officer in the Pacific area. Thus the first of the *States* editors with *Times-Picayune* training was Frank Clinton Allen. Allen, a skinny, red-headed native of Alabama, didn't have the price of a meal in his pockets when, on November 28, 1929, he landed a job as reporter on the *Times-Picayune.* He went on the become city editor, an impatient, hard-driving boss with an uncanny instinct for deploying his staff. New Orleans never knew a more dedicated newsman, nor a more able one. Allen left the *Times-Picayune* in 1941 to go to the Hattiesburg *American.* He was called back on May 29, 1942, to join the *States* as city editor and to begin an association that continued until his death on December 10, 1963. On October 9, 1942, he became acting managing editor when Fitzpatrick departed for war service. Allen took over as editor pro tem as well as managing editor upon the death of Crown. His dual responsibility continued until the return of Fitzpatrick on November 12, 1945.

Fitzpatrick came back from duty aboard aircraft carriers in time for the latter stages of the political campaign in which deLesseps S. (Chep) Morrison rallied the city's reform elements for a surprising victory over Mayor Robert S. Maestri in the 1946 primary election. He and Allen teamed up to direct coverage that brought the *States* its second Sigma Delta Chi Courage in Journalism award. Fitzpatrick also was responsible for the only Pulitzer Prize won by the *States.* He was given the award in 1951 for editorial writing as the result of a series published in 1950 headed "Government by Treaty." The editorials attacked the Genocide Convention and Covenant on Human Rights on the grounds that they endangered the Bill of Rights in the United States Constitution. The theme underscored the conservative policies followed by the *States* when the paper was a me-too carbon of the *Times-Picayune.*

A native of New Orleans, Fitzpatrick worked for the *Item* while he was attending Tulane University. He joined the *Times-Picayune* in 1935 as a reporter and later became picture editor. In May, 1940, he moved over to the *States* as city editor in succession to Hebert. He became managing editor in November, 1941. Fitzpatrick resigned on June 15, 1952, in order to go to the *Wall Street Journal* as associate editor. His departure saddened the staff which delighted in his informality, felt secure in his never-failing efforts to back them up, and respected his vast abilities.

Fitzpatrick was succeeded by Carl McArn Corbin, another former *Times-Picayune* newsman. A native of Mansfield, Louisiana, where he was born on November 22, 1914, Corbin was one of seven Louisiana State University students who were dismissed in December, 1934, when they defied censorship of the student newspaper, the *Reveille,* by the administration of Huey Long. After graduating from the University of Missouri, he was hired by the *Times-Picayune* in 1936. He left in 1941 to join the army. Corbin married Eleanor Nicholson, the daughter of Yorke P. Nicholson, vice-president of the Times-Picayune Publishing Company. He joined the *States* in 1949 as an editorial writer at the invitation of John F. Tims, the general manager, a fact that had its ironic aspects as will be seen. Corbin had the makings of a maverick and would have effected considerable changes in policy had he not been reined in by higher authority.

Fitzpatrick, Allen, and Corbin. They deplored the secondary role ordained for the afternoon paper. Despite their conditioning to *Times-Picayune* practices, they privately longed to lead the *States,* and the *States-Item,* into unplowed ground. But management looked at the afternoon edition as a sort of blocking back assigned to run interference for the *Times-Picayune.*

On January 24, 1964, in the month after Allen's death, the *States-Item* was drawn more closely into the *Times-Picayune's* arms. George W. Healy, Jr., editor of the morning paper, was made executive editor of both dailies. The embrace almost smothered the *States-Item.* Healy, a 1926 graduate of the University of Mississippi, joined the *Times-Picayune* on November 17, 1926. As a young reporter, he absorbed the newspaper's way of doing things, and as city editor, managing editor, editor, treasurer, vice-president, and director he was influential in the evolvement of style and policy. The *Times-Picayune* was his kind of paper. The less conventional, more flamboyant afternoon edition disturbed him, and he could not be accused of concealing his sentiments. In conferences with *States-Item* editors, he sometimes commented: "We plan to do it this way." "We" was the *Times-Picayune.* Whether or not he intended to put a damper on the afternoon staff, he did just that. Under Healy's executive editorship, the *States-Item's* role was unequivocal: Conform.

Then came June 2, 1969. Thirty-five years, ten months and sixteen days after the take-over by the *Times-Picayune.*

That's another chapter.

11

The Rise and Fall of Jim Thomson

A climb to the summit, a skid to the brink of bankruptcy.

That was the script for the *Item* after Dominick C. O'Malley exited behind the scenes and James M. Thomson took his place on stage. At first the sobersided Thomson found O'Malley's shenanigans an easy act to follow. Up went circulation, up went advertising revenue, until the *Item* had no close rival. But Thomson never learned to compete with the journalistic nemesis that came with the merger of two morning papers. His own shortcomings contributed to his eventual downfall.

Yet he controlled the destiny of the *Item* for thirty-four years, the longest tenure of a New Orleans newspaper proprietor in the twentieth century.

Once his *Item* withstood an attempted invasion by soldiers of the United States Army.

Read on.

In the late spring or early summer of 1906 a tall, emaciated, red-headed native of the Shenandoah Valley paid his first visit to New Orleans. His name was James McIlhany Thomson. His gauntness was the result of ill-health which shortly before had caused him to sell the Norfolk, Virginia, *Dispatch.* "I was a kid with more money than I knew what to do with," he acknowledged. And that was the reason he found himself in New Orleans. Charles M. Palmer wanted to unload his majority ownership of the *Item.* Knowing that Thomson was financially able to swing the deal, Palmer enticed him to make a visit and look over the property.

Later Thomson would talk about his early impressions — his surprise when tepid, muddy Mississippi River water flowed out of the bathtub faucet in his St. Charles Hotel room, his discovery that in order to talk business with the minority owner of the *Item* he would have to go to see him in prison.

The escapades of the minority owner, Dominick C. O'Malley, determined Palmer to sell his stock and end his connection with the *Item.* Palmer's experience as owner of the St. Joseph, Missouri, *News-Press* and as developer of the New York *Journal* had not prepared him for the headaches of association with a newspaper dominated by an O'Malley. From July 21, 1894, until May 1, 1902, O'Malley was sole owner of the *Item.* Then he sold two-thirds of his interest to a company headed by Harry S. Thalheimer.[1] Thalheimer, a nephew of Adolph S. Ochs of the New York *Times,* previously had been connected with the Philadelphia *North American* and the Philadelphia *Record.*

H. B. Gruning of Cincinnati was brought in as treasurer of the *Item* and placed in charge of the advertising department. The managing editor was W. J. Leppert, a newsman of seventeen years' experience, who had been city editor of the *Times-Democrat* until August, 1901, when he was hired away by

O'Malley. For some reason, not now explained, Thalheimer chartered two companies using the *Item* name before the purchase took place. On March 13, 1902, the Recorder of Mortgages entered into the books the charter of the Item Publishing Company, Ltd. The capital stock of $100,000 included one thousand shares, of which Thalheimer owned 795. Leppert, Hewes T. Gurley, Edgar Mayer Cahn, and Lyle Saxon* had one share each. On April 29, 1902, the charter of the Item Company, Ltd., was recorded. Its capital of $50,000 represented five hundred shares of stock. Thalheimer had 395 shares; Gurley, Leppert, S. S. Prentiss, and George W. Moore one each. This was the company that actually took over the *Item* from O'Malley.

After May 1, 1902, O'Malley was shoved into the background for nearly a year. Then, unexpectedly, on April 16, 1903, Thalheimer's name disappeared from the masthead. Hermann B. Deutsch wrote in the *Item* of June 11, 1937, that Thalheimer had been laid low by a sudden illness, could not get downtown in advance of the deadline for making an installment payment to O'Malley, and found when he finally was able to reach the office that O'Malley had taken over his desk in accordance with a forfeit clause in the sale contract. W. J. Leppert later gave a similar account in conversations with his son, George M. Leppert, New Orleans attorney.[2] At this point Charles M. Palmer comes onto the scene. In some way he acquired Thalheimer's share of the *Item*. Whether he purchased it from Thalheimer directly, or whether he bought it from O'Malley after forfeiture by Thalheimer, records do not show. Thalheimer left New Orleans, later becoming publisher of the Toledo *Blade*.

Palmer was an absentee proprietor; O'Malley made the day-

* Lyle Saxon was a New Orleans attorney, the uncle of the author of the same name.

to-day decisions. He was running the *Item* as though it were his own paper during the period when he was battling Mayor Martin Behrman and the other newspapers over the appointment of Edward S. Whitaker as police inspector. It was while he was serving his sentence for libeling Behrman that Thomson visited him in his prison apartment at the old Criminal Courts Building at Tulane and South Saratoga streets.

O'Malley told Thomson he did not want to sell his one-third interest. He was not much impressed by his youthful visitor's prospects as a publisher in rowdy New Orleans. He growled to someone else the prediction that within weeks Thomson would be "full of holes and over the levee."[3] Nevertheless, Thomson was intrigued by the thought of directing the *Item*'s competition with the four other English-language dailies: the *Picayune, Times-Democrat, Daily News,* and *States.* He arranged for the New York advertising agency Smith and Thompson to put up the money for a minority share. On January 9, 1907, a month before Thomson's thirtieth birthday, the *Item* announced that he had bought controlling interest from Palmer.

If Thomson expected interference from O'Malley, his fears proved groundless. After a few months O'Malley sent word that he was ready to sell, and Thomson bought his shares. Meanwhile, the Smith and Thompson advertising agency was dissolved, and Frederick I. Thompson became owner of the firm's stock in the *Item.* Thompson moved to New Orleans and took an active part in the newspaper's affairs, but tired of it and after about a year sold out to Thomson.[4]

Thomson was born at Summit Point, West Virginia, in the Shenandoah Valley, on February 13, 1878. His physician father wanted him to be a lawyer and sent him to Johns Hopkins University, from which he was graduated in 1897. He entered the law office of General John E. Roller at Harrisonburg, Virginia, preparatory to taking the bar examinations.

But since boyhood he had suppressed a desire to be a newspaperman, and in 1898 he quit the law office and took a job as a cub reporter on the Washington *Post.* The energetic youth soon formed his own news service, the Interview Syndicate, from which he made enough money to buy the Norfolk *Dispatch* in 1900. He attributed a breakdown in health to the hard work demanded by the *Dispatch.* His discouragement over his physical condition caused him to sell the paper in 1906.

At Johns Hopkins, Thomson was friendly with Zadok Marshall Ballard, a year younger and a member of the class just behind Thomson's. After graduating, Ballard was a reporter for the Baltimore *American* and Baltimore *News.* He was also a friend of H. L. Mencken. Ballard's primary interest was in chemistry. He had returned to Johns Hopkins for graduate study when, in 1900, Thomson summoned him to Norfolk to be editor of the *Dispatch.* The two began an association that lasted for forty-one years. As soon as Thomson knew the deal for the *Item* would go through, he sent Ballard ahead to become familiar with the newspaper and the city. On January 9, 1907, Ballard became editor. Later he would acquire a minority interest.

Thomson's search for a counterpart to Ballard, one who could direct the advertising operation as Ballard did the editorial activities, finally ended on September 9, 1911. He had reached high and picked out Arthur Grover Newmyer, director of advertising for Frank A. Munsey's chain of newspapers. Newmyer broke into the business as a reporter for the Washington *Times,* then switched into advertising. He was one of the first, if not the first, salesmen to present prospective advertisers with suggested copy for their displays. He served Munsey as an executive in Boston, Philadelphia, and Baltimore before moving to New York to direct advertising sales for the chain. Thomson lured him to the *Item* with a stock offer.[5] Thomson also brought in his own brother, Paul Jones Thomson, younger by six years, as a vice-president and assistant business manager. But it was the threesome of Jim Thomson, Newmyer, and Ballard that made the decisions from 1911 until Newmyer left at the end of 1934.

Thomson's debut as a publisher in New Orleans made a big splash. The ripples subsided as the years went by. He came on the scene at a moment when an imaginative and ambitious proprietor, one who could win and hold public confidence, had an opportunity of towering over Newspaper Row. From O'Malley, Thomson inherited an *Item* which, although irresponsible and sensation-mongering, nevertheless had the greatest circulation and advertising linage in the city. He took over at a time when competing dailies were vulnerable.

The *States* was making little headway while its owner, Robert Ewing, turned his energies into political channels. The days were numbered for Ewing's anemic *Daily News,* which finally expired in 1911. A stodgy *Times-Democrat* was in the doldrums, and the venerable *Picayune* was an overripe plum, ready to fall into the hands of anyone who wanted to shake the tree. Thomson nearly doubled the *Item's* circulation in his first seven years, going from 23,725 to 44,014, a figure which in 1914 exceeded the combined distribution of the *Times-Democrat* (20,129) and the *Picayune* (19,000). In 1912 the *Item* printed 6,165,908 lines of advertising, compared with 5,375,-748 for the *States,* 3,838,912 for the *Times-Democrat,* and 3,373,884 for the *Picayune.*

The climactic year was 1914. Owners of the *Picayune,* caught in a tightening financial squeeze, looked around for a deal that could save the paper. They worked out a merger with the *Times-Democrat,* and on April 6, the first issue of the combined paper appeared. Stockholders of the *Times-Demo-*

crat received a $500,000 interest in the new company. *Picayune* owners settled for shares valued at $200,000. Thomson later told associates he negotiated with the *Picayune* interests and made an offer that fell only a few thousand dollars short of a figure which they would have accepted. He should have dug deeper into his pocket or borrowed whatever he needed. If the then-thriving *Item* had acquired the *Picayune* and given battle on two fronts, against the *States* in the afternoon and *Times-Democrat* in the morning, the outcome would have been different. As it was, the wedding of the two morning papers proved to be a business coup. Almost from the first the *Times-Picayune* began capturing more and more of the market. By 1924 the morning paper had taken a substantial circulation lead over the *Item* — 79,085 to 61,229.

Ten years too late, Thomson decided to challenge the *Times-Picayune* in its own field. On the advice of Newmyer, he launched the morning *Tribune* on December 16, 1924. "We put the plant on a 24-hour basis because we could sell news and advertising that way twenty-five per cent cheaper than anyone operating on a single unit basis," Newmyer recalled.[6] The theory was logical. The trouble was that by then the *Times-Picayune* was too strong to be assaulted successfully. For fifteen years the *Tribune* was an albatross around the *Item*'s neck. Its peak circulation was 44,324, less than one-half of the *Times-Picayune*'s, and when on January 12, 1941, Thomson gave up and junked the paper, by now a puny tabloid, the distribution had dwindled to 22,522, hardly one-sixth of the other morning paper's.

The mistake known as the *Tribune* was costly, but Thomson's eventual demise as a publisher resulted from his failure to establish for the *Item* a reputation of incorruptibility. He did not learn from the lessons offered by his competitors. It should have been obvious to him that Robert Ewing was damaging the *States* by tying the paper to his political interests. Yet Ballard was allowed, by his own account, to mastermind Martin Behrman's mayoral comeback campaign.[7] And in 1924 Thomson put the news, editorial, and advertising facilities of the *Item* to work in behalf of the unsuccessful candidacy of his wife, Genevieve, for Democratic nomination as representative in Congress from the Second District. Mrs. Thomson, to whom the publisher was wed on June 30, 1915, was the daughter of Champ Clark, the iron-fisted Speaker of the House, and the sister of Bennett Champ Clark, later United States senator from Missouri. There was nothing subtle in the *Item*'s advocacy of Mrs. Thomson's ambitions. Over the years newspaper endorsements of political candidates have been part of the democratic process. But when the interest is patently selfish, when a publisher raises his editorial voice to promote the fortunes of himself or a member of his family, his paper loses a degree of its acceptability.

The *Item*'s shield was smudged in 1930 when it was revealed that Ballard had been paid a total of $5,500 in the 1924-1926 period by the Public Belt Railroad Commission, a governmental agency with a public relations problem. The editor had undertaken the assignment when the commission wanted to float a bond issue to finance a proposed Mississippi River bridge. One of his duties was to prepare press releases. Thomson said Ballard did the job with his knowledge and approval. "The money was paid for expert services by Mr. Ballard . . . which services were entirely disconnected with his work for the Item Company," the publisher blandly asserted.[8] The incident did nothing for the *Item*'s credibility. An editor or reporter compromises himself whenever he accepts money from a public agency — or a private one, for that matter — about which he writes.

The *Times-Picayune* set an example which Thomson's

failure to follow cost the *Item* standing in the business community. From the beginning, the *Times-Picayune*'s rate card applied to every line of advertising printed. A newspaper demonstrates its integrity by charging all advertisers the same volume rate. But the *Item* — and the *States,* too, in the Ewing days — made under-the-table deals. Secret discounts were offered to favored merchants. Inevitably, the word got around, to the detriment of Thomson's paper and, of course, to the *States* before it was sold.

Other factors worked against Thomson. Between 1914 and 1933 advertising salesmen for the *Item* and the *States* competed directly against each other, and the *Times-Picayune* was the beneficiary. A *States* salesman who failed to land an account told the prospective space-buyer: "Well, if you won't give the business to me, go to the *Times-Picayune.* Don't use the *Item.*" *Item* salesmen took the same line against the *States.* The merger of the morning papers brought together two groups of stockholders both with deep roots in New Orleans business, civic, and social affairs. Names such as Nicholson, Phelps, Howard, Morris, and Hyams had been synonymous with community leadership for many decades. In a stratified hierarchy, Thomson was a Johnny-come-lately, to the disadvantage of the *Item* among the city's movers and doers.

Newspapers with a quarter of the circulation and linage boasted by the *Item* made money. Yet Thomson's journal failed to prosper. He ran the paper with the same business methods that might have been followed by the proprietor of an old-fashioned, crossroads general store. When he wanted a few dollars he dipped into the *Item* till and left a chit. He and Mrs. Thomson charged personal purchases to the paper, and by 1941 the Thomsons owed it $97,932.70. There was no dishonesty involved. All of the transactions were duly recorded, and the board of directors by unanimous resolution approved the practice. Thomson explained that he drew only a nominal salary and was entitled as principal owner to take money from the cash drawer when he wanted it. The arrangement was only tit for tat, he said, because in the early years he frequently was more flush than the *Item,* and made advances from his own funds to pay the paper's bills.[9]

Some employees were less meticulous in dealing with the company. In 1942, when Thomson no longer was owner, an audit revealed that workers in the bookkeeping and accounting departments had systematically embezzled $130,980.50 between 1933 and 1941. The auditors said the thefts actually had started before 1933[10] meaning that the defalcations were greater than the figure reported.

Even in the early 1920s when the *Item* was running a neck-and-neck race with the *Times-Picayune,* Thomson's paper was not showing a profit. In 1921 he gave 250 shares of common stock to Ballard, who already owned 250, and 250 shares to his brother Paul, with the expectation that they eventually would pay him for the stock out of future dividends — which never materialized.

In 1924, in order to finance the inauguration of the *Tribune* in December, Thomson offered a preferred stock to local businessmen at a total price of $257,000.* The issue provided for a 7 percent cumulative dividend, meaning that preferred shareholders had first claim to any profits. No dividends could be declared on common stock until the return promised on the preferred was paid in full. The preferred issue was in default from the first year on. The *Item* was not making any money.

Not since the Dominick O'Malley-C. Harrison Parker gun battle eighteen years earlier had there been such excitement on

* New Orleans Recorder of Mortgages records show that on January 4, 1921, the *Item* charter was amended to provide for capital stock of $650,000, including $500,000 in common and $150,000 in 8 percent preferred shares. On October 30, 1924, another amendment provided for a capitalization of $925,000, including $500,000 in common and $425,000 in 7 percent preferred.

Newspaper Row. It was eight o'clock on the night of July 3, 1917. Marching on Common Street toward the river came 150 of the Louisiana National Guardsmen who had been mustered into federal service for World War I. "Column right, double time!" shouted the leader as the procession reached Camp Street. The soldiers swarmed toward the entrance to the *Item* building at 210 Camp Street. Out of the door emerged an army officer, pistol in hand.

"Halt! Halt!" he ordered. Behind him, to back up his command, was a detail of soldiers armed with machine guns and bayonets. The advancing men hesitated, then began scattering in retreat. At that moment an automobile motor backfired. The startled troopers thought one of the machine gunners had opened fire on them. Quickly they assembled in orderly rows. Then, surrounded by an armed guard, they began marching back to the place whence they came, Camp Nicholls, on Moss Street across Bayou St. John from City Park. After they left, Camp Street was found to be littered with heavy iron bolts. These were the missiles they had intended to use to break every window in the *Item* building while they were wrecking the place.

Only because of the curiosity of the Camp Nicholls commander, Colonel Frank P. Stubbs, was an adequate guard on hand to protect the *Item*. He noticed that the men who had liberty passes for the evening formed into squads and marched away from the camp in a body, an unheard-of procedure for soldiers setting out for a night of fun. Inquiry revealed the destination, and Colonel Stubbs dispatched officers and a score of men in automobiles. They beat the marchers by an hour. Otherwise, the *Item's* only defender would have been the elderly watchman, "Colonel" Audler. Not that he would have yielded easily. When the guard detail told him the troops were on the way, he pulled out his pistol and remarked: "If any man seeking to attack this building crosses that doorstep, he'll never go to France."[11]

The *Item* was indignant. "An astonishing movement of falsely inflamed young men of the Louisiana National Guard against *The Item* office was happily aborted last night by the action of the commanding officers of the First Regiment," said the newspaper. "That bloodshed did not result between these young men and their own comrades on guard or *The Item*'s aged watchman was due solely to fortunate accident. The idea of soldiers of the United States marching in mass against private property of citizens of the United States under the civil law of the land is a new conception in this city." The *Item* accused the *States* of using fakery and falsification to arouse the ire of Camp Nicholls troops against Thomson's paper.

The *Item* had asked for the trouble by publishing a news story on Sunday, July 1. "Investigation about Camp Nicholls made by the camp welfare committee of the Louisiana Federation of Women's Clubs and reported to the Louisiana division of the Council of Defense, disclosed the spreading of immoral influences in the vicinity of the camp," the story began. It said houses of prostitution had been established along Bayou St. John near the camp, and women from the Storyville district were accosting soldiers as they entered the camp. "Large numbers of girls 14 to 17 years old remain in City Park after nightfall visiting with guardsmen in secluded places." Girls reported missing from home were found in rooms near the camp. Social disease was increasing.

The *States* gleefully published the result of an inquiry into the source of the *Item* story. It reported that Miss Eva Wright, who lived at 1530 Felicity Street, was the only member of the "camp welfare committee" of the Federation, that she had no first-hand knowledge — only rumor — to back up allegations of immorality, and that she had given the report to the *Item* in confidence, never dreaming the paper would print the material without confirming its accuracy.[12] The *Item* management squirmed under a public display of righteous indignation. Reported the *Times-Picayune:* "Colonel Stubbs said the attack on the troops was a gratuitous one made by a paper which rarely missed an opportunity to criticize sharply any endeavor made by this country in the war."[13] 'In a July 4 editorial, the *States* said: "The *Item* has been consistent only in its defense of the cause of the Kaiser and Champ Clark; and its consistency has been such, even since the United States entered the war, as to bring this newspaper frequent inquiries as to whether or not its service to Prussian overlordism are not in some way requited and whether or not its quality of patriotism is properly a subject for reference to the Department of Justice."

The *Item* was down, and the *States* couldn't resist the opportunity to kick out a few teeth. "Its foul and cowardly attack on the soldiers of Camp Nicholls having provoked a remarkable demonstration against it by 200 of these soldiers Tuesday night, The *Item*'s efforts to clear its skirts takes a characteristic form. It sets up the preposterous plea that the *States* fomented the demonstration," wrote the editor, J. Walker Ross. "The defense is only less cowardly than the original offense. The *Item*'s plea is utterly, maliciously and wantonly false."[14]

On July 6, over Thomson's signature, the *Item* printed an apology intended to make peace with the soldiers. The paper admitted it had no facts to substantiate the allegations. Crowed the *States*: "No newspaper, within our knowledge, has ever had to make a more humiliating confession of guilt, after first brazenly attempting to justify a slanderous publication.[15]

The taunting by the *States* could not be ignored, and Thomson and Ballard each sued the Daily States Publishing Company, Ltd., and J. Walker Ross for $150,000. Thomson's petition was filed in Civil District Court. Ballard, who commuted from Bay St. Louis and was a citizen of Mississippi, brought action in Federal District Court. They contended they had been libeled in the July 4 editorial which questioned their patriotism.[16] "They do not, of course, expect to get the price of a bar of soap," commented the *States.* "Under their management *The Item* has been an Ishmaelite in New Orleans journalism. It has been the ghoul of the profession, and by the hardened indifference with which it has invaded the privacy of the home and by the recklessness with which it has slandered men of the highest repute, it has drawn more women's tears than any newspaper ever printed in this community."[17]

The hubbub received twenty times the newspaper coverage accorded to the closing of the Storyville red-light district at midnight on November 12, 1917, by order of the Council of National Defense. The *States* devoted a two-column headline and story to reporting the migration of some 750 women from the cribs and mansions in the area where black bands gave early impetus to the development of New Orleans jazz.[18]

For a year and a half Thomson's and Ballard's suits languished in the courts. War fever was beginning to subside when, on January 26, 1919, two months after the armistice ended fighting, Ballard's case finally was called for trial before Federal Judge Rufus E. Foster. For a week New Orleanians who read both the *States* and *Item* might well have had the impression that two trials were in progress, so different were the printed accounts. Both papers drew remonstrances from Judge Foster, who told them from the bench: "I want to say that the evening newspapers will have to stop selling their papers on the strength of this case until the trial is over. There is no necessity for these big headlines, and just as the *States* was at variance with the truth Sunday, so is the *Item* this afternoon. They must stop printing incorrect headlines, and the reporters must not give their opinions in the articles." The judge rebuked the *States* because of a headline which claimed that the *Item*'s editor "Sang German Songs in Rheingold After *Lusitania* Sinking."[19] The news story reported that *States* attorney Henry P. Dart asked Ballard whether at about the time of the torpedoing of the liner *Lusitania* in 1915 he had not regularly met with two German aliens at the Rheingold Restaurant on Common Street, and whether he had not sung "The Watch on the Rhine." Ballard's reply was that he did not know the aliens, that he frequently went to the University Club — "to which most of the lawyers belong" — on the floor above the Rheingold, and that he had joined in the singing of the national airs of several countries. In fact, Ballard recalled, he made Fritz Schroeder, manager of the University Club, stand on a chair and sing "The Marseille." Judge Foster called down the *Item* for a headline which said the *States'* defense was "shattered completely."

Dart summed up the *State's* defense in this manner: "My purpose is to show from the witness' (Ballard's) own statements that he was pro-German, that his writings were pro-German, that his whole sentiments and bearing were pro-German, that he attacked President Wilson and the policies of this country in his writings in practically every issue of the paper. Further than this, I propose showing that even after we entered the war against Germany, his general policies were not changed and that he was in reality pro-German all the way through."[20]

Ballard was the most conspicuous performer. He brought voluminous files into the courtroom and insisted on reading *Item* editorials to refute Dart's intimations. Once the exasperated Dart took exception to the different tones of voice used by Ballard in reciting the editorials to the jury. "When you declaim something which you want to present, I can hear you perfectly," Dart complained. "But when I ask you to read the whole article and cover what you wrote about the German side, your voice is so different I cannot understand a word you say." At another point Juror William K. DePass broke into the proceedings to say: "This jury has been sitting here almost a week, and I, for one, am tired of hearing all this reading." Judge Foster replied that the "only way this case can be presented is by the introduction of editorials." He said he would try to speed up the pace. As the judge spoke Ballard stood up and started to give advice about how the trial could be expedited. "Sit down, Mr. Ballard," said the judge. When Ballard hesitated, Judge Foster repeated, "Sit down, I say. You have a lawyer. Let him do the talking."[21]

"When the United States entered the war," Thomson testified, "Mr. Ballard and I had a conference as to which should go, in case that became desirable. Mr. Ballard told me he was ineligible for military service because of flat feet and practically the loss of sight in one eye."[22] Thomson said he himself offered his services in any capacity. Thomson blamed propaganda in the *States* for talk before the war that the *Item* was pro-German. He told of long-time enmity between the two papers. "What form did the propaganda take?" asked R. H. Marr, the *Item's* attorney.

"It was general and specific," said Thomson. "I recall specifically a paragraph in May that my brother, Mr. Paul Thomson, showed me, which was written by Mr. Aby* and was a direct attack on the *Item*. The paragraph stated the Russians had suffered a severe defeat or something and that is was supposed the news would be a source of great joy to the *Item*. I saw Colonel Ewing about the paragraph as I felt very strongly, told him that if the paragraph was meant as a joke, it was a poor joke, and if it was meant as the truth, I would

* J. C. Aby, *States* columnist.

either have to take the matter up with Aby or him. He said he was responsible for anything that appeared in the paper and seemed inclined to treat the matter as a joke, telling me it was absurd to think that any man in my position could be disloyal. It seemed such a monstrous way to joke that I felt very resentful and made myself very emphatic. I had the understanding he was going to cut out such things and I believe he did up to the time of the libel on which the suit is based."

"What was the attitude of Mr. Ewing toward Mr. Ballard?"

"He was always very hostile to him."

"When does that hostility date from?"

"From the time of the Blanchard administration when Mr. Ballard advocated the abolition of the tax collectors and Mr. Ewing opposed it. Mr. Ewing was one of the collectors."

"They were abolished?"

"Yes."

Thomson said his conversation with Ewing was heated. "I called his attention to the utter absurdity of it. I told him of the number of young men who had gone from my office and of my relatives. I called his attention to the utter monstrosity of a man's not being for his country when it was in a war. He said the *Item* had said rude things about him and it was a matter of give and take." Thomson recalled the *States* reported that he had personally "gone to George W. Perkins and had been paid money* to support the Bull Moose candidate" in the presidential election of 1912.

"Then you and the *Item* were charged with venality with reference to the Parker movement in Louisiana?" asked Marr. John M. Parker, later governor, was the candidate for vice-president on Theodore Roosevelt's Bull Moose ticket.

"Yes. That statement was started by Mr. Lee Emmet Thomas and was widely exploited by the *States*."

* Five thousand dollars.

"You say the *Item* and the *States* have been at odds for a great many years?"

"They are competitors for circulation and advertising. They sell papers in the same field daily and Sunday. The *Item's* chief competitor is *The Times-Picayune.*"

"Is it not a fact," broke in Dart, "that from the time of the Blanchard administration, the *Item* has time and again written editorials against Colonel Ewing and published them?"

"It was never any intention of mine, and the *Item* has never been personal with Colonel Ewing. There is a great divergence in the attitudes of the *Item* and the *States* on public questions. Colonel Ewing is in politics. That makes it entirely correct and proper that his political actions should come under review as much as those of any man in public life."

Thomson complained that the *States* had published a news story saying Ballard had been fired as a result of the Camp Nicholls incident. "Mr. Ballard has no responsibility for that article at all. He was in Bay St. Louis at the time. The article was printed on Sunday and Mrs. Ballard usually goes to Bay St. Louis early Saturday afternoons."[23]

Ross's testimony concluded with the statement: "I believe the *Item* was carrying out a consistent policy of pro Germanism. I believe the *Item's* pro-Germanism was open and very pronounced up to our entrance into the war. Of course, it was not so pronounced after the United States broke off diplomatic relations with Germany."

While it is true that from 1914 through early 1917 the *Item* advocated neutrality, a stand which was increasingly unpopular as public sentiment in favor of the Allies grew, there was not one word of testimony at the trial that the newspaper published any subversive material. Actually, for much of the time the *Item's* views coincided with the public expressions of President Wilson.

On Friday, January 31, Judge Foster dismissed the jury for

the weekend. On Monday, February 3, he smiled from the bench as court was opened and stated:

> Well, gentlemen, the other day when I adjourned this case, I did so because it had occurred to me that I might be able to bring about a cordial understanding between the two parties litigant. They are warm friends of mine, and I for one am thoroughly convinced that all of these gentlemen are loyal American citizens, and it seems to me that this editorial had been written at a time when everybody's nerves were more or less on end — on edge, I should say. We were mixed up in a great war and everyone felt more truculent and intolerant than in normal times, and therefore we were apt to say and do things in our private affairs that we would not do or say at other times, and it seemed to me that there might be some understanding brought about between the parties. I had also in mind the fact that the war was over and we are now entering upon a period of reconstruction where it is necessary that the public press should sink these personal differences, and all work together for the benefit of the city, state and nation, and here was some of the finest editorial talent in the South, if not in the United States, engaged in fighting each other.

Judge Foster said he got the lawyers and principals together, and believed they had reached accord. Dart said the *States* intended no reflection on the character of either Thomson or Ballard and withdrew its imputation of disloyalty. Marr said Thomson and Ballard had no desire to obtain a monetary settlement and were ready to withdraw their suits. Both the federal and state actions were dismissed.*[24]

By early 1941 Thomson's *Item* was about to fade as so many other New Orleans dailies had. The haven of unemployed printers, the strident voice of Dominick O'Malley, the lively journal of the teens was in deep financial difficulty, on the verge of bankruptcy. The paper's plight was no secret. James Hammond, former publisher of the Memphis *Commercial Ap-*

* Memories of the O'Malley days were revived in the heat of the 1925 mayoral campaign when on February 2 the *States* asked editorially: "Has the *Item* again resorted to the trick of bringing in dips and burglars here to discredit Mr. Maloney and help elect Behrman?" Thomson brought a $25,000 libel suit, which he lost in the Louisiana State Supreme Court.

peal, tried to put together a deal that would enable him to take over the paper and try to bail it out. He offered $50,000 cash, a $100,000 note, $500,000 in mortgage bonds, and 10 percent of the profits for twenty years. But Hammond's proposal contemplated a minimum outlay of cash, and the deal fell through.[25]

Meanwhile, the *Item* was deep in debt. The largest single creditor was the sales subsidiary of the International Paper Company, which supplied newsprint. By March 1 the *Item* owed a past-due bill of $85,000 for paper and $15,000 interest. To William N. Hurlbut, vice-president of International, fell the responsibility of protecting his company's stake. "We first had to determine whether this sick customer could be salvaged," he explained later.[26] "The question was whether to let it die, lose our $100,000, or make an attempt to revive it. If we decided to let it die, that was it. There would have been only one afternoon newspaper in New Orleans. I finally arrived at the conclusion, after carefully studying the situation, that it could be salvaged."

Hurlbut was convinced that Thomson would have to abdicate, allowing new management to take over, if the *Item* were to have a chance. He insisted that the Sunday *Item* would have to be scrapped (the *Tribune* had been scuttled in January). By 1940 the Sunday edition had fallen behind the daily in circulation 64,915 against 69,551. "It was the weak sister, dragging down the daily paper," Hurlbut commented. He also emphasized that an infusion of working capital would have to be provided to help the new owner. He estimated that $250,000 to $275,000 would be needed. If the paper company took the lead in the reorganization, it would have to put up cash. "I had the responsibility of recommending that to our Board of Directors," Hurlbut related, "and I naturally would have been criticized if the plan had not been successful."

In February, 1941, Hurlbut visited Thomson in the publisher's tiny office adjoining the cluttered second-story newsroom in the *Item* building at 722 Union Street and broke the news to him: After thirty-four years the *Item* was going to be placed into new hands. If Thomson went along with International's plans, he would receive a price for his interest. The alternative was a bankruptcy proceeding. "Mr. Thomson," said Hurlbut, "I am making my last offer first."[27] As the negotiations continued Thomson demurred mildly over Hurlbut's dictum that the Sunday *Item* must die. "It was his baby he was talking about," explained Hurlbut. At another point Thomson became balky. Hurlbut went to see Samuel Zemurray, the United Fruit Company developer, to whom Thomson owed $30,737 secured by his *Item* stock. "He became very mad," Hurlbut related, "and said he would bring Jim, as he referred to him, back in line. He called him on the telephone and asked him to come to his, that is, Mr. Zemurray's office; and thereafter we proceeded with our deal with Colonel Thomson."

In view of later developments there were ironic aspects to Hurlbut's search for an experienced publisher to whom the International Paper Company proposed to turn over the *Item* without asking for any cash investment. First Hurlbut approached Charles P. Manship, owner of the Baton Rouge *State-Times* and *Morning Advocate.* "He agreed that it was a good opportunity, he concurred in the wisdom of discontinuing the Sunday paper, but said at his age he didn't care to take on additional responsibilities," Hurlbut reported. Hurlbut next made contact with S. I. Newhouse, who then owned several papers in the East. "He agreed with Mr. Manship, but as all of his operations were near New York, he said he didn't want to take on a responsibility so far away." Later Newhouse expanded his newspaper holdings from coast to coast. And in 1962 he paid what then was a record price of $42 million for

New Orleans newspaper properties that included the *Item*. By then circumstances had changed considerably.

Early in his quest Hurlbut offered the *Item* to Leonard K. Nicholson, president of the Times-Picayune Publishing Company, which already owned the *States*. "He said he did not want a monopoly in New Orleans, that he preferred to have a happy competitor." Seventeen years later, after Nicholson's death, the *Times-Picayune* purchased the *Item* for $3,400,000. Judgments which were valid in 1941 no longer applied in 1958. The *Item* had soared over the 100,000 mark in circulation and was a product vastly different from the anemic journal which was barely alive in 1941. Television had become a competitor for the advertising dollar, a rival which newspapers could battle most effectively by presenting a united front. And by then three commercial television stations in New Orleans (there later would be four) offered news coverage and editorial opinions. A merger of newspapers no longer meant the kind of monopoly on the dispensing of information that Nicholson wanted to avoid.

In April, 1941, Richard Doane of the International Paper Company telephoned Ralph Nicholson, co-owner of the *Tampa Times*, and asked whether he still were interested in acquiring another paper.[28] Nicholson was, and Doane invited him to come to New York for a conference. In that discussion and in subsequent meetings in New Orleans, details were worked out under which Thomson yielded the *Item* to Nicholson on June 27, 1941.

It was a rare, can't-lose proposition for Nicholson. A new corporation, The Item Company, Inc., was formed and took over the assets and liabilities of Thomson's The Item Company, Ltd. The proceeds from $500,000 of first mortgage bonds bought by the Jefferson Standard Life Insurance Company were used to buy outstanding stock. Second mortgage bonds in the face amount of $400,000 were issued to Thomson. Nicholson obtained all of the common stock of the new company at a price of $400,000. He did not put up a cent of his own. The paper company lent him the $400,000 on a ten-year note secured by the stock, with the understanding that the interest would be payable only out of the *Item's* earnings. Nicholson testified that he did not even have to sign the promissory note. The $400,000 was deposited to the *Item*'s account in the Whitney National Bank, and Nicholson issued a check to pay the indebtedness to the paper company subsidiary which by now was $125,000. Nicholson discontinued the Sunday *Item* after the issue of July 27, 1974.

Thomson owned 3,300 shares of common stock, his interest in the *Item* being 73 percent of the total. He received $90,000 in cash, from which he was required to pay the $30,737.50 debt to Zemurray and $10,256.14 to the Whitney bank. He also received promissory notes for $65,000, in addition to the $400,000 in second mortgage bonds. Further, the $97,932.70 debt which the publisher and his wife had run up at the *Item* over the years was, for all practical purposes, forgiven. The arrangement was that Thomson would receive an annual advisor's fee of $7,500 from the new company and that the amount would be credited against the debt, and that Thomson would be obligated to make no other payments on the account, and the entire debt would be canceled upon his death.

The other eighty-four stockholders were paid $50 a share for their common stock and $100 for the preferred. Ballard came out of the sale with $93,950. The heirs of Paul Thomson, who died on October 15, 1938, received $17,500 for his 350 shares of common.

Nearly two years after the sale, Mrs. Cecil Guy Robinson filed suit against James Thomson, contending that he received $195.45 per share for his stock, whereas she was paid only $50 per share for 500 shares which she had inherited from her brother, Lynn H. Dinkins, president of the Interstate Bank and Trust Company. Thomson's response was that Mrs. Robinson actually had a better deal than he did because she was paid in cash, whereas he received unsecured promissory notes and second mortgage bonds, and "inasmuch as the old corporation operated at a loss there was a strong likelihood that the new corporation would be unable to make a better showing."[29] Thomson won in both the Civil District and Louisiana State Supreme courts.

In 1944 Thomson qualified as a candidate for Congress from the Second Louisiana District, but withdrew before the campaign was in full swing. He died on September 25, 1959, at Berryville, Virginia.

The *Item's* turn-around was almost immediate once the soft-spoken, coolly efficient Nicholson took charge, thus vindicating Hurlbut's judgment. In the first fiscal year of his regime the company showed a profit, before federal income taxes, of \$13,586. In subsequent years the earnings were \$114,054; \$345,144; \$284,846; \$171,453; \$201,626; \$150,140; \$137,271. The profits belonged to Nicholson, who also paid himself a salary.

Nicholson had the benefit of the booming World War II economy and a time when advertisers came knocking at newspaper doors. He also was a hardheaded publisher and efficient businessman. What would have happened had someone with Nicholson's acumen, instead of the inept Thomson, taken over the *Item* in 1907?

12

Angling for the Kingfish

In 1911 a youthful Louisianian asked editor Marshall Ballard for a job as reporter on the *Item.* "I know the politics of this state frontward and backward," the confident applicant said. "I've been knocking on every door in North Louisiana." He explained he had been selling cottonseed oil.

"What makes you think you can write?" asked the editor.

"Try me out. Want me to write an editorial for you?"

"Let's see what you can do."

A few minutes later Ballard was handed an article on a political campaign. He looked it over, and commented: "I'll give you a job as our over-the-river correspondent to start, covering the news of Algiers and Gretna."

"At how much?"

"Ten dollars a week."

"I've been used to making twenty-five dollars a week

and expenses. I wouldn't even try to live on ten dollars a week. No, thanks."*

In the years ahead the young man would put a reverse twist on the adage. In his case it became: If you can't join 'em, lick 'em.

His name was Huey Pierce Long.

The seven-year era during which Huey Long was the czar of Louisiana provides a lively and revealing chapter in the history of the two afternoon newspapers which later were merged into the *States-Item*. At a critical point, the *States* came through with an endorsement sought by Long as important to his political career. Soon the newspaper turned on him and, after his death, exploded the scandals that riddled his dynasty. On the other hand, the *Item* began by opposing the Kingfish, then succumbed in a surrender that was costly in terms of public confidence and contributed to the eventual failure of the James M. Thomson ownership.

In 1924 Long, while serving on the Public Service Commission, entered the statewide political arena with a convincing third-place finish in the balloting for Democratic nomination as governor. Most of his voting strength was in the country parishes, and he believed it was necessary for him to establish a beachhead in the populous wards of New Orleans in preparation for future campaigns. In advance of the 1925 New Orleans municipal primary election, Long formed an alliance with two of the city's politicians — Old Regular ward leader Paul Maloney and New Regular boss John P. Sullivan — and also with Robert Ewing, who, in addition to being a politician

* The source for this account is an article by Hermann B. Deutsch which appeared in the *Item's* sixtieth anniversary edition of July 11, 1937. Dr. T. Harry Williams, author of the Pulitzer Prize-winning definitive biography of Huey Long, does not recall finding any reference to the incident while doing his research. However, Deutsch wrote the article at a time when he shared an office with Marshall Ballard and obviously was in position to check on his material.

himself, was publisher of the *States*. An arrangement with Ewing appeared especially desirable because he also was owner of the Shreveport *Times*. The union with Ewing obviously was a marriage of convenience, for Ewing as well as for Long. Of Ewing, historian T. Harry Williams writes: "What he wanted now was influence — in the city government and, more so, in the state government; He wanted to be able to call in a governor and tell him what to do."[1]

When the test came in the municipal primary, the Long-Ewing-Sullivan-Maloney axis proved formidable, although Maloney was beaten for mayor by Martin Behrman, who made a comeback after the administration of Andrew McShane. Behrman won by only 2,100 votes, and Long had reason to look forward with increasing confidence to the 1928 statewide test of strength, when he would make his second run for the governorship. Long's opponents in the January primary were Governor Oramel H. Simpson and Congressman Riley J. Wilson. The *Item* supported Wilson,[2] while Ewing's *States* applied all of its persuasiveness in behalf of Long. "The Issue is Clear," was the title of the *States*'s preelection editorial:

> The only hope of the people of Louisiana to escape the twin evils the candidacies of Mr. Wilson and Mr. Simpson foreshadow is by the nomination and election of Mr. Long, WHO FROM EARLY MANHOOD HAS FOUGHT UNDEVIATINGLY AND WITH HIGH COURAGE AGAINST THE SYSTEM AND WHO IS PLEDGED TO SMASH IT AND TO RE-ESTABLISH DECENT GOVERNMENT IN LOUISIANA. . . . All over Louisiana militant organizations of the people are standing with Huey Long and the Cause he represents — organizations so general and so strong, that both of his opponents concede him long leadership in the result of Tuesday and are now only fighting for a chance to meet him in a second primary. THERE OUGHT TO BE NO SECOND PRIMARY . . . DON'T WASTE A VOTE ON WILSON. HE CANNOT WIN. DON'T WASTE A VOTE ON SIMPSON. HE CANNOT WIN. Vote for Long on Tuesday — don't wait to cast your vote for him in the second primary. Finish the job at one time.[3]

The editorial writers of the day liked to emphasize their thoughts with long sentences in capital letters.

After two decades of experience in Louisiana politics, Ballard should have known better than to put himself and the *Item* into the ridiculous position in which they found themselves while the tabulation of votes proceeded. Voting machines and instant, computerized returns were refinements that lay far in the future. The lengthy paper ballots had to be tabulated by hand. As always, in the rural precincts the votes in local races were counted first. Weary poll commissioners turned to the state office contests only after the results of local races were known. Meanwhile, Congressman Wilson drew heavy support in New Orleans, where the ballots for governor were counted with more dispatch. As a result, on Thursday after the Tuesday election, Simpson showed a statewide plurality of about 10,000 votes on the basis of unofficial tabulations while the count in the country continued.

Ballard wrote in a page-one editorial in the *Item*[4] that Long's defeat was inevitable, that he should withdraw and concede Wilson's triumph without the necessity of a second primary. "So far as Mr. Long is concerned his ambitions were foredoomed to failure," said Ballard. "He merely put a double seal on the fate that foreshadowed him when he chose his city affiliation. Neither New Orleans, nor the state of Louisiana, will ever consent to be governed by an obligarchy that reeks with the odor of the race track, the farobank and the roulette wheel."* The editor said Long would need a plurality of 30,000 in order to have a chance. "My judgment is that if he can get a plurality of 9000 or 10,000 over all, he is doing surprisingly well."

The *States* scoffed. "Who ever heard of such an attitude

* John P. Sullivan had racetrack interests. Senator Huey P. Long charged that Sullivan was connected with gambling house operations, an accusation that Sullivan vigorously denied.

when the vote has not been counted?"[5] The *Item*'s embarrassment was complete when the late rural returns sent Long's edge to 40,000 votes, and it was Wilson, rather than Long, who pulled out of the runoff primary.

It was only a question of time before the Long-Ewing honeymoon would end in a falling out of incompatible partners. Both were domineering, impatient personalities who had no intention of yielding the center of the stage. Dr. Williams said Ewing "assumed he was a kind of prime minister, who would determine every important decision the young governor made."[6] Long did not have that kind of role in mind for the publisher. Before many months had passed after the inauguration, Long in private was Ewing "Colonel Bow Wow," and then the break was in the open. Long pointed out that Ewing's *States* had not been an effective vote producer anyway. He was right. Long collected 12,187 votes in New Orleans in 1924, and only 18,053 in 1928 when he had the *States*'s support. He was badly beaten in the city both times.

In August, 1928, Governor Long secretly mobilized National Guardsmen and sent them to raid the Arabi and Jai Alai clubs in St. Bernard Parish where unconcealed and illegal gambling was being conducted. The *States* applauded the move. "Gov. Long, reluctant as he must be to supersede the local authorities in any community, seems to have had no alternative but to resort to the drastic course he adopted Sunday morning to put an end to the flagrant violations of the gambling laws of the State in St. Bernard parish," said an editorial.[7] By February 2, 1929, Ewing and Long had split and the *States* was saying Governor Long "gives no evidence of a return to normalcy. His feet are still off the ground and his head in the clouds. His delusions of grandeur and dictatorship continue. His capacity for loose statement seems unimpaired." And when Long again used the militia to raid gambling houses, Ewing's indignation showed in big headlines and stern editorials.

"Strip Women on Orders of Long," said a headline over a news story which began: "After being stripped of her clothing and searched by two matrons at Jackson Barracks Thursday morning on orders of officers of the Louisiana National Guard, who said they acted upon an order from Gov. Huey P. Long, Mrs. Fred Kriss, of Detroit, wife of a wealthy owner and breeder of thoroughbred race horses, became hysterical in her apartment in the Jung hotel and Mr. Kriss summoned a doctor to her side."[8] The story shared space on page one with an account of the St. Valentine's Day gangland massacre in Chicago.

"In none of the places raided on Wednesday night was gambling found to be going on, even if the games had been in operation before the appearance of the militia," the *States* editorialized. "Yet men and women dining in the restaurants were seized when they were violating no law; they were searched. . . . Other women who protested were subjected to the indignity and humiliation of being stripped to the skin in a similar search. . . . We are not living in the time of imperial Russia." The *States* followed up with a widely discussed news story, an exposé capsuled into this headline: "Long's Wild Night in Vieux Carre on Eve of Strip Raid. In Sworn Affidavits Entertainers Describe High Didos Cut There, with Governor of Louisiana in Stellar Role Dances Alone With Glass Held High, Liquors up with Highballs, and Finally Leaves to Manage Gambling Drive of Troops."[9] The account was of a party at 510 St. Louis Street.

Both the *States* and *Item* gave lengthy and prominent coverage to the impeachment move against Long in the spring of 1929. Both were disappointed when the attempt collapsed because fifteen senators signed a round robin petition saying they would not vote to convict the governor no matter what the evidence was against him, because they considered the impeachment proceedings illegal. "No senator who signed the document but will rue the day when he thus became a dupe of Huey P. Long," snarled the *States.*[10] The *Item* commented: "It was, in other words, much as though a man accused of murder, or any other crime, had fixed three or four members of the jury in advance to say they would not convict him regardless of proof."[11]

In the first years of Long's regime the *Item* was, according to Dr. Williams' definitive biography, "perhaps the bitterest of anti-Long papers." Not only did Ballard attack the governor on the editorial page, but Thomson also got in his licks. He was one of a group of influential men who went to Baton Rouge in May, 1930, to urge the removal of Long's ally, John B. Fournet, as Speaker of the House.[12]

On September 8, 1930, William G. Wiegand, an *Item* reporter, attempted to interview Long in the latter's suite in the Roosevelt Hotel. Long called him a son of a bitch or bastard — the papers termed it an unprintable insult — and the husky Wiegand unloosed a right-hand punch to Huey's mouth, bringing blood. Wiegand laughed at the governor's retaliation, a light blow to the cheek administered after one of Long's armed bodyguards came to his side.[13]

It was in considerable surprise that readers learned in 1931 of an about-face by the *Item,* a change of position which was opposed by Ballard.[14] Thomson liked Long's proposal for a cotton-planting moratorium to deal with a sharp price decline. Obviously, he also became aware of the business manna which could be showered by the state administration on a friendly newspaper. At any rate, in the 1931 election, the *Item* supported O. K. Allen, the henchman picked by Long to be governor while Huey himself was expanding his activity into the national scene as a United States senator.

The rewards were not long in coming. Soon the *Item* became a beneficiary of the notorious deduct system under which public employees found a portion of their wages withheld, whether or not they agreed, for such purposes as campaign contributions or enterprises helpful to Long. The procedure was explored by General S. T. Ansell, counsel for a United States Senate committee which held hearings in New Orleans in February, 1933, on Long's political practices. "We have evidence," Ansell related, "to prove that employees of certain state departments have had to take so many subscriptions to the *Item* and have the cost of those subscriptions deducted from their pay by the officials of those departments and turned over to the *Item.*" From one department alone, he said, about $2,000 was collected for the *Item.* When employees were paid they were given slips showing deductions for the newspaper, Ansell added. Long readily agreed that the deducts were made. "We help those who are with us," he told the senators.

Robert S. Maestri, state conservation commissioner (and later mayor of New Orleans), was a witness.

"Now, Mr. Maestri, about those newspapers," said Long. "We have to switch every now and then, don't we?"

"Yes, we do."

"The *States* was with us and we all subscribed to it?"

"Yes."

"Then nobody was with us and we started one of our own — the *Progress*?"

"Yes."

"And then the *Item* came with us, didn't it?"

"Yes, sir."

Maestri added that the Long organization held a meeting at Daigre's Hall and "got some subscriptions for the *States.*" He said James L. Ewing, Robert's son who became publisher of the *States,* made a speech at the meeting.[15]

In late 1931 the Old Regular City Administration headed by

Mayor T. Semmes Walmsley was allied politically with Long, and city employees also were pressured to repay the *Item* for its editorial favors. The *Times-Picayune* reported a caucus at the Choctaw Club at which Old Regular war leaders were told each would have to meet a quota of *Item* subscriptions. At about the same time New Orleans policemen and firemen were soliciting subscriptions to the *Item*'s little brother, the *Tribune.* Motorists reported being stopped by uniformed motorcycle police and asked to buy subscriptions. Police Superintendent George Reyer conceded that the practice was against regulations, but said he would not halt the campaign because individual members of the City Police Board had no objection to it.[16]

The friendship with Long resulted in advertising plums, as well as subscriptions, for the *Item.* In the fall of 1931 Dr. Arthur Vidrine, superintendent of Charity Hospital and dean of the Louisiana State University Medical Center, wrote a letter to be used by salesmen in rounding up advertisements for a special section fo the *Item-Tribune* published in connection with the dedication of a medical center building. "Our relations with you have been such that we feel justified in suggesting that you extend your cooperation in this section," Vidrine wrote.[17] It was the kind of appeal that could not very well be ignored in the political environment.

In 1933 A. P. Tugwell, chairman of the State Highway Commission, was angered because the Baton Rouge *State-Times* and *Morning Advocate* published letters to the editor criticizing highway department payments for rights-of-way in Livingston Parish. The commission circulated a notice that advertising for bids on construction projects and materials would be transferred from the Baton Rouge papers to the *Item.* J. A. Kinkead, office engineer, wrote in the circular that "news items" about commission activities would be published exclusively in the *Item.*[18]

Long's pet reporter was Charles E. "Chick" Frampton of the *Item*. Dr. Williams related how the association began. Soon after Long became governor he was in New Orleans. He telephoned the city editor of the *Item*. Reporters in the newsroom could hear his voice on the receiver. "I'm getting damn tired of these reporters following me all the time," Long said. "Have you got one man over there that's got any sense at all that I can talk with and I'll clear everything with this one man." The city editor said Frampton would be designated. "Put that son of a bitch on the phone," Huey ordered. Frampton came on the line and said: "Now look. Before we go any further, I don't want you to use that kind of language to me." "You'll do," said Long. "Come on over here."[19]

On October 14, 1931, Long, in New Orleans, put a pistol into his pocket and announced to Frampton that they were driving to Baton Rouge to head off any attempt by Lieutenant Governor Paul N. Cyr to seize the Capitol. Frampton recalled a perilous ride in which Long pushed the automobile to speeds of greater than ninety miles an hour on the narrow road.

On July 1, 1932, Frampton was put on the state payroll at $300 a month as statistician for the attorney general's office while he continued to be a reporter for the *Item* and *Tribune*. "The *Item-Tribune* had nothing whatsoever to do with my getting the job," Frampton said when the *Times-Picayune* exposed the arrangement.[20]

Whatever the short-term financial bonanza Thomson derived from his relations with Long, the arrangement was ruinous ultimately. The road for Thomson's *Item* was all downhill after 1931. The *Times-Picayune*, the *Item*'s competitor, enjoyed its finest modern journalistic hours in the thirties. A talented and aggressive news staff was too much for the *Item* to cope with. In the business office — and it is true that a newspaper with a strong business office and weak newsroom has a better chance for survival than a paper with brilliant reporters and bumbling management — the advantage of the *Times-Picayune* was even more one-sided. Long sneered at the "lying newspapers," but the *Times-Picayune,* his principal foe, had the grudging respect even of his adherents because the paper's news accounts were known to be accurate.

It is not a question of whether Huey Long was right or wrong. Some of his ideas are now deeply rooted in the social and economic structure, and the state still reaps benefits from his projects. His bitter opponents tended to be reactionary stand patters. He was a demagogue whose cynical views of governmental morality influenced his followers for years, yet his "every-man-a-king" thesis strikes a responsive chord in the American psyche. The cancer that ate upon Thomson's *Item* was the suspicion with which its operations had to be viewed — by the independent reader who knew of the affiliation with Long as well as by the unhappy public employee who had to spend part of his pay for a newspaper he did not want.

On Sunday night, September 8, 1935, Senator Long was in the House chamber of the new Capitol in Baton Rouge for the opening of a special session of the legislature. He paused at the press table to speak with Frampton. Then he took a seat on the dais beside Speaker Allen J. Ellender, while Frampton went to the governor's office to make a telephone call to his news desk in New Orleans. He was asked to obtain comment from Long on the deaths of scores of World War I veterans who had been killed in a hurricane while quartered, by the Franklin D. Roosevelt administration, in a camp on the Florida Keys. Frampton kept a line open to New Orleans while from another telephone he put in a call to Long in the sergeant-at-arms' office near the House dais. "Wait there, I'm coming to see you," Long told Frampton. Moments passed, and Frampton opened the door to the corridor outside the governor's office to see whether Long was approaching. He looked out just in time to watch from a distance of a few feet as Dr. Carl Weiss went up to Long and shot him with a pistol.

After giving a flash over the still-open line to New Orleans, Frampton ran to Our Lady of the Lake Hospital, near the Capitol, where he found Huey lying on a hospital cart in a corridor. "Chick," asked Long, "who was that that shot me?" "Don't you know?" responded Frampton. The reporter was one of those who ringed the operating room that night while Dr. Vidrine performed surgery which failed to save Long's life.[21]

On a June morning in 1939 F. Edward Hebert, city editor of the *States,* received a telephone call in the newsroom at 601 North Street. He summoned Meigs O. Frost, veteran reporter, and Wilfred L. d'Aquin, a young photographer, to his desk. He gave them instructions and sent them out on an assignment which they turned into the most memorable journalistic feat in the history of New Orleans newspapers.

The call to Hebert was a tip from James A. Noe, a state senator and former lieutenant governor. Noe had been a favorite of Huey Long. After the assassination, however, Long's followers split into factions, and Noe found himself on the opposite side of the political fence from the group of Long's heirs headed by Richard W. Leche, who was elected governor in 1936. Suspecting skullduggery, Noe hired private detectives to uncover evidence. From his sources he learned that window sashes fabricated in the carpentry shop at Louisiana State University were being shipped in an LSU truck to be used in a private residence under construction in Metairie, New Orleans suburb. Noe told Hebert the truck was enroute. Hebert's problem was to substantiate the delivery and produce photographs to prove it, all without the knowledge of the truck driver or the men who were building the house.

D'Aquin obtained a telephoto lens for his bulky, impossible-to-conceal Graflex camera. He and Frost got into an automobile. On a street corner in the business district they picked up Raymond F. Hufft, assistant manager of Noe's radio station, WNOE, in accordance with arrangements made by Noe and Hebert. Hufft could recognize the unmarked LSU truck. The three drove out the old Airline Highway. Before long Hufft spotted the truck approaching. D'Aquin wheeled into a U-turn and followed the truck as it rolled onto Metairie Road, then turned on Livingston Avenue into the Oak Ridge Park area. The truck came to a halt in the yard of a house being built for James McLachlan, a colonel on Governor Leche's staff, on West Livingston Avenue.

D'Aquin drove on, in order not to arouse suspicion, then turned the car around and moved past the house again. The three men noted weed-grown vacant lots back of the house and decided they probably could stop the car on the next street without being noticed. D'Aquin drove to the selected spot and headed the car in the direction for a getaway if they were discovered. Frost, who was elderly and partly crippled, moved behind the wheel and kept the engine running.

Hufft and d'Aquin crept through the weeds toward the truck. They could hear the workmen talking as the window sashes were unloaded. Finally, from a spot about a hundred feet distant, d'Aquin arose to a crouching position which would enable him to focus the clumsy camera. A horse tethered in the yard near the truck kept watching d'Aquin, who feared the animal's actions would direct the attention of the workmen as he clicked away from his exposed position. He shot several pictures, including one on which the numbers of the license plate could be read, and thus identified as an LSU plate.

In later years, whenever Hufft and d'Aquin met, they would chuckle as they recalled how jittery they were until they returned to the car and drove away.[22] Hufft became the most-decorated Louisiana serviceman as a result of his exploits in World War II. He later became adjutant general of the Louisiana National Guard. Hebert left the *States* and won election as United States representative from the First Louisiana District, serving in the House longer than any other Louisianian in history. D'Aquin served more years as a photographer and later was picture editor of the *States-Item*.

On June 9, 1939, the *States* published Frost's news story and d'Aquin's pictures. The disclosure touched off the Louisiana Scandals, and federal investigators moved in. In succeeding months Leche resigned and was sent to prison for his part in the wholesale corruption in state government. James Monroe Smith, president of LSU, was only one of the members of the Long old guard who went to prison. In the next year the reform ticket of Governor Sam H. Jones swept the Long remnants out of office.

The *States* won the Sigma Delta Chi Courage in Journalism award for its coup. Some wondered why the Pulitzer Prize was not forthcoming, but there would be another day when the *States* would be recognized by the Pulitzer awards committee.

The *States* had a part in starting the Huey P. Long era and also a major part in ending it.

13

Antitrust Backfires

In the hushed splendor of the chamber of the Supreme Court of the United States on May 25, 1953, Associate Justice Tom C. Clark read an opinion. It outlined the reasons for a five-to-four decision, a landmark ruling for the newspaper industry in an antitrust action. One vote made the difference. Had the court leaned the other way, there would be no *States-Item* today.

The black-robed justice was announcing, in effect, a death sentence for the *Item* as a separate newspaper competing with the *States.* Five years later the two dailies would be merged into the *States-Item.*

Developments began in 1949 with the purchase of the *Item* from Ralph Nicholson by David Stern III and a group of associates.

Newly arrived from Florida, Ralph Nicholson showed up at the *Item* in 1941, in his early days as publisher, wearing red linen suits and other resort garb which caused some head-turning in a New Orleans where conventional business attire was the norm. He soon caught on, and toned down his appearance. A few days after taking over from James M. Thomson, he called the news staff into a meeting in the city room. I'm going up and down the street visiting advertisers, he said. I'm going to tell them that the *Item* will be covering the spot news. But I'm going to say that we also will publish stories of the *Reader's Digest* type. He meant human interest and background articles such as were featured in the mass circulation magazine. He urged reporters and editors to cooperate in producing a paper with a diversified appeal to readers. To outsiders, Nicholson was a cold, unemotional, aloof figure who could inflict psychic wounds with soft-voiced sarcasm. His employees knew him as an approachable boss, one who never failed to say hello to janitor or editor alike.[1]

Nicholson told John W. Fanz, the business manager, to take charge of the internal operations of the paper. Nicholson himself went out to sell space. One of his first problems was to placate some merchants who were miffed by Thomson's willingness to offer under-the-table discounts to favored advertisers. In Nicholson's time, the *Item's* rate card was followed.[2]

Nicholson was a winner, an opportunist who made it to millionaire status on his own wits and energy. He came to the *Item* with a wealth of varied experience surprising for a man only forty-two years of age.[3] He was born at Greenfork, Indiana, on February 12, 1899. At twelve he borrowed seventy-five dollars from his father and bought a carrier's route on another *Item,* the Richmond, Indiana, *Item.* He kept the route until he was a freshman at Earlham College, a small Quaker School at Richmond. When the *Item* changed from an afternoon to a morning paper, Nicholson sold his route and became a part-time reporter. In the summers he was a book and automobile salesman. He enlisted as a naval aviation cadet in World War I. When the fighting ended he returned to college, graduating a month and a half early in order that he might, at the age of twenty-one, take a job offered by Carl Ackerman, who was establishing a foreign news service for the Philadelphia *Public Ledger.* Ackerman later became dean of the Columbia University School of Journalism.

After a few months in London, Nicholson went to Ireland, where he became a friend of Terence McSwinney, the lord mayor of Cork, whose fast unto death in behalf of Irish freedom was a major news story of the twenties. Transferred to Berlin, Nicholson used his ingenuity to obtain an exclusive interview with Grover Cleveland Bergdoll, the draft dodger, who revealed how he had bribed his way out of the United States. Nicholson sent word to Bergdoll that he had a message for him. When Bergdoll took the bait, Nicholson said the "message" was from his editor, saying the people wanted the fugitive's own story. The result was a notable exclusive. Nicholson spent a year at Harvard University, where he earned a master of arts degree. He returned to the *Ledger* as a reporter, then joined Ackerman in a public relations firm before becoming production manager for the New York *Evening Post.* Next he appeared in Tokyo as general manager of the *Japan Advertiser,* and after a year returned to New York as production manager of the *Telegram.* Ackerman hired Nicholson as manager of the public relations department of the General Motors Corporation. In 1933, Nicholson and David E. Smiley acquired ownership of the Tampa *Times.* Then came the opportunity of taking over the *Item* without investing a dime of his own money. After leaving the *Item* in 1949 Nicholson served in Frankfort as a member of the cabinet of John J. McCloy, high commissioner of the United States zone of occupation in Germany. He was director of the office of public affairs. Upon his return to the United States in 1950, he busied himself with newspaper investments. He spent a period as president and publisher of the Charlotte *Observer,* joined with the Lykes Brothers steamship and land interests of Tampa in buying the St. Petersburg *Independent,* and later took on the Dothan, Alabama, *Eagle;* Troy *Messenger;* Brundidge *Banner;* and the Pascagoula, Mississippi, *Chronicle.* He sold his half-interest in the Tampa *Times* and two radio stations to Smiley for $825,000. Nicholson died at Tallahassee, Florida, on July 10, 1972. Both before and after his tenure in New Orleans, he followed an instinct which led him into profitable situations and, more importantly, told him when it was time to move on.

At first Nicholson left the editorial and news operations of the *Item* in the hands of Ballard and holdovers from the Thomson regime. By 1944 Ballard was getting old, and the publisher decided to bring in outside talent. He recruited Clayton Fritchey, a special writer for the Cleveland *Press* who had worked previously for newspapers in Baltimore and Pittsburgh. On July 17, 1944, Nicholson announced the employment of the thirty-nine-year-old Fritchey as executive editor. Inflation was a worry that lay in the future, and Fritchey accepted the post for $200 a week, a salary that by 1970 would have been scorned by a journeyman reporter. Nicholson also agreed to sell Fritchey an interest in the paper ranging from 2 to 10 percent. When he disposed of the *Item* Nicholson paid Fritchey $22,000 in discharge of the obligation. The bright and restless Fritchey never felt at home in New Orleans, though he remained until 1950. He dressed up the *Item* typographically and carried out Nicholson's ideas of presenting magazine-type features. But his impact was minimal, although he became editor after Ballard retired on January 7, 1947, after forty years on the paper. Ballard died on March 24, 1953.

Increasingly, Fritchey's interest was in national politics. He left the *Item* to become head of public relations for the Defense Department in Washington, served a stint in the White House as an administrative assistant to President Harry S. Truman, was a deputy national chairman of the Democratic party, edited the party's magazine, the *Democratic Digest,* and was press representative of Adlai Stevenson, Democratic nominee in the presidential campaign of 1956. Fritchey later wrote a nationally syndicated political column.

In *Times-Picayune* executive office conversations, Nicholson was referred to as "Cousin Ralph." It was an in-joke, with a double meaning. It was a not-so-sly reference to the fact that he shared a surname with Leonard K. Nicholson, president of the Times-Picayune Publishing Company, and Yorke P. Nicholson, vice-president. He was no kin to the brothers. But in New Orleans slang "cousin" has a connotation all its own. "Patsy" is the word used elsewhere, meaning an opponent that a man knows he can conquer. Cousin — pronounced in South Louisiana as koo-zan — has the additional sense that the opponent won't compete too determinedly because of ties. Nicholson learned that he could make money at the *Item* without challenging the preeminent position of the *Times-Picayune.* There was enough advertising and circulation for his paper. He did not have to wage war on the well-entrenched rival. Nicholson took no initiative toward upsetting the status quo, although he did imbue the *Item* with a professionalism and sense of integrity lacking during Thomson's ownership. The terms of his deal with the International Paper Company forbade publication of a Sunday *Item* for ten years or until the $400,000 note was retired. He might have refinanced the note, discharged his obligation, and been free to go after a share of the lucrative Sunday business. He didn't, and future experience confirmed that his decision was sound. At any rate, for eight years Nicholson was content to get fat on the crumbs, the advertising and circulation leftovers. By 1949 he realized the postwar boom had peaked; the fortuitous circumstances which made the *Item* profitable to him were changing; the time had come to take his winnings and get into a new game.

Once he decided to sell, Nicholson approached Leonard Nicholson and offered his paper to the rival company. "He said he didn't want it. It would be too monopolistic," Ralph Nicholson recalled.[4] He began looking in other directions, and newspaper brokers were told the property was on the market.

It was at a time when David Stern III was footloose and searching for a daily into which he could turn his energies and those of associates who had worked with him on other papers. Stern is the son of J. David Stern, once owner of the New York *Post,* Philadelphia *Record,* Camden, New Jersey, *Courier-Post,* and other dailies. The younger Stern, born at Philadelphia on September 2, 1909, started as a cub reporter on the *Courier Post.* He served apprenticeships in various departments to prepare himself for later assignments as publisher of the *Record* and of the Camden papers. The Sterns scrapped the *Record* as the result of a strike, and in 1947 sold the *Courier Post.* David Stern wrote fiction, including a mystery novel entitled *Stop Press! Murder!* under the nom de plume Peter Stirling, and in his own name was author of books on Francis, the talking Army mule with a gift for military and political strategy. In 1948 Stern spent months in Hollywood preparing the script for Francis' motion picture debut. Afterward he knew he wanted to return to newspaper publishing. He checked the profit and loss statements of available papers across the country. At one point he purchased the building and presses with the idea of acquiring the Seattle *News.* But the deal fell through and Stern was on the lookout again when brokers suggested the *Item.*[5]

Stern began to make inquiries and found that the *Item* passed his preliminary tests. An old friend of the Stern family was

Albert M. Greenfield of Philadelphia, who as chairman of the Bankers Security Corporation controlled City Stores. Maison Blanche, the New Orleans department store, is part of the City Stores chain. "Mr. Greenfield had some knowledge of the New Orleans publishing scene," Stern recalled. "He recommended that we buy the *Item.* He gave assurances he would support us with his advertising." Negotiations with Nicholson were moving toward completion when Stern made the first visit of his life to New Orleans. He was excited by the "stimulating, interesting, cosmopolitan city." He was not frightened by the high mortality of dailies in the city. He had made money on the *Record* in Philadelphia, another graveyard for newspapers. The prospect of competition with the *Times-Picayune* and *States* did not deter him. "I felt I knew how to run a newspaper. I don't mean as a crusader, but as a businessman. I had professional associates, people I felt could operate any newspaper. I was used to competitive battles in New York and Philadelphia. I was used to having an underdog newspaper. If I had had more sense, I would have had more qualms."

Nicholson sold for $900,000 in cash and a $100,000 note. He paid off the paper company debt and took a profit of $600,000.[6] Stern's group put up about $2,000,000, which they raised by obtaining an $850,000 loan from the Jefferson Standard Life Insurance Company, $1,000,000 from the sale of debentures and $1,250,000 from the sale of stock.

On June 29, 1949, the Item Company was chartered in Wilmington, and on June 11 Nicholson's company was merged into the former. The new company was headed by David Stern as president. Eberhardt P. Deutsch, New Orleans attorney, was vice-president and George W. Nelson, a Stern associate, secretary-treasurer.[7] J. David Stern was chairman of the board. The younger Stern owned just over 50 per cent, and other members of his family held another 5 or 6 per cent. Nelson, Irvin M. Orner, Harry Saylor, and George Chaplin, all colleagues of Stern's on other papers, had minor holdings.

Stern was anxious to have local participation in the ownership for the sale of good business relations in the community. He sold an interest of about 20 percent to 15 New Orleanians with gilt-edged credentials in financial and legal circles. Those who invested up to $30,000 each were Eberhardt Deutsch, Monte M. Lemann, Morris Newman, Richard W. Freeman, Edgar B. and Edith Stern, Robert E. Craig II, John Minor Wisdom, Leon Irwin Jr., Albert Meric, Herman Kohlmeyer, Edgar A. G. Bright, Lester F. Alexander, A. Quistgaard Petersen, and J. Freyhan Odenheimer.

Stern did not enter New Orleans with any idea of playing second fiddle. The sweet music of the Nicholson-*Picayune* waltz became an echo quickly drowned out by the dissonance of competition. The Stern management opened up the *Item*'s pages to present more news and features, fortified the staff, and went after advertisers with hard-sell aggressiveness. If there had been any misunderstandings about Stern's purpose, they were resolved three months after the purchase when on October 18 the *Item* announced it would publish a Sunday paper beginning on March 5, 1950.

Then the realities began to become evident. In the first few months, Stern explained, "we spent too much money and we had to retrench. I realized that we couldn't continue to be so lavish because the advertising wouldn't support the expenditures. We had to compromise. We had to cut the garment to fit the cloth." One disappointment was the Maison Blanche linage. The account fell below Greenfield's promise. "I saw Greenfield frequently but was unable to persuade him to live up to what he said he would do," Stern recalled. "I was upset, but I couldn't tell him that I wasn't going to talk to him any more. MB was important to us even if the business did fall short of expectations."

The bare-knuckle fighting in Philadelphia and New York had not prepared Stern and his associates for competing in the city where the Times-Picayune Publishing Company for years had provided an effective advertising medium for merchants. Ironically, it was the *Item* which set a precedent for a practice used to advantage by the rival publishing house. When James Thomson launched the morning *Tribune* in 1924, he instituted a system under which classified advertising was sold only as a unit for publication both in the *Item* and the *Tribune.* Two years after buying the *States,* the Times-Picayune Publishing Company adopted the same plan for selling classified advertising in its publications. In order to have a want ad in the widely circulated morning paper, the advertiser was required to run the same copy in the *States.* Later the company instituted an arrangement whereby an extensive retail or general advertiser in the *Times-Picayune* would be allowed the cheaper volume rate for linage placed in the *States.* Stern found the plan hard to compete against.

As early as 1948 executives of the Times-Picayune Publishing Company had been debating the question of whether to institute the unit, sometimes called forced combination, rate for general (national) advertising.[8] By December 1, 1949, a decision had been made, and it was announced that the unit rate would become effective for general advertising on February 1, 1950. In order to advertise in the *Times-Picayune,* a national business also would have to buy the same space in the *States.*

The move caused consternation at the *Item.* Eberhardt Deutsch, attorney for the company, advised Stern to bring an antitrust suit against the Times-Picayune Publishing Company. The possibilities were too advantageous to be ignored.

First, a victory would result in restrictions on the rival and make the *Item* more competitive. Second, antitrust law provided triple damages for victims of monopolistic practice, offering a potentially rich prize for Stern and his colleagues. Stern said he notified the United States Justice Department that the suit was planned. He was invited to Washington for a discussion. As Stern relates the conversation, Herbert A. Bergson, assistant attorney general, said the government was interested in proceeding against the publishing company. If Stern would drop his suit, Bergson promised, the Justice Department would pick it up. "We were delighted," said Stern. "We really didn't have the money to do it ourselves. It would cost a lot."

Justice Department agents appeared at the *Times-Picayune* and demanded access to the books and correspondence files. *Item* executies helped in the assembly of evidence. On June 14, 1950, the government filed a complaint in the United States District Court for the Eastern District of Louisiana. Defendants named were Leonard K. Nicholson, president of the company; John F. Tims, Jr., vice-president and general manager; Aubrey F. Murray, advertising director, and Donald W. Coleman, circulation manager. They were accused of using the dominance of the company to establish a monopoly and to injure or destroy the *Item*. Illegal acts allegedly included the purchase of the *States* with a goodwill provision in 1933, the institution of the combination rate on classified advertising in 1935, the granting of volume rates in the *States* on the basis of *Times-Picayune* linage, and the adoption of the unit rate on general advertising in 1950. The government charged that the International Paper Company made a deal with Ralph Nicholson in 1941 to scrap the Sunday *Item* in return for which the Times-Picayune Publishing Company entered into a ten-year contract for the purchase of newsprint.

The suit sent a tremor throughout the newspaper world. No fewer than 180 publishers in the United States used the unit rate. There had been rumors that the administration of President Truman was contemplating antitrust proceedings against the Kansas City *Star* and *Times.* Now it was certain that the practice would be tested in the courts. The results could be far-reaching.

The suit threatened the Times-Picayune Publishing Company's preeminent position in New Orleans. It presented the gravest crisis to arise since the company was created by merger in 1914. By force of circumstance, the responsibility for the company's defense and its future welfare were placed into the hands of a thirty-six year old attorney. He was Ashton Phelps, member of a family which had ties with the *Times-Picayune* and its predecessors dating from the late 1870s or early eighties. His great-grandfather, John, was a cotton dealer who came to New Orleans in 1848. His grandfather, also Ashton, appeared in the news in 1881 as one of those involved in the amalgamation of the *Times* and the *Democrat.* He wrote a daily cotton column for the *Times-Democrat,* always beginning with a quotation from Shakespeare. He also was the de facto manager of the paper by the time of the merger with the *Picayune* in 1914, and became the first president of the Times-Picayune Publishing Company. He died on December 12, 1919. His son was Esmond Phelps, a lawyer and a director who exerted great influence on the policies of the publishing company in the period of its ascendency. Esmond Phelps was general counsel for the company, and it was he who began in the summer of 1950 to prepare the defense against the antitrust suit. He died of a heart attack in his office on October 18 of that year, and the stunned directors turned to his son to take the burden of trying to save the company from a serious setback. The name of Ashton Phelps will be found on many pages of the closing chapters of this book. He was to make a decision which changed the course of history for the *States-Item*.

From April 30 until May 17, 1951, the case was tried in New Orleans before District Judge Herbert W. Christenberry. Phelps with Charles E. Dunbar, Jr., a member of his law firm, made the chief presentation for the defense. He was joined as counsel by Henry N. Ess, James C. Wilson, and C. A. Peterson of Kansas City. Since the basic question of the legality of the unit rate was to be answered, the Times-Picayune Publishing Company had invited other publishers who used the rate to join in the defense. An informal group of publishers banded together to employ the Kansas City attorneys.

The chief government attorney was Victor H. Kramer. As the trial proceeded he arose to answer what he said was a suggestion that "we are trying a case which will demonstrate specific damage to the *Item*." "This is not our purpose," he said, "and I am not sure that we could do it if we tried. For example, there has been talk that the *Item* has not been doing well. . . . It is entirely possible. I don't know the answer and am unable to contend either way that that has been due to management problems, that it has nothing to do with the unit rate. For example, they may have lost advertising, may have been wasteful in their expenditures on salaries; I don't know. I am not going to try to answer it. If the *Item* feels it has some grievance against the *Times-Picayune* and it is brought to legal battle then some court, some day, will have to decide it. I am completely uninterested."[9]

He did not introduce into evidence an affidavit by *Item* officials which claimed the paper was losing $400,000 a year.

The government contended that the Times-Picayune Publishing Company operated the *States* at a loss in order to hurt the *Item*. Tims testified that company records showed before-tax profits in 1947 of $2,673,953.73 for the *Times-Picayune* and $476,068.61 for the *States*; in 1948 of $2,698,639.19 and $327,521.40; in 1949 of $3,026,556.64 and $247,836.68. But the Justice Department brought in accountants who said the figures were based on arbitrary allocations, and other bookkeeping methods would prove the *States* to be a loser.

The *Times-Picayune* and *States* were pictured by the government as separate newspapers and by defense counsel as morning and evening editions of the same paper. The government introduced advertising agency representatives who testified that the adoption of the unit rate caused them to place general advertising in the *States* instead of the *Item*. Local automobile dealers and real estate brokers said the unit rate on classified advertising worked to the advantage of the *States* over the *Item*. The government tried to elicit testimony to show that the International Paper Company required Ralph Nicholson to scrap the Sunday *Item* in 1941 as part of a scheme to obtain a ten-year newsprint contract from the Times-Picayune Publishing Company. Both Nicholson and William N. Hurlbut, paper company vice-president, refuted the government version.

On May 27 Judge Christenberry held all of the defendants except Coleman guilty of violating the Sherman Antitrust Act. He dismissed the charge against Coleman.

"These papers are separate and distinct and have always been considered so by defendants," Christenberry wrote. He noted that after the unit rate was instituted, general advertising in the *States* increased by more than 30 percent in 1950. "Some advertisers completely abandoned use of the daily *Item*, while others reduced their linage in that newspaper, as a result of the forced unit rate on general advertising." The judge said, "The corporation is able to enforce the unit rate only because of the dominant position which the *Times-Picayune,* the tying product, occupies in New Orleans and in the New Orleans trading area."

"It was also the intention of the defendants," he ruled, "to restrain general and classified advertisers from making untrammeled choice between the afternoon newspapers in purchasing advertising space, and also to substantially diminish the competitive vigor of the *Item,* the *States'* only competitor in the afternoon field."

On two points, the defendants won. "I find nothing in the evidence which would indicate, much less establish, that the *States* at any time was operated at a loss," said Judge Christenberry. The government also failed to convince him that there was a plot to force abandonment of the Sunday *Item.* He did not mention this allegation in his opinion.

The judge ordered the *Times-Picayune* Publishing Company to abandon the unit rate and to sell space in either of its papers at the choice of the advertiser, without any tie-ins.

While Phelps prepared an appeal to the United States Supreme Court, the company's directors began planning the adjustments that would be made if the lower court were upheld. It was decided that the *Times-Picayune* would be operated as an all-day, around-the-clock newspaper. This is a daily with morning and evening issues in which the same advertising is presented but news content and features are changed in succeeding editions. An all-day *Times-Picayune* would have meant the end of the *States* and, of course, the *States-Item* never would have been published. The *States* staff would have devoted its energies to the task of producing the evening editions of the *Times-Picayune.*

At the *Item* the Christenberry opinion was greeted with elation. Stern talked with attorney John Minor Wisdom about filing a triple damage suit once the Supreme Court acted.

Later Stern expressed the belief that the reins placed by the judge on the rival company would have been more important to the *Item* than a triple damage award. "If his opinion were allowed to stand it would have changed the picture. It would have let us compete."

Stern watched and listened as the appeal was argued in Washington on March 11, 1953, before the justices of the Supreme Court. "I wanted to hear the proceedings because it was an important decision. I thought the *Times-Picayune* would lose."

To Phelps fell the task of convincing the court that the district judge erred in his conclusions. He contended that the unit rate was a reasonable and desirable trade practice. He was supported in an argument by John T. Cahill, representing ninety-eight publishers in twenty-five states whose own business practices were in jeopardy. Robert L. Stern, assistant to the solicitor general, made the appearance for the government. Edward O. Proctor, attorney for the Boston *Post,* supported the Justice Department's views.

On May 25, two and a half months after the arguments, Phelps answered the telephone in his office in the United Fruit Company building at St. Charles and Union Streets. "You won!" boomed the voice of George W. Healy, Jr., editor of the *Times-Picayune,* relaying an Associated Press bulletin. Not more than a hundred yards away, in the *Item* building at 722 Union Street, Stern was informed at about the same time of the news that the Supreme Court had overturned Judge Christenberry's decision. "I was amazed. It was a tragedy to the country. It was the last blow to competitive journalism, and competitive journalism is healthy in a democracy," said Stern. The action ended dreams of a triple-damage windfall. It also signaled the beginning of the end of the *Item* as an independent newspaper competing with the *States,* although five years would pass before Stern bowed out.

Justice Tom C. Clark, who once had been the Justice Department's prosecutor in antitrust cases, wrote the Supreme Court's five-to-four opinion. The last paragraph made it clear that Phelps had picked his way through a legal minefield in persuading the justices. "This record does not establish the charged violation of Section 1 and Section 2 of the Sherman Act," said Clark and the four justices who concurred. "We do not determine that unit advertising arrangements are lawful in other circumstances or in other proceedings. Our decision adjudicates solely that this record cannot substantiate the government's view in this case. Accordingly, the district court's judgment must be reversed." In other words, the unit rate as administered by Phelps's client was permissible. Long afterward, a consent decree in a Kansas City *Star* case set restrictions on concessions that may be offered in unit rate situations. And as Stern remarked in 1975: "It's a moribund question now. There's not enough competitive journalism left in the United States for it to make any difference."

Justice Clark's opinion said: "Here . . . two newspapers under single ownership at the same place, time and terms sell indistinguishable products to advertisers; no dominant 'tying' product exists (in fact, since space in neither the *Times-Picayune* nor the *States* can be bought alone, one may be viewed as 'tying' as the other); no leverage in one market excludes sellers in the second, because for present purposes the products are identical and the market the same. . . . In short, neither the rationale nor the doctrines evolved by the 'tying' cases can dispose of the publishing company's arrangements challenged here." The court noted that the *Item* sold general display space to more advertisers in 1950 than in 1949. "The *Item* flourishes. . . . The *Item,* the alleged victim of The Times-Picayune Publishing Company's challenged trade practices, appeared, in short, to be doing well."

Repercussions from the suit persisted. Phelps had earned a

place in the inner circle of policy makers to which his grandfather and father belonged. Leonard K. Nicholson died on October 19, 1952, while the appeal was pending. Conscious of the approaching end, Nicholson wrote what amounted to a deathbed memorandum in which he suggested that Phelps succeed him as president. Phelps declined. He was enjoying his law practice, and he felt that John F. Tims was fully capable of heading the company and had earned the opportunity to do so. There would be another opportunity, another time, for Phelps.

Members of the *Item* news staff crowded around a teletype printer while it clicked out the story of the Supreme Court's decision. Then they scattered to their desks, or out of the building to search for headlines. They had no time to mope, even though they read the news with foreboding. Deadlines were approaching for new editions, each one a skirmish in a circulation war that had been waged against the *States* every working day since Major Henry J. Hearsey put the first issue of the competing journal onto the streets on January, 3, 1880.

Competition had intensified since Stern appeared on the scene. Salaries were better, standards higher. The *Item* had come a long way since the James Thomson ownership when a reporter heading out for an interview was handed fourteen cents for round-trip streetcar fare.

Stern and Fritchey got a taste of Louisiana politics in June, 1950, when the state Senate cited them for contempt as the result of an *Item* editorial that said legislators "have about as much independence as trained seals. When their trainer barks, they jump." The two were haled before a Senate committee and subjected to belligerent questioning. Memories of more violent days in New Orleans journalism were evoked when one senator clinched his fist and started to swing at Fritchey, only to be restrained by others. Once tempers cooled, the Senate voted not to jail the publisher and editor, to "leave it to the subscribers, the advertisers, the stockholders and to the good, plain citizens of Louisiana to deal with Mr. Stern and Mr. Fritchie."[10]

A few weeks later Fritchey resigned. George Chaplin moved up from managing editor to editor. Chaplin began an association with Stern during World War II. He was editing a Pacific edition of *Stars and Stripes* in Honolulu, and Stern was assigned to his staff. Chaplin was the leader of the *Item*'s news and editorial forces during the last eight years of head-and-head competition with the *States* for street sales and home-delivered circulation.

It was a spirited contest, one of the last confrontations in the dwindling list of cities where rival afternoon dailies were published. Editions of both papers were scheduled to reach vendors simultaneously. The goal in both city rooms was an intriguing headline that would catch the eye, never mind the substance of the news story on which it was based

For the early editions, the ones designed for street sales, the battlefield more often than not was police headquarters, where both papers centered their search for a salable story. The *States* depended on veteran reporter Richard J. (Jack) Dempsey, who knew almost every officer on the force by his first name, to provide the first tip on a major crime, and then to follow through with inside information from detectives and beat men. The *Item*'s counterpart was Benjamin Franklyn (Ben) Hay, a wily operator whose sources were as numerous as Dempsey's. Dempsey's first act, long before dawn, was to deliver coffee and doughnuts to the crew in "65," the complaint room. They were the officers to whom he looked for the first word that something was happening. No secretary of state ever conducted foreign policy with more secrecy than that with which Dempsey and Hay covered their maneuverings. Both reporters used subtle persuasion to load their stories with the names of policemen, catering to the vanity of old-fashioned officers who liked to be quoted, or at least mentioned. New rewrite men on the *States* were startled to discover that notes dictated by Dempsey contained the identities of more policemen than criminals. Nothing was more fleeting than the first edition sensation of a holdup, shooting, or automobile accident. Sometimes a news story which rated scare type across the top of page one at 9 A.M. was shunted to the want-ad section in the more sedate home-delivered edition, if indeed it found a place at all. On an unusually dull day the story might be resurrected for the final edition, when headlines again were needed.

Dempsey was a sometimes prizefight announcer and radio reporter with a voice like thunder. He liked to regale listening policemen with a dramatic rendition of the facts as he telephoned an account to the city desk, beginning with an order to "stop the press" and directions to "put it on page one with stars around it." "Better than 'Dragnet,'" murmured one rookie officer after hearing a performance.

Chaplin emphasized bright writing and offbeat features and also sent his reporters on investigative missions which resulted in exposes. One of his ploys was to work with free-lance investigator Jack Richter, who turned up damaging information against individuals in a scandal-ridden police department. Chaplin imported Mickey McDougall, a gambling detective who told readers of the crooked dice and marked cards used at illegal gambling establishments in New Orleans and the suburbs.

At the *States,* Frank C. Allen, managing editor, and Walter G. Cowan, city editor, stressed the coverage of hard news. The *States* always peaked on a day when there was a disaster or startling political development to report. Allen's paper dug up its share of government scandals and was a long-time watchdog that signaled the periodic outbreak of gambling.

In the two presidential elections held during the Stern-Chaplin administration, the *Item* endorsed Democratic nominee Adlai Stevenson. The *States* followed the lead of big-brother *Times-Picayune,* broke the Hearsey-Ewing Democratic tradition, and backed Republican Dwight D. Eisenhower. The *Item* attacked the witchhunt of Senator Joseph McCarthy. Chaplin was proud of the fact that no prosegregation editorial was printed during his editorship. All in all, the *States* was more conservative, undoubtedly more faithfully reflected prevailing community attitudes, and as a result probably was held a little more credible in the eyes of the average New Orleanian.

It was a newspaper atmosphere straight out of *The Front Page.* To get a story first was a triumph. And to humble the other paper — by exploiting an angle that eluded the opposition — was the ultimate. Tenseness built up in the *States* city room as the time neared for a runner to deliver the newest edition of the *Item.* When he appeared, the comparable *States* was on the press, and it was too late to recoup if the *Item* had an exclusive, although sometimes frantic telephone calls would produce a face saving bulletin in a replate edition. A page-one story, no matter how trivial, that the *States* could not match sent Frank Allen striding in frustration across the room to the water fountain six times in ten minutes. Hilarity prevailed after hours in the Marble Hall bar across Lafayette Street from City Hall if the *States* stole a march. The mood at Abadie's, on Carondelet Street, reflected the *Items* fortunes for the day. It was a time of snap judgments, of making decisions under deadline pressure. An editor often had to assess fragmentary information and give an order that later would make him look ridiculous if his instinct failed him. An opportunity for calm reflection was a luxury enjoyed only occasionally. It was a time of exultation or despair. It was a cliff-hanging existence in which fascinated newsmen of both papers reveled.

It also was the closing innings of the game that began in 1880 — although the players themselves did not realize it then. The energetic rivalry of the news staffs was only a spinning of the wheels. Neither side won a clear-cut advantage, but that didn't really matter. The issue already had been decided in the courts and in the business offices. Justice Clark's decision shattered Stern's hopes.

The fate of the revived Sunday *Item* was a straw revealing that the wind was blowing against Stern. Brought out on March 5, 1950, as a regular Sunday paper printed on Saturday night, the first issue had seventy-two pages in addition to thirty-two pages of comics — "The World's Biggest Comic Section" — and the *American Weekly* magazine. The price was fifteen cents. By December 17 the size had shrunk to fifty pages, plus an eight-page Hadacol advertising section, the comics, and the *American Weekly.* It was the last gasp for a regular Sunday *Item.* On Saturday, December 23, at the regular edition times for a Saturday afternoon paper, the *Item* produced a "weekend edition" that bore a Sunday dateline. It had only thirty-six pages, plus comics and magazine, and was offered at ten cents. Even before the antitrust suit was filed, Stern had failed in his attempted invasion of the Sunday market.

The extent of the Sunday paper debacle is measured by the figures for the first fiscal year of Stern's operation. For the period ending June 30, 1950, the company lost $367,571. In the next fiscal year the deficit was $175,910. Then followed annual profits of $75,633, $04,417, $114,983, $117,043, $162,818 and $68,348, the last figure being for the year ending June 30, 1957.[11]

As the years went by Stern began to find the pressures intolerable. Rising costs hurt. "We had all of the unions; the opposition did not," Stern recalled. "The opposition paid the same salaries, but that was only the tip of the iceberg. We had to deal with nine unions. There was constant agitation, arbitration and negotiation. The cost of maintaining these was a major factor. I kept telling the unions that they were going to destroy the weaker paper, but they wouldn't pay any attention." The share of advertising revenue that Stern was able to capture had to cover mounting expenses. The *Item* was handicapped because local display advertising could be bought in the *States,* with a comparable circulation, at a volume rate earned by using space in the *Times-Picayune,* admittedly the essential medium for a New Orleans merchant. "There was a question of whether the *Item* could continue to exist with the *Times-Picayune* in control and rigging rates," said Stern. "They could have forced out any competition. Maybe somebody who wanted to operate a newspaper as a crusade could continue. But I didn't have that kind of money. I made my living as a publisher."

By the middle 1950s television had developed in New Orleans as a rival to newspapers, both as an advertising outlet and as a claimant to public attention. Station WDSU-TV had been on the air since December 18, 1948, and was prospering to the point where there was a scramble to obtain licenses to open stations on other channels. The Times-Picayune Publishing Company competed unsuccessfully for Channel 4, which the Federal Communications Commission awarded in 1957 to Loyola University. Eventually there would be four commercial stations and one public television station in operation. The impact of television not only added to the problems of the *Item,* but also made it obvious, from a business standpoint, that one morning and one evening daily, under joint ownership, best could compete with the new electronic gadget in the living room. There was nothing unique about the situation in New Orleans. Throughout the land, competition among newspapers either had ended or was destined to cease. In city after city, one publishing company had supplanted all others.

Monopoly? In a sense. An evil? Not necessarily, not in the eyes of merchants who fail to advertise in a competing journal or readers who neglect to subscribe to it when by doing so they could keep it alive. What kind of newspaper can be trusted to keep a capitalistic society informed except one that exists as a business venture and profits because it has earned the confidence and support of a community? The alternatives are journals subsidized by government, political party, or special interest — all much more concerned with persuading than with dispensing information. Monopoly? Not when five television stations and a dozen or more radio stations load the air all day and most of the night with news reports, editorials, and advertising, as well as entertainment.

The flight to the suburbs had begun in New Orleans as in the rest of the country. In the years ahead the bedroom communities of Jefferson Parish, particularly, and also of St. Bernard and St. Tammany parishes would boast a multiplying population while the census count of the city itself remained static. Shopping centers inevitably sprang up amidst the suburban residential developments. In the major metropolises promoters already had demonstrated the profitability of shopping guides, free weekly papers that are distributed to all families in a designated area. They are not mere handbills, but are papers which sugar-coat the advertisements with news and features. It would not be long before the throwaways blanketed the larger New Orleans suburbs. No longer did urban dailies have a monopoly on the distribution of printed advertisements — by far the most effective medium for retail merchants because they alone allow the listing of prices on a wide range of products. On television or radio a recitation of prices is a dreary exercise that results in quick knob-turning.

The changing population pattern and economic developments presented circulation problems not encountered by the distribution of the early *Item* and *States*. In the late nineteenth-century, New Orleans, because of drainage and flood control necessities, had a dense population in a small geographic area. By 1958 residential neighborhoods sprawled over vast stretches of former swampland on both banks of the Mississippi. The mechanics of getting papers thrown onto the front porches of subscribers had grown complicated and expensive. Traditionally, afternoon newspapers have been delivered by schoolboys who make their rounds between the end of classes and suppertime. They can handle only small routes in the two or three hours available. Income potential is restricted because the price of the product is small. By the fifties the competition for the services of boys in the carrier age range was intensified. Supermarkets, for instance, need baggers.

The migration of middle-class white families to the ranch houses and breathing room of the suburbs was accompanied by the pressure from the burgeoning black population. Inevitably, the character of neighborhoods changed. Blockbusting was quickly followed by the substitution of black for white faces. The Supreme Court's school desegregation decision of 1954 was much too recent to have affected the level of education of blacks. Newspaper reading habits vary on the basis of schooling. College graduates depend on the printed word much more than do the dropouts, who look to television and radio for whatever knowledge they have of current events. The subscribers on whom the *States* and *Item* had depended were moving to the subdivisions where they were harder to reach. It would not be too long in the future before marauding toughs added to the difficulty of enlisting carrier boys for once-serene routes.

Meanwhile, wages and newsprint prices, the chief costs in the newspaper industry, spiraled ever higher.

Within three years of the Supreme Court decision in the antitrust case, it became obvious to directors of the Times-Picayune Publishing Company that the reluctance shown in previous years to acquisition of the *Item* was out of date. At the same time, the figures in the ledgers weakened David Stern's resolve, although he wanted to stay in New Orleans. The cost of operating the *Item* was $50,000 a week when Stern took over in 1949. By 1958 expenses ran to nearly $100,000 a week.[12] Newsprint cost $104 a ton in 1949 and was up to $134 in 1958. Stern also had a personal problem which kept him away for frequent periods. His wife, Louise, became ill, was disenchanted with New Orleans, and moved to Princeton, New Jersey. Stern often went to Princeton to be with her. His absences were not an overriding factor, however. His associates believe it would not have saved the *Item* had he spent every day calling on Canal Street merchants.

By the end of 1956 directors of the Times-Picayune Publishing Company were discussing the advantages that might accrue from the purchase of the *Item* and its merger with the *States.*

At the same time, Stern was seeking a way out. He talked with Ralph Nicholson, who offered a million dollars more for the *Item* than the figure for which he sold it, provided that he also could buy the *States.* A newspaper broker told Stern that S. I. Newhouse would pay $4 million or more for the *Item,* but only if the *States* also could be purchased. Stern explored the possibility of acquiring the *States* himself and was told that the Times-Picayune Publishing Company had turned down all offers. The *States* was not for sale.

In August, 1957, while the news, advertising, and circulation staffs of the *States* and the *Item* were continuing to wage their unending warfare, secret talks were begun to discuss an amalgamation of the two papers. The negotiators were Stern and Tims. Tims, for the second time in his life, was representing the *Times-Picayune* in the purchase of an evening daily. He had also acted as the go-between in 1933 when the morning paper acquired the *States*.

Tims and Stern set up a preliminary meeting in the privacy of a room at the Roosevelt (now the Fairmont) Hotel. It was the first of numerous conferences held in the hotel, where the publishers could get together in secrecy with little chance of exciting curiosity. Stern described the first session as casual. "At the time I didn't regard it as a momentous moment," he said.

Memories of the antitrust suit had not faded, and Tims insisted from the start that the purchase would have to be cleared by the *Item* with the Justice Department. It would be Stern's responsibility to qualify the *Item* as a failing newspaper, justifying the sale to a competitor as an alternative to bankruptcy. The Times-Picayune Publishing Company would take no part in dealings with the department.

The *Item* management approached the Justice Department early in 1958 with a presentation to show that Stern's position had become untenable.[13] The talks continued, and by June attorneys could cite figures to show that the paper indeed was in jeopardy. The operating loss for the first five months of the calendar year 1958 was $70,473.[14]

Since the *Item*'s outlook was gloomy, it was unlikely that any outsider would become a prospective purchaser. The higher the asking price, of course, the less likely it was that any feelers would be received from others. Stern's bargaining point in talking with Tims was the nuisance value of the *Item* to its competitor. In the prevailing circumstances it made business sense for Tims's company to operate without a competitor.

The *Item* would be a more valuable asset to the Times-Picayune Publishing Company than it could be to an independent proprietor.

On the evening of July 13, 1958, Chaplin went to his home at the corner of Octavia and South Rocheblave streets feeling depressed over a secret to which he was privy as a director and as editor of the *Item*. The family's television set was tuned to Channel 6 for the newscast of William B. Monroe, a former *Item* editorial writer. Among his stories was a report that the *Times-Picayune* was about to buy the *Item*. "What is going to happen to us?" wailed the Chaplins' young daughter, Jerri. After a near sleepless night, Chaplin drove to the French Quarter, parked his automobile near the St. Louis Cathedral, and sat for an hour. He recalled some of the high points of the *Item-States* competition in which he had been a combatant for nine years. But mostly he sorrowed at the thought of leaving New Orleans, a city he had taken to his heart. Chaplin then went to Eberhardt Deutsch's law office in the Hibernia Bank Building and joined the other *Item* directors in signing papers for the provisional sale of the *Item* and its assets.[15]

The price was $3,400,000 cash, out of which all obligations of the *Item* had to be paid. At the insistence of the Justice Department, the transaction was approved with one stipulation. For sixty days the *Item* had to be offered for sale at the same figure to any other bidder who could finance the deal and also was willing to reimburse the Times-Picayune Publishing Company in the amount of up to $75,000 to cover the company's expenses in negotiating the purchase. It was, of course, a futile gesture which reflected the Justice Department's sensitivity to the provisions of the antitrust laws. Who else would pay $3,475,000 for a paper with the *Item*'s prospects?

The Justice Department also required the Times-Picayune

Publishing Company to agree that it would not impose the unit rate on general advertising for a ten-year period, "except in the event of changed conditions of such magnitude as to constitute a substantial handicap." The company was allowed to grant reasonable discounts on advertising voluntarily placed in the morning and evening editions.

For two months the 425 employees of the *Item* managed to carry on business as usual while most of them were searching elsewhere for jobs. All would receive severance pay in accordance with union contracts. Hardly a corporal's guard would be taken on by the already fully staffed *States* and the *Times-Picayune.* Stern's management set up an employment bureau. By the time the waiting period was over, some 90 percent of the workers had been placed. There were a few sidelights to an otherwise grim routine. Columnist Hermann B. Deutsch, believing he would not be taken on by the *States,* began a "farewell" series of reminiscences, only to make an awkward switch in tone when he learned that his column would be picked up.

The charade on which the Justice Department insisted finally was acted out on September 14 without a nibble from another prospective publisher. In a farewell statement published on page one of the last *Item* under his control, Stern cited union troubles, rising costs, and the antitrust decision as having contributed to his decision to sell. He also mentioned merchants. "In the past several years many advertisers have not felt that their stake in competitive journalism was sufficient to warrant fair support of the *Item.* An increasing portion of their advertising expenditures is going to media other than newspapers." The last solo issue was number eighty-two of he *Item*'s eighty-second year.

On Monday, September 15, the first issue of the *New Orleans States-New Orleans Item* was produced in the plant of the Times-Picayune Publishing Company at 601 North Street. Before long the cumbersome title would be reduced to the *New Orleans States-Item* and eventually to *The States-Item.*

New name notwithstanding, the paper still was basically an afternoon edition of the *Times-Picayune.* Judge Christenberry had ruled that the *Times-Picayune* and *States* were separate papers. Employees knew better. Long years still remained before the afternoon paper would be allowed to go its own separate editorial way.

14

A House Divided

New Orleanians stared in surprise at a headline when they unfolded the Red Flash, the home-delivered edition of the *States-Item*, on Tuesday, May 29, 1962. "Offer Made to Purchase T-P Stock," said the two-column line over a news story reporting that S. I. Newhouse, owner of a group of sixteen newspapers, had bid more than the market price for a majority of shares in the company that published the *States-Item* and the *Times-Picayune*.

The disclosure brought into the open a splintering conflict in the company ownership. One of the corporate takeover fights so prominent in the business world in the 1960s was being staged in New Orleans. This one attracted special attention, not only locally but nationwide as well. Newhouse's offer was the largest ever made until that time for a newspaper property. Even by the standards of the conglomerate era it was a deal of respectable size. More important, in generating local interest, were the personalities involved. The families in control of the Times-

Picayune Publishing Company has had interests in the city's newspapers ever since reconstruction times — the Nicholsons, Howards, Phelpses, Hyamses, Morrises — big names in a city where tradition counts not only socially but also in business.

There was an additional facet to titillate those who understood the maneuvering. It was a showdown between some of the major stockholders and management, between owners and employees. Suspenseful days followed.

By the early 1940s the highly profitable *States* and the *Times-Picayune* became obvious prizes for outside publishing interests with an eye on expansion. The company was particularly vulnerable because large parcels of stock created in the 1914 merger of the *Times-Democrat* and the *Picayune* were held by half a dozen owners. In a few key transactions, a majority of the shares could change hands. Leonard K. Nicholson and other directors with New Orleans roots were worried over the possibility of losing control. They set up an impregnable defense by forming a voting trust, dated December 27, 1943. The effect was to put the company into the keeping of a group of trustees, and to prevent the sale of trust shares to outsiders. A majority of the stock was pledged to the trust, which was approved by the Securities and Exchange Commission. The original trustees were Leonard K. Nicholson; Yorke P. Nicholson and his wife, Amie Boyd Nicholson; George H. Terriberry; Edgar B. Stern; Esmond Phelps; Mrs. Alvin Pike Howard; Edith Allen Clark; John A. Morris; C. H. Hyams III and Ira B. Harkey. Leonard Nicholson was elected chairman at the first meeting of the trustees on April 10, 1944.

The original trust was supplanted on June 12, 1952, by a new trust which again included a majority of the stock. The new trust had a provision, as did the old, that it would continue for a term of ten years and could be extended for an additional ten years by action of the owners of a majority of shares included in the trust. The establishment of a new trust required approval of owners of a majority of all the stock issued by the company. But an extension of ten years could be obtained by the vote of just over one-half of the shares already in the trust. In effect, the owners of about one-fourth of all the stock would have the power to keep the trust alive from 1962 until 1972. The provision would take on extreme importance a decade later.

Since the original trust had made the company safe from assault, Leonard Nicholson was mindful of its effect, on May 16, 1952, when he drew up a will designating his son, Jerry K. Nicholson, as his principal heir. "I request, but do not require, my executor and or my trustees to vote the said Times-Picayune Publishing Company stock in favor of any new voting trust, or of the continuation of the present voting trust," he wrote in the will.[1] Five months later, on October 19, 1952, he died.

Cracks began to develop in the trustee structure even before the new trust was formed. Yorke P. Nicholson had died on February 23, 1948, and his elder daughter, Eleanor, later Mrs. Carl McArn Corbin, was elected a trustee in his place. Until her marriage she served on the *Times-Picayune* staff as a reporter, drama and motion picture critic, and amusements columnist. She asked no favors because of her family connections, had a mind of her own, and became imbued with the idealistic newsroom philosophy that sees a newspaper primarily as an agency to inform and advise the public rather than as a profit-making enterprise. In her view, and also in the opinion of her mother, management was putting too much emphasis on the business side of the operation. They complained that the Times-Picayune Publishing Company was losing face in New Orleans.

They directed much of the blame at John F. Tims, Jr., the

executive vice-president and general manager, who moved up to president and publisher upon the death of Leonard Nicholson. Longstanding personality differences may have influenced their feelings. Tims had been close to Leonard but not to Yorke Nicholson. As the years went by Leonard more and more looked to Tims for counsel, sometimes calling him in for conferences at which Yorke, a company vice-president, was not present.

A century of New Orleans journalism has produced no success story to rival the rise of Tims. Office boy to chairman of the board, he made the climb on his own legs. His career spanned the period from the time the *Times-Picayune* was formed from the amalgamation of the two ailing morning newspapers until the company had absorbed its last rival and stood unchallenged in the New Orleans field. His contribution to the success was acknowledged by his employers, who gave him promotions and policy-making powers.

Tims was hired by the Nicholson Publishing Company in 1910 to be an office boy at the *Picayune.* By the time of the 1914 merger he was an advertising solicitor. As a salesman and then advertising director, he was on the firing line in the critical late teens and early twenties when the *Times-Picayune* was establishing its mastery over James M. Thomson's *Item.* Effective as he was as a space salesman, Tims had even more skill as a manager in charge of the overall operation of the morning paper and after 1933 the evening paper as well. He won a reputation in the newspaper industry for his acumen. He knew how to get maximum output from men and machinery, how to hold down costs, how to keep step with improvements in production methods. To employees whom he considered loyal and hardworking he was a benevolent boss. He had little patience with those regarded as shirkers or agitators, yet he fired few men in his lifetime. His policy was to pay competitive wages and to expect performance. His long-time lieutenant, Robert E. Gough, was his alter ego, his eyes and ears, a sponge able to soak up details which could be used to advantage in the company's operations. Tims was a product of the business office. The news and editorial functions admittedly interested him less than the profit-and-loss statements. He was not unique in this respect. For every reporter who emerges as a top executive on a newspaper, there are half a dozen, and maybe a dozen men, who make their way up through the advertising, circulation or production channels. There has to be a financially sound showcase for displaying the brilliance of editorial gems. Gifted editors often neglect to acquire the know-how for running a business.

Tims did not fit into the staid mold perhaps expected of *Times-Picayune* executives by his critics. Most mornings a discreet employee delivered to his desk a copy of the *Racing Form* concealed in a photo envelope. He would pick his horses and send out his bets, all the while taking care of his business duties. He sat in on high-stake poker games at the New Orleans Athletic Club with cronies, most of them members of the newly prosperous segment of the business community. The son of a city tax assessor, Tims never lost his zest for politics. He operated with the instincts of a politician: reward friends and punish enemies. He was accessible to politicians, from governor down to ward heeler. Mayors, senators, congressmen, and legislators sought his advice and prized his comradeship. Dignified, affable, well-groomed, recognized for his civic efforts, he was, nevertheless, not invited to join the clubs in which the stock-owning hierarchy of his company circulated. Perhaps it was a penalty he paid for being born in New Orleans into a political family. Newcomers with fewer credentials were accepted into membership. In New Orleans, family background is important; this is a heritage both from the Creoles and from its Solid South geography.

The unanimity with which the voting trustees habitually

functioned was broken on November 19, 1951, when Mrs. Yorke Nicholson and her daughter Eleanor opposed a motion to allow the board of directors to purchase company stock with company funds and to hold it as treasury shares or to reissue and dispose of it. "My opposition is to the broad scope of the power with its absence of controls and limitations," said Mrs. Nicholson. "This could provide an opportunity for a future board to abuse the interests of the stockholders — an opportunity that has not existed in the past. I feel that the proposed undefined authority to purchase for no specific purpose is unwarranted." Clearly, Mrs. Nicholson and Mrs. Corbin were suspicious of managements' motives. The vote was nine to two against them.[2]

By 1959 Ashton Phelps had been elected chairman of the voting trustees whom he had joined as a member after the death of his father. Other new members included Jerry Nicholson, in place of his father; Mrs. Ashton J. Fischer, the former Elizabeth Nicholson, younger daughter of the Yorke Nicholsons, succeeding her mother, who resigned; and Alvin H. Howard, in place of his mother, Mrs. Alvin Pike Howard, who resigned. At a meeting on February 12, 1959, the trustees were scheduled to elect a successor to trustee Robert G. Robinson, who had died. During this session came the break which in the end resulted in the dissolution of the trust. The selection of Tims was foreordained. But Mrs. Corbin offered a written motion in which she said:

> I feel that the position of Voting Trustee is vastly different from that of an employee. Because as the prospectus says: "The control of the Trust is vested in persons who are in control of the Corporation because of their ownership of a large part of the stock thereof." . . . I feel that the chances of this Voting Trust being continued into the future depends on us, the Voting Trustees, choosing a person on whom we can agree. . . . For the protection of the Voting Trust — and even more important for the protection of the respected position this newspaper has always occupied in this community — I feel that the man who replaces Mr. Robinson should be a

man like Mr. Sunny Jim Robinson — and like you other Voting Trustees here today. He should be a man with a reputation for integrity. A man who is respected by the other leading citizens of New Orleans.[3]

Mrs. Corbin nominated Sam Israel, Jr. There was no second. The vote was nine to one in favor of Tims, whose own holding of 607 shares was small but who was a trustee for the estate of Leonard K. Nicholson which included more than 25,000 shares. Ballots in favor of Tims were cast by Jerry Nicholson and Elizabeth Nicholson Fischer.

Tims was incensed over Mrs. Corbin's statement. Ashton Phelps suggested to Mrs. Corbin that in the interest of harmony she withdraw her remarks from the minutes. She refused to do so. The exchange set the stage for an explosive meeting of the trustees on November 16, 1959, which turned into a confrontation between Mrs. Nicholson and Tims. Perhaps no bridges were burned that day, but the sparks were flying.

Tims had the floor first, to read a statement starting with an expression of appreciation for his election. "I feel that this is an expression of confidence in me; in my integrity and in my devotion to this publishing company, which I soon will have served for half a century. I feel that it bespeaks your confidence in the respect in which I am held by the leading citizens of New Orleans." He noted that Leonard Nicholson had demonstrated confidence in him, citing a letter written by the latter on June 20, 1939, when Nicholson was going on a month's vacation. "I have left Mr. John F. Tims Jr. in charge of the newspapers," Nicholson had said. Tims reminded that Nicholson had assigned him to negotiate for the purchase of the *States* in 1933. "I was led further to believe that I enjoyed the respect and confidence of Mr. Nicholson when he named me one of the trustees in his will for his son, Jerry." Tims continued:

To the best of my knowledge the present board of directors had implicit

> faith in my ability from August, 1957, through May, 1958, the period during which I negotiated for purchase of the *New Orleans Item.* During the many months of these negotiations I made a full disclosure to members of our board of directors of discussions between Mr. Stern and myself. . . . I feel, in all modesty, that I played some part in establishing this trust, as it was out of discussions between myself, Mr. Nicholson, Mr. Phelps and a few others that it was born. I feel that the voting trust is the greatest safeguard we have against these newspapers falling into undesirable hands.

Tims concluded by quoting a letter from John D. Ewing, who said: "Certainly if it had not been for your square and friendly competition with the *States* it could not have been purchased from me in 1933."[4]

Next it was the turn of Mrs. Nicholson, appearing with the proxy of Mrs. Corbin, who was unable to be present. Mrs. Nicholson read a prepared statement:

> I had considered asking to speak before you, even if she had been able to come, for I have been so shocked and indignant at the pressure brought on Eleanor to retract her vote opposing the new trustee, Mr. John F. Tims Jr., and to have her statement taken out of the minutes, that I wanted the opportunity to join her in this statement, and to say that had I still been on the voting trust, there would have been two no's to record, and an even stronger statement. I want to explain that this opposition is not personal, but instead Eleanor's vote was a matter of principle, and stemmed from her conviction that the election of Mr. Tims as a trustee would not be for the ultimate good of the publishing company.
>
> As such her opinion should have been respected, and her vote allowed to stand. That some of you were so concerned about this obscure record, with its opposing vote, and so persistent in trying to have it changed, raises in my mind the question of whether you also aren't doubtful about your choice — and its effect on the stockholders. In my opinion you have not chosen wisely, but with expediency — and have turned from the high ideal of regarding a newspaper as a public trust, to being satisfied, and even gratified, with a successful commercial organ, a good money-making enterprise.
>
> I do hope I have been able to make you feel and understand that it is the paper we are thinking about — both papers, *The Times-Picayune* and the *States-Item*. It is their interest we have at heart. Eleanor was thinking of

them as she cast her vote, especially of *The Times-Picayune*. She was remembering her grandmother, her grandfather, her father, her Uncle Leonard, and how long the name Nicholson has been associated with this newspaper. She felt she had been handed a high trust, and that what she decided or did could only be with her honest convictions. Would you have wanted her to have done anything else? Should she be penalized for that, and subjected to all this pressure to retract her vote?

That she has been, is conclusive evidence to me that from now on, there will be no freedom of opinion or choice on the voting trust. I feel I have been grossly misled. My confidence has been sorely shaken. I have been made to regret that I ever entered into the voting trust agreement.[5]

Phelps said he had told Mrs. Corbin he thought it would be in the best interests of all concerned if she agreed to delete from the minutes the statement she made about the election of Tims. At no time, Phelps added, had he asked Mrs. Corbin to change the minutes with respect to her vote or her nomination of Israel.

Heated as was the exchange between Mrs. Nicholson and Tims, it did not prove to be the climactic event in the eventual breakup of the trust. A year later, on November 21, 1960, the voting trustees held their annual meeting. Those present discussed the question of whether the existing trust should be renewed for ten years or whether a new trust should be formed with a potential life of twenty years. The minutes reflect no dispute, saying it was the consensus that a new trust was preferable. Since the support of a majority of holders of all the stock would be needed for a new trust, it was obvious that at the time no major opposition was expected.[6]

Phelps, Tims, Jerry Nicholson, and Alvin Howard began to do the groundwork necessary for the formation of a new trust. Tims and Phelps went to New York in an effort to persuade Mrs. Chapman H. Hyams, Jr., owner of 21,700 shares, to join in a new trust. Mrs. Hyams, who had kept her stock out of the existing trust, told Phelps and Tims she would not go along with the new plan. But the two were more successful when they arrived in Washington to talk with the eighty-four-year-old Miss Edith Allen Clark, who with 28,340 shares was the largest individual stockholder. Miss Clark received her stock as an inheritance from her father, Charles S. Clark, a New York newsprint broker who died in 1926. According to company legend, Clark acquired an interest in the *Times-Democrat* or one of its predecessors in payment of a $4,000 bill for newsprint. It was an investment with Midas-like results. In 1961 alone, his daughter received $127,530 in dividends from the Times-Picayune Publishing Company. Miss Clark participated in the original trust and the new trust of 1952, and indicated she would pledge her holdings to the trust proposed by Phelps, Tims, and the others.[7]

A twenty-two page document with terms of the proposed trust was drawn up and presented at a routine meeting of the company's finance committee at International House. Phelps, Tims, and Howard were flabbergasted when Jerry Nicholson commented: "Have you checked this with Miss Clark? I understand she will not sign it." It was the first intimation that Nicholson would not be a party to a new trust or an extension of the existing one.[8] Months later, at a meeting of the trustees on November 20, 1961, he read a statement explaining his position. He said he intended no reflection on Tims, "who has managed our company very effectively and his record speaks for itself." He said he did not believe anybody would be able to buy the newspapers as long as management was fair to stockholders, "and I believe there is less danger of a sale now than there was previously." The company faced no "excessive competitive abuses," he wrote. He commented that the intent of the first trust was to "insure perpetual control by large stockholders" and that the proposed trust did not accomplish this purpose. He complained that the trust depressed the price of company stock, adding that management and trustees should be directly responsible to stockholders.[9]

The other trustees learned that sometime in advance of the finance committee meeting Nicholson had gone to Washington and spent several hours with Miss Clark. They believed he had asked her to oppose the trust. Nicholson said, "Actually, she persuaded me." He explained that her attorney had asked the advice of officials of the National City Bank of New York, "and they were against the trust."[10]

Without the participation of Miss Clark and Nicholson, the future of the trust was clouded. Mrs. Yorke Nicholson already had made it clear that her side of the family was disenchanted. The holdings of Miss Clark, Jerry Nicholson, and the Yorke Nicholson family added up to a total of 87,424 shares, almost one-third of the company's total issue of 280,000 shares. The prospects of pulling together the 140,001 shares needed for a new trust became nearly hopeless. The two Nicholson branches owned 69,084 shares of the 180,557 in the existing trust. Unless Miss Clark would go along, there apparently would not be enough stock even to extend the trust for ten years.[11]

The change of heart by the thirty-one-year-old Jerry Nicholson caused consternation. Tims wrote that Nicholson had indicated he preferred a new trust but would support an extension, and his announcement was "an immense surprise to all of us." "Whether this is because of his ambition to receive assurances that he will be the next president of the company, or for some other reason, we do not know, but it seems that he is desirous of some commitments which the present directors certainly feel, in the light of his present state of readiness, are not justified." Howard was even more emphatic. "I for one would think it is high time that we stopped playing the role of a bunch of nursemaids for this boy," he wrote. "If we ever let somebody like this ever get control of the paper we had better bail out fast."[12]

A breakup of the trust would, of course, open the way for a

reshuffle of the directorate and management. Most of the trustees had substantial investments in the company which they wanted to protect. Tims's own career hung in the balance. Large stockholders were opposed to him.

At this time, and later, Jerry Nicholson disclaimed any burning desire to be president of the company.[13] Apparently he felt, however, that Tims, Howard, and Phelps were making decisions without consulting him as the owner of 27,099 shares, the second largest block. There was no indication that the two Nicholson branches ever would pool their holdings and present a united front. They were not close socially and did not always see eye to eye on company policy. Except in the period immediately preceding the deadline set by Newhouse on his offer to buy the stock, the two branches operated independently. The side headed by Mrs. Yorke Nicholson regarded Jerry Nicholson's break with Tims as an attempt by him to gain control. Mrs. Nicholson wanted neither Tims nor Nicholson in a position of power.

Throughout the spring and summer of 1961 Phelps, Tims, and Howard tried to work out a plan for salvaging the trust. They knew the battle would be won or lost on the decisions of Miss Clark and Mrs. Hyams. With the votes of both, a new trust might be formed without the Nicholsons. With the support of Miss Clark alone, the existing trust might be extended. The key figure was W. Gwynn Gardiner of Washington, Miss Clark's octogenarian attorney. Phelps wrote to remind Gardiner that in 1960 Miss Clark had favored a new trust. Gardiner replied that she had changed her mind. In July a group of voting trustees went to Washington for a conference with Gardiner and Melvin Gordon Lowenstein of New York, Mrs. Hyams' attorney. Although Lowenstein said he would advise Mrs. Hyams to come in, Gardiner listened to the arguments of the *Times-Picayune* representatives and stood pat. He said in a memorandum to Miss Clark: "I have made a thorough investigation and the present management of the *Times-Picayune* is excellent, and should not be disturbed. On the other hand, I have told them that it was cruel to expect you to put your stock in the Hibernia National Bank and permit them to manage it for 20 years without any control over it, and without any right to determine its costs since all of that was vested in the voting trustees." He said if Miss Clark wanted to sell her stock she would get only half-price for it because other trust members had a monopoly and would not bid against each other.[14] Appeals directly to Miss Clark were unproductive. At one point Howard told her the success of the company under the trustees was demonstrated by the fact that in 1961 its net income would exceed the combined profits of all New York City newspapers. In the end both Miss Clark and Mrs. Hyams refused to yield.[15]

After Jerry Nicholson read his statement to the trustees on November 20, 1961, Howard moved that preparations be made for a meeting on June 11, 1962, for the purpose of extending the trust.[16] It was a session that never would be held. The demise of the voting trust was inevitable. Too many people knew about the crisis for it to be a secret. A chain of events was set into motion. It would gather momentum until in a climactic five weeks of activity the voting trust issue would be settled once and for all.

In February, 1962, Jerry Nicholson received a telephone call from G. Shelby Friedrichs, a partner in the investment firm of Howard, Weil, Labouisse, Friedrichs & Company, which was headed by Alvin H. Howard. Friedrichs said he had an inquiry from Allen Kander, newspaper broker who was acting in behalf of S. I. Newhouse. Kander wanted to know whether Nicholson was interested in selling his interest in the Times-Picayune Publishing Company. "My stock is not for sale," replied Nicholson.[17]

The fateful period was begun on May 2. Friedrichs was

attending a directors' meeting in Hot Springs, Arkansas. He was summoned to the telephone to receive a call from New York. Kander was on the other end of the line. He said Newhouse believed the time might be ripe to make a bid for the New Orleans papers. Friedrichs telephoned Howard, and the brokerage firm began to make inquiries to determine whether enough stock could be purchased to give Newhouse control.[18] At the time, the voting trust held a majority of shares out of reach. But on May 8 all of the Nicholson interests and Miss Clark joined in signing an instrument that terminated the trust.[19] The climax had been a long time abuilding; the denouement would be swift and inexorable.

Newhouse came to New Orleans on May 15. He met with some of the large stockholders, promising that if he succeeded in purchasing a majority interest, the papers would remain under local control. Later he wrote to Tims as follows: "Please be assured that you will be continued as president of said company for as much time as you may desire. You are further assured that I will maintain intact the present management and personnel of both *The Times-Picayune* and the *New Orleans States-Item* and that complete freedom of operation of said newspapers will remain in their hands. There will be no change of policy concerning the operation of said newspapers without your approval."[20]

The Times-Picayune Publishing Company in 1961 netted $2,482,907.14, a return of $8.87 per share out of which dividends of $4.50 were paid. In two years the price of the stock on the over-the-counter market had ranged from a low of $110 bid to a recent high of $135. Newhouse discussed with Friedrichs the price to be offered. He finally settled on a figure of $150 a share. He was told that Mrs. Alvin Pike Howard had acquired her shares when the price was much lower and would have to pay a whopping capital gains tax. At $150 she could pay the tax and still realize a return approximating the recent market price. Friedrichs told Newhouse a canvass indicated that at least 51 percent of the stock could be purchased at the $150 figure.[21]

Jerry Nicholson later said his first inkling of the Newhouse offer came from Mrs. Hyams, with whom he had an agreement that each would notify the other if approached. On the day before the *States-Item* printed the first news story about the proposed purchase, the board of directors met. Nicholson read a statement in which he referred to rumors that he was trying to acquire control. "It seems logical to believe," he said, "that these have been instigated by persons who are interested in getting control at the lowest possible price. I am having these false allegations investigated." He insisted that "no changes in management were contemplated or thought necessary by those who elected to terminate the trust." He continued: "I am angered to hear rumors that the management approves acquisition of our papers by Mr. Newhouse. I have talked to most of the major stockholders and the majority do not want to sell. I do not wish to sell." He moved that the president be instructed to write to all stockholders stating that management has not recommended the sale. Stockholders who did want to sell would be asked to offer their shares to the company. A committee would be formed to determine the desirability of having the company buy any stock offered. If the directors then decided in favor of allowing an outsider to take over, competitive bids would be asked. Nicholson said a price of $150 a share was too low.[22] Carl M. Corbin, editor of the *States-Item* and Eleanor Nicholson's husband, seconded Nicholson's motion, although he had not known about it in advance of the meeting. The vote against the proposition was seven to two.[23]

Ashton Phelps was introduced to Newhouse for the first

time shortly before the purchase offer was publicized. He urged the publisher to buy all of the stock tendered rather than a mere majority. Newhouse agreed to do so. Phelps expressed his thoughts in a letter to a stockholder who asked his advice about selling:

> I am thoroughly satisifed, having met Newhouse, that local autonomy will be maintained. Naturally, a man with a $40,000,000 investment is bound to make some suggestions as to business management, but I do not believe we will be confronted with any curtailment of editorial prerogative. . . . I have felt that it was inevitable that someone would buy up several of the large blocks of stock outstanding and control the company. My principal hope was that, when this occurred, the present employees, who were so responsible in building the property, would also be protected. The interests of my family at the time of my grandfather's death was worth about $13,000. Today it is worth over $1,000,000. I cannot help but feel a tremendous sense of responsibility to those who made this possible. Their protection is a paramount consideration. My feeling therefore is that it would be preferable, if control must pass from the present owners, to see it go to a responsible publisher, of a high type, who has committed himself to protect the employees and small stockholders.[24]

Phelps added he had no assurance from Newhouse as to his own continuation as general counsel for the company.

Newhouse's formal offer, made public on May 29, set a deadline for acceptance as of 2 P.M. Monday, June 4. New Orleanians watched with fascination the maneuvering that ensued. The Nicholson family, sometimes united and sometimes going separate ways, made a last-ditch campaign to persuade stockholders to keep their shares. Allied against the Nicholsons were most of the voting trustees and company directors.

Mrs. Yorke Nicholson, her two daughters, and Jerry Nicholson sent a letter to stockholders in which they said they terminated the voting trust because they "came to realize that it had become controlled by only a small percentage of stockholders."

> The effect of this termination has been to return to the individual stockholder his right to vote his stock and to be heard in the councils of the

company. We now understand that those very voting trustees and directors who urged continuance of the Voting Trust in order, so they claimed, to keep the control of the policies of the papers in local hands are now urging the sale to Mr. Newhouse of Newark. . . . It is a matter of common knowledge that policy is dictated by ownership rather than management. We are firmly of the opinion that the interests of the stockholders generally can be protected only on two conditions: first, a full disclosure of financial information concerning the company, and second, an explanation of the facts and circumstances by those directors, who heretofore desired to continue the voting trust for the stated purpose of preserving local control, which now cause them to favor a sale to Mr. Newhouse.[25]

Their point about full disclosure of financial information referred to the fact that the company's treasury contained stocks and bonds worth about $12 million. The sale of these liquid assets would reduce the cost to Newhouse for all 280,000 shares from $42 million to $30 million.

The crisis came at a time before the proliferation of newspaper chains, a day when the thought of absentee proprietorship raised a specter of a politically ambitious multimillionaire with his own philosophies to peddle, an arrogant press lord who knew little about community problems and cared less. Another decade would pass before Knight-Ridder, Gannett, Chicago *Tribune,* New York *Times,* Los Angeles *Times* — and Newhouse himself — would expand their holdings into city after city, and group newspaper operation would prove to be not only sensitive to local conditions but even able to provide a caliber of journalism beyond the capacity of most local publishers. Newhouse was offering to pay $42 million — or $30 million if salable assets were subtracted — for the two newspapers. Later he would spend $16 million to build and equip a new plant. The total represents the greatest investment by one man in any one business property in New Orleans. With so much at stake, how could he be unconcerned with the well-being of the area? He was willing to gamble on his ability to produce papers that would appeal to readers and advertisers. He was not buying a monopoly — not with television, radio, and shopping guide throwaways blanketing the city and its suburbs. But in 1962 the idea of newspapers that were not home owned took some getting used to by New Orleanians, and the Nicholsons planned their strategy accordingly.

Time was running out when Newhouse's bid came into the open. Jerry Nicholson called in Ralph Nicholson, the *Item*'s former owner and then publisher of papers in Alabama, to help in the effort to thwart the purchase.[26] The move took the Yorke Nicholson branch by surprise, and was greeted with coolness by that side. All of the Nicholsons came together, however, at a meeting in the office of Garner H. Tullis, securities broker, at which the prospects of enlisting local financiers to form a syndicate to counter the Newhouse bid were explored. Among those consulted were Richard W. Freeman and Darwin H. Fenner. The reception was cordial, but it was apparent that a deal of such magnitude could not be put together in less than a week.

Meanwhile, Friedrichs and his associates were conducting an urgent sales campaign by personal visit, telephone and telegraph. Friedrichs kept a tally showing a steady climb toward the majority sought by Newhouse. Jerry Nicholson and Ralph Nicholson tried in vain to line up holdouts into a new voting trust. Years afterward, Jerry Nicholson said they came within 1 percent of attaining the required majority of stock.[27]

Friedrichs' penciled notes show that at 4 P.M. on Friday, June 1, Tims reported that a total of 2,090 shares owned by company employees could be depended upon. At a point between 4 and 9 P.M., Newhouse's goal was reached. Friedrichs' notes timed at the latter hour show 153,232 shares counted as safe. Friedrichs' total included Mrs. Hyams's stock. At that time Miss Clark had not tendered her holding.

Late in the day, when he was convinced the sale was going through, Friedrichs telephoned Mrs. Jerry Nicholson, the former Harriet Smither. Friedrichs was a long-time friend of her family. He told her the deal was certain, and advised that Jerry sell his shares while Newhouse's offer to buy all of the stock tendered was still in force. A few minutes later Friedrichs received an indignant telephone call from Edward B. Benjamin, Jr., a Nicholson attorney. Why did Friedrichs say that Newhouse had achieved a majority, demanded Benjamin. "Because he has," replied Friedrichs.[28]

The most dramatic meeting of a tense week came on Saturday, June 2. It was an anticlimax, but not all of the participants realized it at the time. Mrs. John B. Hobson III, a New Orleanian who was not a stockholder, but who was upset by the prospect of the loss of the papers by local owners, paid an unannounced visit at about 9 A.M. to the home of Alvin Howard. "Can't you do something?" she asked him. Howard said he would be willing to discuss the situation. Mrs. Hobson made a number of telephone calls, and a session was scheduled at 10 A.M. at the home of Mr. and Mrs. Corbin, 290 Walnut Street. Those who attended included Mrs. Yorke Nicholson and her daughters and sons-in-law. Harry McCall, Jr., one of Mrs. Nicholson's attorneys, was summoned from a tennis game and appeared in playing clothes. N. P. Phillips, another attorney for the Nicholsons, was on hand. Sidney W. Provensal, Jr., attorney for the Ashton Fischers, came from the lake in yachting garb. Howard and Ashton Phelps were present. Jerry Nicholson did not attend. Mrs. Hobson was there for the start, but left before the two-hour conference broke up.

Mrs. Nicholson said she now would be willing to enter another voting trust, even though to do so meant accepting Tims as president of the company. She made it clear that she felt this would be a lesser evil than the alternative of outside ownership. It became clear as the discussion continued that the move was too late; nothing could be done to halt the sale.

That evening Mrs. Nicholson and her daughters sent telegrams to stockholders. "We no longer have a basis for hope that majority control ot The Times-Picayune Publishing Company by Samuel I. Newhouse can be prevented," they said. "Consequently we feel an obligation to inform other stockholders who may have been resisting sale that it is our intention reluctantly to sell our stock on Monday."[29] On Sunday, Jerry Nicholson made the same announcement. "I still believe our newspapers should remain in local hands and are worth more than $150 per share. However it is my sad duty to advise you that I am forced to sell my stock to Mr. Newhouse at $150 a share in order to avoid the untenable position of a minority stockholder with Mr. Newhouse, as majority stockholder, in complete control of our papers."[30] All of the Nicholsons made their decision with the knowledge that Newhouse's policy was not to pay large dividends from his operations.

The action by the Nicholsons ended the opposition. Before the next week ended Newhouse had acquired all but a handful of the 280,000 shares. The Times-Picayune Publishing Company was reorganized as the Times-Picayune Publishing Corporation, totally owned by Newhouse. The success of the old company was reflected in comparative figures. In 1914, when it was organized, seven thousand shares of stock were issued with a value of $100 each. In 1962 the value of each $100 share had grown to $6,000. And over the forty-eight-year span owners had collected rich dividends as well. Newspaper publishing in New Orleans no longer was a nickel-and-dime business.

On Tuesday, June 5, Jerry Nicholson wrote his resignation as treasurer and director.* As he laid the letter on Tims's desk the president looked up. "Wait a minute, I want to talk to you," Tims told Nicholson. "We have nothing to talk about,"

* Ashton J. Fischer, the husband of Elizabeth Nicholson, resigned as an advertising salesman.

replied Nicholson, walking out.[31] On the same day Newhouse visited the plant for a meeting with department heads. Tims introduced Corbin. "You know that I am a member of the family that opposed the sale," Corbin told Newhouse. "It was your privilege to do so," said the new owner, "and I hope you will stay on, both as editor and as a member of the board of directors."[32] Corbin remained until 1965, when he resigned because he felt he was under pressure from Tims. By then Tims had reached the summit. He was, as Newhouse had promised, in complete charge of the two dailies. He was the sole boss, so far as editorial policy and business operations were concerned.

The *States-Item* became part of a conglomerate which includes newspapers, magazines, television and radio stations, and a newsprint plant. Employees seldom see the owner, and many fail to recognize him when he takes a quick tour through the newsrooms and production and business offices on one of his infrequent visits. Newhouse was born on May 24, 1895. At the age of sixteen years he became manager of the Bayonne, New Jersey, *Times*, and turned the faltering paper into a money-maker. He was only twenty-six when he bought a majority interest in the *States Island Advance*, the first acquisition in building what has become the second-largest newspaper group in the United States.

"I am not interested in molding the nation's opinion," he has said in explaining his hands-off policy. "I want these newspapers to take positive stands of their own. I want them to be self-reliant."

His brother, Norman Newhouse, lives in New Orleans and maintains an office in The *Times-Picayune* building. He spends two or three days each week in Cleveland, Ohio, and in Alabama, in connection with his duties with the Newhouse papers.

S. I. Newhouse's offer for the New Orleans papers was

pictured by opponents of the purchase as a bargain basement price. It was a wise investment, as the passing years have shown, but by ordinary business standards he paid at least the going rate. Allowing for the liquid assets, he spent $30 million for a return that in the previous year was $2,500,000 — a price-earning ratio of eight to one. Capital expenditure of $16 million for a new plant and equipment made the ratio even higher. In retrospect, Jerry Nicholson said he believes the sale by local owners to have been inevitable in the light of changing business conditions and the tax structure. He pointed out that dividends are fully taxable, whereas capital can be put into new ventures that provide tax benefits. He said he himself is better off financially than he would have been had the company remained under the same ownership.[33]

The *States-Item,* meanwhile, continued its accustomed place in the shadow of the *Times-Picayune,* endorsing the same political candidates, taking the same stand on public issues, a hapless business example of the younger son under the law of primogeniture. It would not always be thus.

15

Out of the Shadow

"The concept of a William Randolph Hearst sitting in San Simeon and dictating policies as far away as Baltimore, Md., is totally foreign to the Newhouse concept of publishing."

Ashton Phelps had waited for a propitious moment to make an announcement.

"They have some papers which are Republican, some papers which are Democratic, some papers which are liberal and others which are conservative."

He was speaking on February 17, 1968, from the loading platform of the new *States-Item* and the *Times-Picayune* building at 3800 Howard Avenue.

"In Alabama, they have pro-Wallace papers, and they have anti-Wallace papers. But, in any event, in each instance the paper is designed to suit the needs of its own community."

Behind Phelps on the platform sat S. I. Newhouse, owner of the New Orleans papers, and John F. Tims, chairman of the board. Standing on the pavement below were guests at a reception that marked the opening of the $16 million plant.

"Related to this is the thought in which I am sure each of you will be interested. Ever since The Times-Picayune Publishing Company acquired the *Item* the board has had under consideration the desirability, in the interest of the community, of splitting the editorial policies of the morning and evening papers."

States-Item editors and reporters in the audience glanced at each other in sudden realization that Phelps's next words would be fateful.

"Hereafter, the policies of the *States-Item* and the *Times-Picayune* will no longer necessarily be the same."

There it was. Freedom. Emancipation. A chance to venture into uncharted news areas. An opportunity of bringing a fresh viewpoint to metropolitan problems.

"The mechanics of working this out are still under consideration, but the decision has been made, and it is one of the many happy effects of the new facility which permits a separation of the *New Orleans States-Item* and *The Times-Picayune.*"[1]

On October 3, 1967, Ashton Phelps became the fourth president in the fifty-three-year-old history of the company that publishes the *States-Item* and the *Times-Picayune.* The first was his grandfather, the original Ashton Phelps, who held the office from 1914 until he was forced by illness to retire in 1918. Leonard K. Nicholson was president from that time until his death in 1952, when he was succeeded by John F. Tims. Tims held sway for five years after S. I. Newhouse acquired the company. Failing health made it necessary for Tims to give up his active duties and to take an advisory role as chairman of the board. Tims's last public appearance was at the dedication of the new plant. He died on September 2, 1969.

Phelps was born in New Orleans on December 30, 1913. He was graduated, a member of Phi Beta Kappa, from the Tulane University school of law, and he joined the law firm in which his father, Esmond Phelps, was a principal partner. The elder Phelps had close ties to the publishing company, and his son followed in his footsteps.

When the time came for Tims to turn over the presidency, he and Newhouse knew that the logical successor would be Phelps, provided the attorney could be persuaded to take the job. He enjoyed practicing law, and his reputation had been enhanced by his triumph in the antitrust suit against the Times-Picayune Publishing Company, and as a result he numbered large national corporations among his clients. The salary that went with the post being vacated by Tims was substantially less than Phelps's income from the legal profession. Newhouse and Tims were aware that Phelps could have become president in 1952 upon the death of Leonard K. Nicholson, had he been willing at that time to abandon law, his first love. But in 1967, when Newhouse asked him to run the company, Phelps accepted. "I didn't exactly become fired with journalistic zeal at my father's knee," he muses. Yet he was conscious of his family's long-time prominence in the New Orleans newspaper field, and particularly of his father's leadership in the *Times-Picayune*'s fight against Huey P. Long. The persuasive factor was his realization of the importance of the Newhouse dailies to the well-being and progress of the community.

Phelps likes the give-and-take of editorial conferences and sometimes writes an editorial himself for page one of the morning paper when his own slightly right-of-center opinions arouse strong feelings about an issue. Yet his legal training and his sense of fairness make him willing to concede that there are two sides to most questions.

After his announcement at the building dedication Phelps spent a year getting ready to put the editorial divorce into effect. June 2, 1969, was Independence Day for the *States-Item.* Phelps appointed Walter G. Cowan, then fifty-seven years of age, editor with overall responsibility for the news operation. Charles A. Ferguson, thirty-two years old, was made associate editor in charge of the editorial page. George W. Healy, Jr., who had been executive editor of both papers, was reassigned as editor of the *Times-Picayune,* and his authority over the *States-Item* ended. He later stated that he felt relief over this move.

Cowan gained his newspaper experience on the *Item,* which he joined as a reporter in 1936 as a new graduate of the University of Missouri school of journalism, and on the *States,* where he was employed in 1945 after a hiatus as a railroad public relations representative. He was made city editor in 1946 and promoted to managing editor in 1964 but made responsible to Healy. The soft-spoken, low-key Cowan never had an opportunity to put his ideas into full play until Phelps told him to take over the *States-Item* and give the newspaper a character of its own. He responded with a boldness and willingness to innovate that may have taken Phelps somewhat by surprise, but certainly pleased him. Cowan gave the *States-Item* a new look with a six-column format for page one and principal inside pages, instituted a tabloid amusements and television section, called *Lagniappe,* for the Saturday paper, and even changed the formal name to *The States-Item,* dropping New Orleans from the masthead. He bolstered the staff both in numbers and quality, encouraged editors and reporters to forget old taboos and produce a paper relevant to the social, economic and racial revolution that was in progress. No daily in the South was more responsive to the hopes and aspirations of blacks. How Major Hearsey would have suffered had he seen his old journal eliminate demeaning color references, give Negroes equal dignity with whites in news and editorial columns, and campaign for reforms aimed at educational and economic parity!

Charles Ferguson, a graduate of the Tulane law school, served the *States-Item* as reporter and Baton Rouge correspondent before taking a year off to attend Harvard University as a Nieman Fellow. He returned as an editorial writer. In the 1969 reshuffle Phelps told Ferguson to set the paper's editorial course. He responded by veering from the conservative direction followed during the years of *Times-Picayune* domination and earlier during the Hearsey and Robert Ewing ownership. Ferguson has not hesitated to buck the New Orleans establishment on controversial issues. His editorial opposition was a telling factor in the defeat of plans for a Mississippi River bridge with ramps in the Uptown residential area. He came out strongly against the proposed use of public funds for private schools. The *States-Item* was dovish on the Vietnam War and suspicious of President Nixon in the early Watergate disclosures.

The *States-Item* today is a product of its times, just as Mark Bigney's *Daily City Item* and Hearsey's *Daily States* reflected their era. There is no more resemblance of today's paper to its forebears than there is of modern New Orleans to the community that shook off carpetbag rule. Although their resources were limited, Bigney and Hearsey nevertheless had the advantage of the monopoly of the printed word. There was no other way for citizens to get the news. New Orleanians — the ones who could read — were hungry for fact or fancy, for editorial essays that fed their prejudices, for glimpses of the great outside world, for vignettes reflecting the triumphs and tragedies of human beings like themselves. The table set by Bigney and Hearsey offered, by later standards, a starvation ration. But it was better than famishing. A man who wanted even a modicum of information couldn't do without his newspaper. The newspaper brought the first word about a disaster, an election, a legislative session, a baseball game. A publisher could sell his journal by printing the bare facts. As a result, the demands on reportorial skills were limited. It was enough to tell what happened. A young man could make the grade as a reporter if he was inquisitive, aggressive, and literate enough to write for a not-too-demanding readership. This combination of qualities could be hired a century ago for ten dollars a week. Interpretation and backgrounding were the prerogatives of editors, many of whom were apologists for their political factions, a circumstance well understood by subscribers.

The newspaper buyer learned from the news columns that an event had occurred, and from the editorials he knew whether it pleased the Democratic or the Republican party. He was given no clue as to why the event took place, how it related to other developments, or how it might affect his own life. He got no insight into the personalities involved. In short, there was little to guide him in making his own judgments.

Now, in the last quarter of the twentieth century, the *States-Item* has to appeal to New Orleanians who are infinitely more sophisticated, more highly educated, and better informed than the readers to whom Bigney and Hearsey made their pitches. Citizens are bombarded with television and radio news flashes, broadcast with a speed no newspaper printing and distributing system can match. They do not have to depend upon newspapers alone for a knowledge of current events. The challenge to dailies now is to make themselves indispensable by the breadth and depth of their coverage. The surface is skimmed by the broadcast media. The principal function of a newspaper no longer is to provide a bulletin service, to flash the news to readers who get their first information from the headlines. No longer is the cry "Extra! Extra!" heard on the streets. The latest extra issued by the *States-Item* reported the assassination of President John F. Kennedy on November 22, 1963. This does not mean that newspapers can abandon their duty of reporting spot news. Television and radio announcements do not inform anyone who is not tuned in at the moment, and with so many stations vying for the listener's ear, the chances of any one spot broadcast reaching a big segment of the population are slim. Except in events of transcendent importance or interest, newscasts offer only brief synopses. Therefore, newspapers have to be edited not only for those who have not heard the broadcasts, but also for those who were given only the barebone facts and, if they have any intellectual curiosity, want to learn more about cause and effect.

Motion pictures, good roads and a car-in-every-garage, jet travel, television and radio as entertainment sources, the influx of outsiders attracted by job opportunities, pension plans and welfare programs, compulsory school laws, racial integration, the shorter week and the resultant increase in leisure time, labor-saving devices and frozen dinners which give the housewife an opportunity of reading or listening, the proliferation of paperback books — all these developments have made the time of Bigney and Hearsey a Dark Age in comparison.

Under the editorship of Cowan, the *States-Item* became a newspaper designed to appeal to the New Orleanians of the 1970s. Long before the Watergate scandal won public admiration for investigative reporting, Cowan told Bill Lynch, the Baton Rouge correspondent, to leave routine coverage of the Capitol to the Associated Press, and to become a watchdog over state government. Lynch responded with a series of exposés that had repercussions in state government. A new standard for interpretive coverage of government was set by Jack Wardlaw in recording the adoption of a new state constitution in 1974. The paper's first reporter-at-large, Allan L. Katz, made his byline the one most frequently found on page one as he roamed through the fields of politics, economics, crime, and government. A free-wheeling family section directed by Bettye Anding replaced the old society page that had dealt with debutantes, Carnival, and brides. Inhibitions disappeared as Mrs. Anding's reporters explored such subjects as abortion, drugs, prostitution, unmarried mothers, and gynecology. The social scene is narrated with an irreverence not seen before in a New Orleans daily. Jack Davis stepped on the toes of advertisers and public officials alike in his commentaries on the urban environment and architectural trends. Les Brumfield became the state's leading observer of the natural environment and ecological problems. Richard L. Collin, the Underground Gourmet, became the most controversial columnist in the city. His assessments of restaurants infuriated proprietors who received unfavorable reviews and delighted those who saw new diners flocking to the places that earned his praise.

It no longer is enough to report that the city council voted a 5 percent wage increase for city employees. Now the reader must be told how the money will be provided, whether the budget will be unbalanced, how the new scale compares with those in other cities, how it stands up against the pay rates of private industry, how long the recipients can be expected to remain satisfied, what employees will do with the extra money, whether the political hand of the mayor and councilmen is strengthened. Even expert reporting of events no longer is adequate. *States-Item* reporters are expected to spot trends, to warn readers of approaching decisions pertaining to their welfare. It is a time of specialization, of acquiring background and expert understanding of a particular subject — crime, education, business, politics — that will enable the reporter to enlighten readers. The old-fashioned general assignments reporter who can wrap up a disaster, murder, or trial in a burst of frenetic activity is not the star any longer. The bylines belong to the specialists. The reporting of the early *Items* and *States* is as out of date as the handset type that was replaced by typesetting machines, themselves now given way on the *States-Item* to computerized cold-type composition.

Phelps's announcement that the *States-Item* would go its own editorial way was greeted with some public skepticism, a fact which did not too greatly concern the publisher because he expected the true status to become obvious as time passed and the two papers consistently disagreed on issues and candidates. No announcement was made of the fact that an advisory board, composed largely of men who had served as directors of the Times-Picayune Publishing Company before Newhouse bought the company, was told that its counsel would be sought only in matters relating to the *Times-Picayune.* Phelps asked Cowan whether he wanted a similar board of advisors for the *States-Item.* Cown said no. Cowan and Ferguson are responsible directly to Phelps.

The first major difference between the two papers over politics — and the *States-Item*'s initial election triumph in its new-found freedom came in the campaigning for mayor in 1969, within weeks after the new arrangement was announced. In a formidable field, the candidate whose social and racial philosophy most closely agreed with Ferguson's editorial views was Councilman Moon Landrieu. He was a long-shot because most of his support was centered in the black community, and white voters still were more numerous. Meanwhile, the *Times-Picayune* urged support for Councilman John J. Petre. In the first Democratic primary election Councilman James E. Fitzmorris, Jr., ran ahead, while Landrieu barely squeaked into the runoff election and Petre was eliminated. In the runoff, the *Times-Picayune* swung to Landrieu, who won. Landrieu credited the support of the *States-Item* with being decisive. Without it, he said, he would not have survived the first primary.

It was the *Times-Picayune*'s turn to win one in the 1972 campaign for governor, when the papers again parted ways, as they have repeatedly done in minor elections since 1969. The morning daily gave its nod to Congressman Edwin W. Edwards, while the *States-Item*'s choice in the first Democratic primary was Gillis Long. When Long failed to make the runoff, the *States-Item* turned to J. Bennett Johnston. Edwards prevailed. Johnston, however, established himself as a state political power, and before long he was elected United States senator.

If by 1972 there still was any doubt as to Phelps's commitment to an independent *States-Item,* it should have been resolved by his actions in the presidential election.

The choice lay between the Republican incumbent, Richard M. Nixon, and the ultraliberal Senator George C. McGovern, who took the Democratic nomination away from more moderate aspirants. In editorial conferences Phelps made no secret of his low regard for McGovern's capability and of his deep mistrust of the candidate's policies. The Watergate hurricane which later would blow Nixon out of office was only a hard-to-believe whisper of rumors, and Nixon's reelection by a landslide was an obvious inevitability. Nevertheless, Ferguson said that in order to remain true to its liberal posture, the *States-Item* would have to oppose Nixon. Editorial writers David Snyder and Les Brumfield contended that the newspaper, as a matter of principle, should endorse McGovern, even if the editorial were a lukewarm one. In New Orleans and environs, sentiment against McGovern was so deep-seated as to justify a concern that a newspaper which supported him would alienate many subscribers.

Ferguson, on November 1, 1972, wrote an editorial for publication on page one the next day. It concluded: "We still believe there is room in this country for decency, morality and yes, a little idealism. Indeed at this juncture in our history, we can think of no qualities that would stand us in better stead. That is why we support George McGovern for President."[2] Ferguson discussed the editorial with Cowan, then took the typewritten copy to Phelps's office. Later Cowan went to see Phelps. "I know you are apprehensive about this," Cowan said. Phelps studied the editorial, and handed it back to Cowan with the words: "You fellows do whatever you want to do." The endorsement was printed.

It would be difficult to have a more convincing demonstration that Phelps believes community interests are best served by two different daily newspaper voices. He does not dismiss the possibility that an occasion might arise when he would use his veto power. "I would not allow the *States-Item* editors to take an action which I thought would be ruinous," he said. In view of the McGovern decision, it is not likely that the occasion will come up. When outsiders seek to discuss *States-Item* news stories or editorials with him, Phelps refers them to Cowan or Ferguson. "We did away with the executive editor in order to give the *States-Item* its independence," he says. "There is no point in my taking the place of an executive editor." Phelps said the decision to split the two papers editorially was made with the idea of presenting the view of more than one segment of the population. "It has turned out that *The Times-Picayune* is relatively conservative and the *States-Item* liberal. But it was not necessarily seen that way when the separation was planned. The idea was to present two viewpoints. Conceivably the *States-Item* might have been more right-wing than *The Times-Picayune.*" The publisher is of the opinion that the separation is bearing fruit in the public interest. He feels that the racial revolution in New Orleans has been less violent than might have been expected because the *States-Item* has been consistently sympathetic to the hopes of blacks. The principle of editorial independence has become deeply rooted during the Phelps-Cowan-Ferguson era.

Epilogue

No. 39 Natchez Street* to 3800 Howard Avenue — a mile and a half on the map but an astronomical distance in terms of technology, economics and philosophy. The unemployed printers who banded together to establish the *Daily City Item* could not have found jobs on today's *States-Item* unless they had developed new skills. They set type by land, lifting it letter by letter out of the forms before which they stood for leg-numbing hours. Some lived to take part in the transition to typesetting machines, the clatter of which was the predominant sound in newspaper composing rooms for eight decades. Now the Linotypes and Intertypes are gone from the *States-Item,* banished by electronic marvels, computers that transform a reporter's copy to printable form without the turn of a human hand.

As bright and imaginative as he was, Mark F. Bigney left no editorial comment to indicate that he foresaw all of the changes that have occurred in New Orleans since his time.

* Actually, the building at 39 Natchez Street, which was the *Item*'s first home of its own, was demolished long ago, and the site now is part of a parking lot.

The metropolitan area is five times as populous; $100,000 homes stand in areas where alligators waddled. Yellow fever has been conquered; levees and powerful pumps protect against flood. A racial revolution is reflected in the black faces of shoppers on Canal Street and in the advertisements of stores located in shopping centers that sprang up following the white exodus to the suburbs. The *States-Item* runs to fifteen or twenty times the thickness of the four-page paper cranked out by Bigney's staff. Circulation has increased twenty-fold. A top reporter earns in an hour about as much as Lafcadio Hearn was paid in a week.

As the *States-Item* enters the second century of its existence opportunities are magnified, but so are the problems. Bigney and Henry J. Hearsey, in the early issues of the *Daily States,* had to wrestle every day with the specter of failure. Now the wolf is gone from the door, but the producers of the *States-Item* must cope with the problem of printing a profitable and meaningful newspaper amidst the stresses of the late years of the twentieth century.

Superficially, today's generations are the best informed people who ever lived in New Orleans. Morning, noon, and night a twist of the dial brings a breathless voice on radio capsuling world and local events. On television carefully coiffeured anchor men or women touch on the highlights in word and picture. The listener-viewer is sated, his appetite for news jaded by the once-over-lightly fare offered on the air. But many a listener comes to realize that he has been told who, where, what, and when — not why.

For the *States-Item,* as for other evening newspapers, the challenge is to win the reader's attention away from the flickering screen, to be a community force too compelling to be ignored. In the last quarter of the twentieth century, as in the last decade of the nineteenth, there is an opportunity for the

Joseph Pulitzers and the William Randolph Hearsts, men who sense what will sell. The old stereotyped daily — gray, stodgy, predictable, timid, understaffed, unimaginative — is a candidate for oblivion.

The *States-Item* is a youthful centenarian, partly as the result of an infusion of new blood. Ashton Phelps, Jr., was only twenty-seven years old when he became assistant to the publisher, the fourth in his line to be associated with the publishing corporation and its predecessors. Joseph I. Ross became business manager at forty-two, moving up from the advertising staff. Ferguson, as noted, took over as associate editor at thirty-two. Young and talented fingers tap the typewriter keys in the newsroom. The reportorial staff has been almost doubled since Newhouse bought the paper. A resurgence of interest in print journalism as a career followed the triumph of the reporters who unearthed the Watergate scandals, and a pool of promising college graduates is there to be drawn upon. Mounting costs of labor and newsprint show on newspaper balance sheets, but up-to-date production equipment provides offsetting economies, and no publisher has been more ready than Newhouse to install efficient cold-type devices. The *Daily City Item* came out a hundred years ago in time to take advantage of an upswing in the city's economic fortunes. As the *States-Item* observes its centennial, the outlook for the metropolitan area is bright.

A survey in 1976 showed that the newspaper has its greatest readership in college-graduate, upper-income families. The upheaval that attended the racial integration of New Orleans schools in 1960 has been followed by continuing improvement in education levels. As time goes by an increasing proportion of the population, white and black, will be the kind of enlightened citizens who will want the *States-Item*.

It will be here for them.

Notes

CHAPTER 1

1. *Picayune*, April 25, 1877.
2. *Item*, June 11, 1937.
3. *Ibid.*
4. *Ibid*, June 11, 1902.
5. *Ibid.*
6. New Orleans *Times*, June 12, 1877.
7. New Orleans *Democrat*, June 13, 1877.
8. *Item*, June 11, 1937.
9. *Ibid*, June 11, 1902.
10. *Ibid*, June 11, 1917, June 26, 1927.
11. *Ibid*, June 11, 1937.
12. *Times-Democrat*, May 1, 1886.
13. *Ibid.*; *Picayune*, May 1, 1886.
14. *Picayune*, November 30, 1887.
15. *Item*, June 26, 1927.
16. *Ibid.*
17. *Picayune*, December 15, 1883.
18. *Item*, June 26, 1927.
19. *Ibid.*, June 7, 1937.
20. Edward Larocque Tinker, *Lafcadio Hearn's American Days* (New York: Dodd, Mead and Company, 1925), 48.
21. *Ibid.*, 88.
22. *Item*, June 26, 1927.
23. *Ibid.*, May 19, 1924.
24. Daily City Item Co-Operative Printing Company to John W. Fairfax, December 14, 1878, in Papers of Harry S. Michel, Howard-Tilton Library, Tulane University.
25. *Item*, June 26, 1927.
26. Henry E. Chambers, *A History of Louisiana* (Chicago and New York: American Historical Society, Inc., 1925), III, 367-68.
27. Betty Porter, "The History of Negro Education in Louisiana," *Louisiana Historical Quarterly*, XXV (1942), 784.
28. Succession of Julia Kendall, Clerk of the Civil District Court, New Orleans.

CHAPTER 2

1. Berthold C. Alwes, "The History of the La. State Lottery Co.," *Louisiana Historical Quarterly*, XXVII (1944), 969-76.
2. New Orleans *Republican*, January 2, 1869.
3. Alwes, "History of the La. State Lottery Co.," 981.
4. *Ibid.*, 1020-21.
5. *Ibid.*, 986.
6. New Orleans *Democrat*, June 2, 1878.
7. Alwes, *"History of the La. State Lottery Co.,"* 1022.
8. *Ibid.*, 974.
9. *States*, March 27, 1890.
10. Richard H. Wiggins, "The Louisiana Press and the Lottery," *Louisiana Historical Quarterly*, XXXI (1948), 716.
11. New Orleans *Democrat*, March 8, 1878.
12. *Ibid.*, May 15, 19, 21, 1878.
13. *Ibid.*, April 4, 1879.
14. *Ibid.*, April 8, 1879.

15. Wiggins, "The Louisiana Press and the Lottery," 773, 774.
16. New Orleans *Democrat,* December 23, 1878.
17. Wiggins, "The Louisiana Press and the Lottery," 776.
18. *States,* September 25, 1891.
19. Wiggins, "The Louisiana Press and the Lottery," 777.
20. *States,* September 25, 1891.
21. New Orleans *Democrat,* March 12, 1879.
22. Alwes, *"History of the La. State Lottery Co.,"* 1002.
23. Wiggins, *"The Louisiana Press and the Lottery,"* 774.
24. New Orleans *Democrat,* April 24, 1879.
25. *States,* February 17, 1880.
26. *Ibid.*, March 5, 1880.
27. *Ibid.*, March 11, 1880.
28. *Ibid.*, May 6, 1890.
29. Wiggins, "The Louisiana Press and the Lottery," 799.
30. Alwes, "History of the La. State Lottery Co.," 966.
31. Wiggins, "The Louisiana Press and the Lottery," 797.
32. New Orleans *New Delta,* January 13, 1891.
33. Wiggins, "The Louisiana Press and the Lottery," 1095.
34. *Ibid.*, 817.
35. *States,* August 2, 1890.
36. Wiggins, "The Louisiana Press and the Lottery," 821.
37. *Ibid.*, 821, 824.
38. *States,* February 13, 1891.
39. *Ibid.*, February 17, 18, 27, March 2, 1891.
40. *Ibid.*, March 3, 1891.
41. New Orleans *New Delta,* June 30, 1891.
42. Alwes, "History of the La. State Lottery Co.," 824, 825.
43. *Ibid.*, 832.
44. *Item,* September 6, 1894.

CHAPTER 3

1. *States,* January 3, 1930.
2. Crozet J. Duplantier, "A History of the New Orleans *States"* (M.A. thesis, Louisiana State University, 1956).
3. *States,* January 3, 1930.
4. Duplantier, "History of the New Orleans States."
5. *States,* January 3, 1930.
6. *Ibid.*, January 12, 1880.
7. *Ibid.*, January 23, 1880.
8. *Ibid.*, March 11, 1880.
9. Joseph M. Leveque, in Henry Rightor (ed.), *Standard History of New Orleans,* (Chicago: Lewis Publishing Co., 1900), 279.
10. William Ivy Hair, *Bourbonism and Agrarian Protest in Louisiana Politics, 1877-1900* (Baton Rouge: Louisiana State University Press, 1969), 24-25.
11. Edward Laroque Tinker, "Two-Gun Journalism in New Orleans," *American Antiquarian Society Proceedings* (Worcester, Mass., October, 1951), 14.
12. *States,* January 3, 1930.
13. *Picayune,* January 28, 1880.
14. *States,* September 14, 1924.
15. *Ibid.*, September 20, 1883.
16. Succession of Minor M. Elmore, clerk of the Civil District Court, New Orleans.
17. *States,* July 3, 1898.
18. *Ibid.*, September 14, 1924.
19. *Ibid.*
20. *Ibid.*, September 25, 1891.
21. *Ibid.*, August 13, 1907.
22. *Confederate Military History* (Atlanta: Confederate Publishing Company, 1899), X, 399.
23. *States,* April 26, 16, 1887.
24. *Mascot,* April 30, 1887.
25. *States,* June 7, 1882.
26. Charter of the Daily States Publishing Co., Ltd., Recorder of Mortgages, New Orleans.
27. Succession of George W. Dupre, Clerk of the Civil District Court, New Orleans.
28. Succession of J. Pinckney Smith, Clerk of the Civil District Court, New Orleans.
29. Succession of Robert Ewing, Clerk of the Civil District Court, New Orleans.
30. Charter of the Daily States Publishing Co., Ltd.
31. *States,* March 29, 1882.
32. Issues are in bound volumes at the Louisiana State Museum Library.
33. *States,* January 1, 1895.
34. *Picayune,* January 22, 1895.
35. *States,* January 26, February 6, 1895.
36. *Ibid.*, January 12, 1883.
37. *Ibid.*, November 25, 1896.

CHAPTER 4

1. George E. Waring and George W. Cable, *History and Present Condition of New Orleans, Louisiana,* Tenth Census of the United States (Washington: Government Printing Office, 1881), 5.
2. Joy J. Jackson, *New Orleans in the Gilded Age* (Baton Rouge; Louisiana State University Press, 1969), 22.
3. Norman Walker, in Henry Rightor (ed.), *Standard History of New Orleans,* (Chicago: Lewis Publishing Co., 1900), 100-101.

4. John S. Kendall, *History of New Orleans* (Chicago: Lewis Publishing Co., 1922), I, 407.
5. Thomas Ewing Dabney, *One Hundred Great Years: The Story of the Times-Picayune from Its Founding to 1940* (Baton Rouge: Louisiana State University Press, 1944), 270.
6. Waring and Cable, *History and Present Condition of New Orleans,* 64, 65.
7. Kendall, *History of New Orleans;* I, 401-403.
8. *Ibid.*, 438-40.
9. Waring and Cable, *History and Present Condition of New Orleans,* 5, 85, 5.
10. *Item,* April 8, 1904.
11. Bussiere Rouen, "*L'Abeille de la Nouvelle-Orleans,*" *Louisiana Historical Quarterly,* VIII (1925), 586. Circulation figures in this chapter are those listed in the appropriate editions of *N. W. Ayer and Son's Newspaper Annual.*
12. Joseph M. Leveque, in Rightor (ed.), *Standard History of New Orleans,* 277-79.
13. *Evening News,* May 24, 1879, Vol. I, No. 37, in Howard-Tilton Library, Tulane University.
14. *New Orleans Reference Journal,* April 9, 10, 1883, in Howard-Tilton Library.
15. *Mascot,* September 1, 1888.
16. *Evening Chronicle,* June 13, 1883, Vol. I, No. 73; October 23, 1886, Vol. IV, No. 215, in Howard-Tilton Library.
17. Leveque, in Rightor (ed.), *Standard History of New Orleans,* 282.
18. *States,* February 23, 1885.
19. *Mascot,* May 21, 1887.
20. *States,* January 17, 1887.
21. *L'Opinion,* January 9, 1887, Vol. I, No. 11, in Howard-Tilton Library.
22. *L'Orleanais,* July 8, 1892, Fifth Year, No. 791, in Howard-Tilton Library.
23. Leveque, in Rightor (ed.), *Standard History of New Orleans,* 282.
24. *Evening News,* August 25, 1890, Vol. I, No. 274, in Howard-Tilton Library; Soards' city directory, 1892.
25. Dabney, *One Hundred Great Years,* 313.
26. Leveque, in Rightor (ed.), *Standard History of New Orleans,* 282; *Daily Truth,* March 17, 1894, in Howard-Tilton Library.
27. *Daily Crusader,* July 10, 1894, in Howard-Tilton Library.
28. *States,* February 1, 1898.
29. *Evening Telegram,* February 7, 1900, Vol. XI, No. 127, in Howard-Tilton Library; *States,* June 21, 1900; *Item,* April 4, 1902.
30. *States,* July 3, 1896.
31. *Daily News,* October 9, 1905; Edward Larocque Tinker, "Two-Gun Journalism in New Orleans," in *American Antiquarian Society Proceedings* (Worcester, Mass.: October, 1951), 20-21.
32. *New Orleans America,* October 4, 1905, Vol. I, No. 83, in Howard-Tilton Library.
33. *Picayune,* January 1, 1912, January 18, 1908.
34. *Times-Picayune* and *Dixie Magazine,* July 24, 1960, August 27, 1933.
35. Bound volumes of *Daily Call* in Howard-Tilton Library.
36. Bound volumes of the *Republican* in Louisiana State Museum Library.
37. *States,* August 31, 1887.

CHAPTER 5

1. *States,* March 18, 1891.
2. *Picayune,* July 8, 1881.
3. New York *Herald,* article reprinted in *Item,* November 5, 1890.
4. *Ibid.*
5. John S. Kendall, "Who Killa de Chief?" *Louisiana Historical Quarterly,* XXII (1939), 499.
6. *States,* March 18, 1891.
7. *Picayune,* July 17, 1881.
8. Kendall, "Who Killa de Chief?" 501.
9. *Picayune,* July 8, 1881.
10. *Ibid.*
11. *Ibid.*, July 16, 1881.
12. *States,* July 18, October 1, 1881, May 11, 1882.
13. Kendall, "Who Killa de Chief?" 501; *States,* March 18, October 25, 1891.
14. *States,* October 25, November 7, 1881.
15. *Picayune,* October 14, 1881.
16. *States,* October 14, 1881, April 18, 1882.
17. Herbert Asbury, *The French Quarter* (New York; Alfred A. Knopf, 1936), 405, 406.
18. John E. Coxe, "The N.O. Mafia Incident," *Louisiana Historical Quarterly,* XX (1937), 1106; *Item,* October 18, 1890.
19. *States,* March 17, 1891.
20. Kendall, "Who Killa de Chief?" 511; *Item,* May 7, 1891.
21. *States,* March 6, 7, 1891.
22. *Picayune, Times-Democrat, States, Item,* October 16, 1890.
23. Coxe, "The New Orleans Mafia Incident," 1076.
24. *Item,* October 16, 1891.
25. Coxe, "The New Orleans Mafia Incident," 1076.
26. *Item,* May 7, 1891.
27. Coxe, "The New Orleans Mafia Incident," 1076.

28. *Times-Democrat,* March 1, 1891.
29. *States,* February 21, March 1, 1891.
30. *Ibid.,* March 3, 8, 1891.
31. *Ibid.,* March 5, 1891.
32. *Ibid.*
33. *Ibid.,* March 7, 1891.
34. *Ibid.,* March 8, 9, 1891.
35. *Ibid.,* March 1, 3, 1891.
36. *Ibid.,* March 5, 1891.
37. *Ibid.,* March 2, 6, 8, 10, 1891.
38. *Ibid.,* March 10, 11, 1891; *Item,* April 4, 1891.
39. *Item,* March 6, 1891.
40. *States,* March 12, 1891; Coxe, "The New Orleans Mafia Incident," 1084.
41. *Item,* March 14, 1891.
42. *Mascot,* March 21, 1891.
43. Coxe, "The New Orleans Mafia Incident," 1088.
44. *Ibid.,* 1088.
45. *States,* June 13, 1909 (reproducing Orleans Parish Grand Jury report of May 5, 1891).
46. *Item,* March 14, 1891.

CHAPTER 6

1. *Picayune,* October 30, 1874.
2. *Ibid.,* December 27, 1874.
3. *Ibid.,* September 27, 28, 29, 1886.
4. *States,* January 26, 1890.
5. *Picayune,* March 19, 1891.
6. *Mascot,* March 28, 1891.
7. *Item,* June 7, 1891.
8. *States,* October 20, 21, 1903.
9. *Item,* June 3, 1904.
10. *Picayune,* January 18, 1908.

CHAPTER 7

1. *Item,* May 7, 1891.
2. *Ibid.,* October 12, 1890.
3. *States,* March 6, June 13, 1905.
4. *Item,* May 7, 1891.
5. *Ibid.*
6. *States,* June 13, 1905, March 19, 1891.
7. *Ibid.,* June 10, October 9, 1891.
8. *Ibid.,* March 14, 1891.
9. *Item,* May 7, 1891.
10. *Ibid.,* March 21, 1891.
11. *Ibid.,* March 24, April 3, May 7, 1891.
12. *States,* April 3, 1891.
13. *Item,* November 27, 1920.
14. *States,* June 23, July 15, 1881.
15. *Ibid.,* January 6, 1882.
16. *Ibid.,* May 22, 1883.
17. *Ibid.,* September 9, 1895.
18. *Picayune, Times-Democrat, States, Item,* January 1, 2, 1888.
19. *States,* May 14, 1896.
20. *Ibid.,* January 14, March 13, 1897.
21. *Mascot,* April 22, 1882.
22. *Picayune, Times-Democrat, States,* August 15, 1897.
23. *States,* April 20, 1900.
24. *Picayune, Time-Democrat, States,* October 11, 1899.
25. *States,* January 24, 1900.
26. Succession of D. C. O'Malley, Clerk of the Civil District Court, New Orleans.
27. *Times-Democrat,* October 11, 1899.
28. *Picayune,* October 11, 1899.
29. *States,* October 12, 1899.
30. *Item,* November 27, 1920.
31. Soards' and R. L. Polk & Co., *New Orleans City Directory,* 1881 *et seq.*
32. *Item,* June 11, 1937.
33. *Times-Picayune,* December 3, 1922; *Item,* November 17, 1920.
34. *Item,* November 27, 28, 1920.
35. *Times-Picayune,* October 3, 1922.
36. *Picayune,* February 9, 1888.
37. *Times-Democrat,* January 24, 1894.
38. *Item,* November 27, 1920.
39. *States,* March 30, 1891, April 2, 1906.
40. *Ibid.,* June 5, 1899; *Item,* April 2, 1906.
41. *States,* April 12, 1906.
42. *Item,* April 12, 1906.
43. *States,* February 10, 1887.
44. *Times-Democrat,* January 11, 1894.
45. 45 *States,* May 27, August 19, 20, December 25, 1896.
46. *States,* May 29, 1897, June 4, 8, 9, 1897.
47. *Item,* April 13, 1906.
48. *States,* March 6, 1891.
49. *Item,* April 4, 1891.
50. *States,* March 26, 1881.
51. *Ibid.,* March 28, April 4, 1881.
52. *Mascot,* April 28, 1882.
53. *States,* July 9, December 8, 1885.
54. *Ibid.,* December 26, 1885.
55. *Ibid.,* March 7, July 9, August 8, 1885, August 18, 1886.
56. *Ibid.,* March 6, 1891, November 20, 1895.
57. *Ibid.,* June 13, 1905; *Picayune,* May 10, 1884.
58. New Orleans *New Delta,* December 8, 1890.
59. *States,* March 6, 1891.
60. *Item,* April 13, 1906.
61. *Times-Democrat,* May 24, 1905.
62. *Item,* February 7, 1906, November 27, 1920.
63. Edward Larocque Tinker, "Two-Gun Journalism in New Orleans," *American Antiquarian Society Proceedings* (Worcester, Mass.: October, 25, 1952.)
64. *Item,* June 11, 1937.
65. *Announcement of the First Annual Louisiana Industrial Exposition* (New Orleans, 1899).

66. *Item,* June 18, 1905.
67. *Ibid.,* June 11, 1937.
68. *States,* May 5, 1905; *Item,* July 28, 29, 1905.
69. *Item,* June 11, 1937.
70. Tinker, "Two-Gun Journalism in New Orleans," 26.
71. *Item,* July 15, 1894, *et seq.*
72. *Ibid.,* August 14, 16, 25, 28, 1894.
73. *Ibid.,* July 19, 25, 1894.
74. *Ibid.,* August 23, 1894.
75. *Ibid.,* October 27, 1894.
76. *Times-Democrat,* August 21, 1894.
77. *Item,* August 27, 1894.
78. *Times-Democrat,* June 14, 1894.
79. *Picayune,* June 14, 1894.
80. *Ibid.,* August 23, 1894.
81. *Item,* July 25, August 10, 25, 27, 29, December 5, 26, 1894.
82. *Ibid.,* August 12, 15, November 24, December 14, 19, 1894.
83. *Ibid.,* December 26, 27, 1894.
84. *Ibid.,* October 1, November 30, December 28, 1894.
85. *Announcement of First Annual Louisiana Industrial Exposition* (New Orleans, 1899).

CHAPTER 8

1. *Item,* July 19, 1905.
2. *N. W. Ayer & Son's Newspaper Annual* (Philadelphia, 1904), 335.
3. *States,* September 15, 20, 1904.
4. *States,* September 15, 1904.
5. *Item,* June 7, 1905.
6. *States,* April 2, 3, 1906.
7. *Ibid.,* April 2, 3, 1905, April 2, 3, 1906; *Item,* April 3, June 16, 1905.
8. *Item,* June 18, 1905.
9. Edward Larocque Tinker, "Two Gun Journalism in New Orleans," *American Antiquarian Society Proceedings* (Worcester, Mass.: October, 28, 1951).
10. *Item,* June 18, 1905.
11. *Ibid.*
12. *States,* May 8, 1883, May 23, 1899, June 18, 1905; *Times-Democrat,* January 17, 1884, January 19, March 13, 1894.
13. *Item,* June 7, 1905.
14. *Ibid,* June 13, 1905.
15. *Ibid.,* July 8, 1905.
16. *Ibid.,* May 24, 1906.
17. *States,* May 5, 1905.
18. *Ibid.,* June 10, 1905.
19. *Ibid.,* June 12, 1905; *Item,* June 6, 1905, March 29, 1906.
20. *States,* June 12, 1905.
21. *Ibid.,* June 14, 1905.
22. *Ibid.* June 14, 1905.
23. *Item,* June 16, 1905.
24. *Ibid.,* June 19, 1905.
25. *Ibid.,* June 16, 1905; *States,* June 17, 1905.
26. *Item,* June 29, 1905.
27. *Ibid.,* June 19, 1905.
28. *States,* June 20, 1905.
29. *Item,* August 14, 1905; *States,* February 2, 1906.
30. *Item,* June 11, 1937.
31. *Ibid.*
32. *Ibid.,* November 27, 1920.
33. *Picayune,* February 19, 1908; *Item,* January 6, 1912.
34. *Item,* November 27, 1920.
35. Succession of D. C. O'Malley, Clerk of the Civil District Court, New Orleans.
36. *Item,* November 28, 1920.

CHAPTER 9

1. *States,* November 8, 1885.
2. *Picayune,* September 12, 1874, December 26, 1883.
3. Benjamin Kaplan, "A Study of Newsboys in New Orleans" (M.A. thesis, Tulane University, 1929), 39.
4. *States,* November 8, 1885.
5. *Ibid.,* December 3, 1895.
6. *Item,* November 26-27, 1894.
7. *Picayune,* January 14, 1885.
8. *States,* January 21, 1897.
9. *Item,* December 25, 1917; *Times-Picayune,* October 5, 1946.

CHAPTER 10

1. *Harlequin,* April 12, 1906.
2. *States,* December 29, 1902.
3. *Item,* January 1, 1903.
4. *Harlequin,* August 23, 30, 1906; *States,* August 25, 1906.
5. *Harlequin,* April 5, 12, 1906; *States,* April 8, 1906; *Item,* April 10, 1906.
6. *States,* January 3, 1930, April 28, 1931; John S. Kendall, *History of New Orleans* (Chicago: The Lewis Publishing Company, 1922), II, 788.
7. Margaret Ann Martin, "Colonel Robert Ewing, Louisiana Journalist and Politician" (M.A. thesis, Louisiana State University, 1964), 56, 62.
8. Transcript of Record, *United States of America* vs. *The Times-Picayune Publishing Co.,* Federal District Court, New Orleans, 191 *et seq.*
9. Philip Guarisco, interviews, 1975.
10. Transcript, *U.S.* vs. *Times-Picayune Publishing Co.,* 191 *et seq.*
11. Thomas Ewing Dabney, *One Hundred Great Years: The Story of the Times-*

Picayune from Its Founding to 1940 (Baton Rouge: Louisiana State University Press, 1944), 463-64.
12. *Ibid.*, 301-302.
13. Crozet J. Duplantier, "A History of the *New Orleans States*" (M.A. thesis, Louisiana State University, 1956), 118.

CHAPTER 11

1. *Item*, June 11, 1937.
2. George M. Leppert, interviews, 1974-75.
3. *Item*, June 11, 1937.
4. *Item's Book of Louisiana* (New Orleans, 1916.)
5. *Item*, September 9, 1931.
6. *Ibid.*
7. *Ibid.*, June 11, 1937.
8. *Times-Picayune*, January 29-30, 1930.
9. Transcript of testimony, *Mrs. Myriam Dinkins Robinson* vs. *James M. Thomson*, Clerk of Civil District Court, New Orleans.
10. Record of proceedings, *The Item Company Inc.*, vs. *C. G. Robinson and Company*, Clerk of Civil District Court, New Orleans.
11. *Times-Picayune, States, Item*, July 4, 1917.
12. *States*, July 3, 1917.
13. *Times-Picayune*, July 5, 1917.
14. *States*, July 4, 1917.
15. *Ibid*, July 7, 1917.
16. *Item*, July 9, 1917.
17. *States*, July 10, 1971.
18. *Ibid.*, November 13, 1917.
19. *Ibid.*, January 26, 1919.
20. *Ibid.*
21. *Ibid.*, January 29, 31, 1919.
22. *Ibid.*, January 30, 1919.
23. *Item*, January 30, 1919.
24. *States, Item*, February 3, 1919.
25. Transcript, *Robinson* vs. *Thomson*.
26. Transcript of Record, *United States of America* vs. *The Times-Picayune Publishing Co.*, Federal District Court, New Orleans, 577 *et seq.*
27. *Ibid.*, 580 *et seq.*
28. *Ibid.*, 599 *et seq.*
29. Transcript, *Robinson* vs. *Thomson*.

CHAPTER 12

1. T. Harry Williams, *Huey Long* (New York: Alfred A. Knopf, 1969), 224.
2 *Item*, January 16, 1928.
3. *States*, January 16, 1928.
4. *Item*, January 18, 1928.
5. *States*, January 18, 1928.
6. Williams, *Huey Long*, 341.
7. *States*, August 13, 1928.
8. *Ibid.*, February 14, 1929.
9. *Ibid.*, February 16, March 3, 1929.
10. *Ibid.*, May 17, 1929.
11. *Item*, May 17, 1929.
12. Williams, *Huey Long*, 445, 535.
13. *Times-Picayune*, September 9, 1930.
14. Williams, *Huey Long*, 535.
15. *Times-Picayune*, February 9, 1933.
16. *Ibid.*, October 26, December 13, 1931.
17. *Ibid.*, November 21, 1931.
18. *Ibid.*, May 21, 1933.
19. Williams, *Huey Long*, 455.
20. *Times-Picayune*, December 18, 1932.
21. Williams, *Huey Long*, 863 *et seq.*
22. Wilfred L. d'Aquin, interviews, 1974.

CHAPTER 13

1. Walter G. Cowan, interviews, 1974-75.
2. John W. Fanz, interviews, 1974.
3. *Item-Tribune*, June 29, 1941.
4. Transcript of Record, *United States of America* vs. *The Times-Picayune Publishing Co.*, Federal District Court, New Orleans, 609.
5. David Stern III, interview, February 5, 1975.
6. Transcript, *U.S.* vs. *Times-Picayune*, 609.
7. Charter of The Item Company Inc., Recorder of Mortgages, New Orleans.
8. Transcript, *U.S.* vs. *Times-Picayune*, 87.
9. *Ibid.*, 202-203.
10. *Item*, June 13, 1950.
11. The *Item's* financial records were made available through the cooperation of David Stern III.
12. *Item*, September 14, 1958.
13. Memorandum presented to the Justice Department, February 24, 1958, on behalf of the *Item*. Made available by David Stern III.
14. Memorandum to Justice Department, June 19, 1958. Made available by David Stern III.
15. George Chaplin, correspondence with author, 1975.

CHAPTER 14

1. *Item*, October 24, 1952.
2. Minutes of the Voting Trustees, The Times-Picayune Publishing Company, November 19, 1951.
3. *Ibid.*, February 12, 1959.
4. *Ibid.*, November 16, 1959.
5. *Ibid.*
6. *Ibid.*, November 21, 1960.

7. Correspondence files of Times-Picayune Publishing Co.
8. Interviews with Jerry K. Nicholson and Ashton Phelps.
9. Minutes of Voting Trustees, November 20, 1961.
10. Correspondence files of Times-Picayune Publishing Company; interview with Jerry K. Nicholson.
11. Records of Voting Trustees.
12. Correspondence files of the Times-Picayune Publishing Company.
13. Interview with Jerry K. Nicholson.
14. Correspondence files of the Voting Trustees.
15. *Ibid.*
16. Minutes of Voting Trustees, November 20, 1961.
17. Interviews with Jerry K. Nicholson and G. Shelby Friedrichs.
18. Interview with G. Shelby Friedrichs.
19. Notice of Dissolution to Securities and Exchange Commission, May 8, 1962.
20. *States,* May 30, 1962.
21. Interview with G. Shelby Friedrichs.
22. Statement of Jerry K. Nicholson to Board of Directors, Times-Picayune Publishing Co., May 28, 1962.
23. Minutes of Board of Directors, May 28, 1962.
24. Correspondence files of Voting Trustees.
25. *States,* May 31, 1962.
26. *Ibid.*
27. Interview with Jerry K. Nicholson.
28. Interview with G. Shelby Friedrichs.
29. *Times-Picayune,* June 3, 1962.
30. *Ibid.*, June 4, 1962.
31. Interview with Jerry K. Nicholson.
32. Interview with Carl M. Corbin.
33. Interview with Jerry K. Nicholson.

CHAPTER 15

1. Transcription of recording of Ashton Phelps's remarks.
2. *States-Item,* November 2, 1972.

Index